ALL THINGS FLEE THEE FOR THOU FLEEST ME

A Cry to the Churches and Their Leaders to Stop Running from the Nonviolent Jesus and His Nonviolent Way

(Rev.) Emmanuel Charles McCarthy
—Third Revision: November 2018—

For Printed Copies or Additional Information Contact:

Center for Christian Nonviolence • Wilmington, DE
E-Mail: ATFT@centerforchristiannonviolence.org

Other resources Available at:

CenterForChristianNonviolence.org

Contents

Preamble vii

Dedication ix

Prologue xv

1 To Teach What Jesus Taught: A Call to Accountability
    Calculated Inattentiveness 1.1
    Evasion by Seminaries 1.2
    The Grand Illusion—The Christian State 1.3
    The Temptation of Power 1.5
    Christian Violence: Unbelief Made Flesh 1.6
    To Not Teach What Jesus Taught Is Evangelical Sterility 1.8
    The Ultimate Norm of Christian Life 1.8
    Toadies to the Father of Lies 1.9
    Trustful Fidelity Can Achieve the Impossible 1.10
    The Ordained Tactics—Ignore, Mock, Trivialize 1.10
    The Enfeebled Fruits of Dishonest Shepherding 1.11
    The Moral Mantra 1.12
    Ruling Religious Elites Selectively Shroud the Story 1.13

2 *Quo Vadis, Domine?*
    Consistency 2.2
    Sanctity 2.3
    Heroism 2.3
    Secularization 2.5
    Survival 2.6
    The Nonviolent Follower of a Nonviolent Leader 2.7

3 Violent Monotheism: Truth or Falsehood
    Cannot Serve Two Masters 3.2
    The Martyr 3.3
    The Gospel 3.4
    When 3.4

    The Enemy 3.5
    Worship. 3.6
    Other Divine Expectations. 3.7
    Institutional Christianity 3.8
    Distrusting Jesus 3.9
    Hopping Christians 3.10
    "X" or Not "X" 3.11

4   He Does Not Break the Bruised Reed: Capital Punishment and Christian Mercilessness

    Waldorf Astoria 4.1
    Christ's Messianic Program 4.2
    Advocate vs. Accuser 4.3
    Radical Evil. 4.3
    Renaming Mercilessness 4.4
    Philosophy or God's Will 4.4
    Praise the Lord and… 4.6
    Life that Outlasts Time 4.6
    WWJD. 4.7

5   Calling Down Fire: Lost Sheep and Lost Shepherds

    Holy Communion in the Service of Homicide and Enmity 5.2
    Eucharistic Fratricide 5.3
    Unenlightened Shepherding. 5.3
    Non-Empathic Shepherding 5.4
    Moonshine Shepherding 5.5
    Immature Shepherding 5.6
    Jesus or Elijah 5.7

6   The Nonviolent Trinity

    Beyond Reason to Revelation and Faith. 6.1
    The Perfect Icon of God 6.2
    God Is One 6.2
    Violent Monotheism—Vesting a Lie. 6.3
    Betrayal of the Nonviolent Trinity 6.4
    Divine Conscription as Spiritual Fraud 6.5
    Worshipping and Following the True Image of God 6.5

7 Patronizing God

- Rejection of Violence and Enmity... 7.1
- Simultaneous Adoration and Rejection 7.3
- One Is Known Only by Words and Deeds 7.3
- Spiritual Schizophrenia—Praise God and Pass the Ammo 7.4
- Church Teaching Reflects Paucity of Faith in Jesus.................... 7.5
- The Aberrational Transition from Cross to Sword..................... 7.5
- Anti-Evangelization in the Extreme... 7.6
- Liturgical Pampering of the Holy One Is Not Enough 7.7
- Clerical and Academic Disdain for the Nonviolent Jesus 7.7
- True Praise of God is Abandonment to Nonviolent Love 7.8

8 Will the Reformed Church Be a Peace Church?

- The Head of the Church 8.1
- Means and Ends 8.2
- Secularization of the Church 8.2
- Bartering Away Jesus' Legacy 8.4
- Which Power Saves? 8.5
- Eternity, Sanctity, Church 8.6

9 To See God Face to Face

- St. Peter and St. Paul 9.1
- Mahatma Gandhi... 9.2
- The Kingdom of God Is Within You....................................... 9.2
- A Follower of Jesus.. 9.3
- Realpolitik and the Sermon on the Mount 9.4
- The Master Question... 9.4
- John Paul II and Gandhi 9.5
- The Medium and the Message.. 9.6
- The Corollary 9.7
- *Opus Dei* 9.7

10 Follow the Nonviolent Jesus OR Follow the Nonexistent Jesus

- Peace and Salvation 10.1
- Peace: the Self-Communication of God 10.2
- Peace: The End and the Means to the End............................... 10.2
- Repentance and Praxis, Praxis and Repentance 10.4

"Follow Me!" "Come Back to Me!" 10.4
Fidelity Needed, Not a Crowd 10.5
Pacifism: An Imprecise Christian Term 10.5
Coming Back from Moral Dwarfism 10.6
The Evil Person? 10.6
A Time of Temptation 10.8
Violence and Enmity Are Contagious 10.9
The Practice of the Presence of the Loving Parent of Each and of All 10.10
Be a Realist 10.11
A "2 by 4" World 10.11
The Word of the Cross, The Words from the Cross 10.11

11 The Refusing Churches and New Testament Scholarship
Does Air Exist? 11.2
Constantinian Christian Missionaries and Scholars 11.3
"X and not X" 11.3
Doublespeak and Solipsism 11.4
Theology as Atheism 11.5
The Color of Jesus' Hair 11.6
Jesus is not a Vacuum 11.7
"Jesus, I don't Trust You." 11.8
A Transmogrified Proclamation 11.8
Medicinal New Testament Scholarship and Remedial Truth 11.8
Pusillanimity and Perfidiousness 11.10

12 The Nonviolent Spirituality of St. Maximus The Confessor
A Life and Death Struggle 12.1
The Perduring Embrace of Love Engenders Deification 12.2
Deification—Synergy between Divine Will and Human Will 12.3
To Love as Christ Loves is the Entire Law of the Gospel 12.4
SIN—Choosing Freely to Revolt Against Love 12.5
The Discipline of Love 12.7
The Problem of Violence 12.7
The Voluntary Relinquishing of Violence 12.9
Separating Passions from Representations 12.9
The Refusal to Abandon Christic Love 12.11
A Nonviolent Mindstyle and Lifestyle Invite the Cross 12.12
The Rejection of All Violence—Internal and External 12.13

    Building an External Commonwealth of Love for All 12.14
    The Human Mind—The Holy Place, the Temple of God. 12.15
    Dropping Allegiances That Are Impediments to Love 12.15

13 Behold The Nonviolent Lamb of God
    The Lamb 13.2
    Hebrew Scriptures. 13.2
    New Testament 13.3
    Baptism 13.4
    Eucharist 13.5
    Church. 13.5
    Social Responsibility 13.6

14 The Nonviolent Eucharistic Jesus: A Pastoral Approach
    The Ultimate Norm of the Christian Life 14.1
    New Commandment Contains the Entire Law of the Gospel 14.2
    Liturgical and Operational Indifference 14.3
    A Eucharistic Prayer that Embodies Nonviolent Love. 14.4
    Maundy Thursday—A Mandate to Love as Christ Loves. 14.5
    Emaciated Revelatory Remembrance Subverts Divine Love 14.6
    Amnesia About Truths in the Suffering and Death of Christ 14.6
    The Key to Eucharistic Unity and Christian Unity 14.7
    New Time of Christian Agapé 14.8
    Betrayal of Baptismal and Eucharistic Unity. 14.9
    Disunity Emanates from Separation of Divine Mandates. 14.10
    A Pastorally Truth-Filled Eucharist 14.11

15 The Nonviolent Eucharistic Jesus: A Scholarly Approach
    Encounter with God 15.2
    Principal Witness and Mundane Specifics 15.2
    No Toleration of Ambiguity. 15.3
    Virulent Plague 15.5
    Power Made Visible. 15.5
    Universal Public Education 15.6
    Undeveloped Remembrance in the Acting Person. 15.8
    Harmfulness of Incomplete Expression. 15.10
    Evasion of Unwanted Truth. 15.11
    Way and Purpose 15.13

Knower and Known	15.14
Mandatum for Change	15.15
Eucharist: The Arena of Struggle	15.17
The Civilization of Love and the Banality of Evil	15.17
A Priority Task	15.19
The Catalytic Factor Awakens Possibilities	15.20

Epilogue A.1

Biography A.7

A Christian Parent's Pledge to All Mothers and Fathers A.9

PREAMBLE

WHAT IS GOSPEL NONVIOLENCE ALL ABOUT?

"Fear Not!" The God of Jesus, the God who is Jesus is not going to hurt you—no way, nowhere, no how. The God who is Jesus is love (Greek: agapé), unconditional, everlasting, irrevocable love. If Jesus is who the New Testament and the Churches say He is, then "He is the image of the invisible God" (COL 1:15). If Jesus knows what He is talking about, then God is a God of nonviolent love. God is nonviolent love because Jesus, who teaches that He is one with the Father (JN 10:30) and that to see Him is to see the Father (JN 14:9), is nonviolent love made flesh. This is great, great news. For those who have faith in Jesus it is the good news because it is now certain that "Nothing can separate us from the love of God made visible in Christ Jesus, Our Lord" (RM 8:39).

No longer is there a need or a justification for human beings to feel insecure in existence, regardless of the fact that we humans appear to be totally perishable beings on a totally perishable planet in a totally perishable galaxy. No longer is there a need to fight and kill to try to do the impossible—to preserve the intrinsically impermanent in order to have security and peace. Peace and security, eternal survival and everlasting love are given to us because we, all of us without a single exception, are the immortal and infinitely cherished sons and daughters of a Parent who is immortal Life and Love Itself. As St. Edith Stein expresses it a few years before her death at Auschwitz:

> *I know myself held, and in this I have peace and security—not the self-assured security of a man who stands in his own strength on firm ground, but the sweet and blissful security of the child which is carried by a strong arm.*

The person who believes in Jesus is called upon and yearns to proclaim, glorify, and magnify the true God to the rest of humanity by imitating his or her Divine Parent and not hurting anyone, anywhere, anytime for any reason. This yearning exists because he or she fathoms that God longs for each of His sons and daughters to be at peace and because of all the things human beings need in order to be at peace— the first and most important is the awareness that God loves them forever and will never, ever abandon them or hurt them. The Christian's model for the proclamation of this great news is Jesus. Christ is the perfect imitation of the Father, who "makes his sun rise on the bad and the good, and causes rain to fall on the just and the unjust" (MT 5:45). The Christian, who desires to help reveal the true God to humanity, must then imitate the nonviolent Jesus who loves friends and enemies even unto physical death. Authentic evangelization is primarily imitation that magnifies the real God, so that others may "see" their Beatific Parent and know peace. It is in understanding the depth of love that God has for each person that peace on earth will be realized.

Since there is no violence or enmity in the true God and since there is no violence or enmity in Jesus, violence and enmity are always and everywhere and under all circumstances unholy, unChrist-like, contrary to the will of God. Because of who and what the true God is there is never a need for violence nor is there ever a reason for enmity. Because of who and what the true God is, violence and enmity are always the work of a false God or a false understanding of God and His Way. They are always the work of the Evil One, who spreads lies about God, who is a killjoy and who wants no one to live in the perpetual peace that comes from realizing that he or she is in the never-ending embrace of a Parent of Unconditional Love. Satan, the Accuser, the Adversary, the Divider, the Spirit of Mercilessness, the Father of the Anti-Christ is the crazed one who is out to destroy the sense of total security that people should have in God and thereby destroy people's peace as God's beloved. The Evil One ferociously engages in this labor of wickedness because it is inevitable, that once the peace of absolute security in the Father's/Mother's love is lost, this will undermine the security and hence the peace people have within themselves and among themselves. Human beings will then fear and fight each other over the possession or over the loss of possession of illusionary substitutes for that security and peace that can only come from understanding that each and everyone is held dear forever in the arms of their Heavenly Parent.

All this and the stream of personal and social implications and imperatives that flow from it are what Gospel Nonviolence is all about.

DEDICATION

†

To those countless millions
of Christian men and women
who killed and were killed,
who maimed and were maimed
in war over the last 1700 years,
and who were denied knowledge of
the Nonviolent Jesus of the Gospel
and His Way of
Nonviolent Love of friends and enemies
by their bishops, priests and ministers.

&

To the hundreds of millions
of mothers, fathers and children
murdered and maimed
in soul, spirit and body
over the centuries
by Christian Just-Warists.

†

In Memoriam

A Twenty-Four Year Old Icon

Visible reality is but a speck of reality. Most of what is most important in life takes place on the invisible side of existence. Each life is an icon, a visible image of invisible realities. The clenched fist or the open hand does not exist in history without something unseen, but very real, within the person causing the hand to either close in hostility or to open in hospitality. So also it is with the tongue and the feet and with every conscious act of every human person at every second. I would like therefore to speak today of the invisible side of John Leary—the infinity behind the face of this *Magna Cum Laude* Harvard graduate and *Summa Cum Laude* Catholic Worker.

Because of some mysterious dynamic, John recognized early in life that outside God's will there was no genuine or lasting life, hope, love, peace or revolution. He realized that if the cacophony of evil and death were to be silenced and an ultimate harmony restored to human existence, then God would have to orchestrate it and John Leary would have to be God's willing instrument. Nothing was clearer to the "invisible John" than the fact that all attempts by an instrument to lead the band were doomed to continue the cacophony. To substitute ones own ideas on how to conquer evil and death for God's revealed Way on how to conquer evil and death was in the strictest sense of the word absurd. With a maturity beyond his twenty-four years he knew the meaning of "Our peace is in Your Will." To this end, each day, for what was to be the last two years of his life, John tried to say with his whole heart the following prayer:

> *Father, I abandon myself into your hands.*
> *Do with me as you will.*
> *Whatever you may do, I thank you.*
> *I am ready for all. I accept all.*
> *Let only your will be done in me*
> *And in all your creatures.*
> *I wish no more than this, O Lord.*
> *Into your hands I commend my soul.*
> *I offer it to you with all the love of my heart,*
> *For I love you, Lord, and so need to give myself,*
> *To surrender myself into your hands*
> *Without reserve and with boundless confidence*
> *For you are my Father.*

For John, the actual content of God's Will was revealed ultimately and definitively by Jesus Christ, the Incarnation of a God who is love (1 JN 16). John took with maximal seriousness Jesus' declarations that "The Father and I are one" (JN 10:30) and "Whoever sees me sees the Father" (JN 14:9). Jesus and His teaching were for John the Way and Will of God to which the Christian was called to be trustfully obedient. Jesus' New Commandment to "love one another as I have loved you" (JN 13:34) was for John Leary not a spiritual platitude to be set aside when adherence to it became difficult. It was a moral imperative for any person who believed Jesus to be who the Gospel said He was, namely, the Messiah of Israel, the Saviour of the world, the Word made flesh.

What was equally important for John was that, since Jesus' Way was the Will of God and not just another piece of human speculation about the will of God, failure to choose according to it was *de facto* a choice for something other than God. This choice required explicit repentance. John repented much in the years I knew him, because he intuited that spiritual disintegration would follow, if he obstinately persisted in what he knew to be unChrist-like thoughts, words or deeds. He was aware that the refusal to acknowledge that an evil had been done would eventually result in calling evil good. He knew that an unnamed sin perpetuated itself indefinitely. We often joked about the fact, that the difference between cultural nurturing and Christ's revelation of the Will of God, was so stark, that the Christian life often seemed like a life of repentance. Yet, the only choices available were to follow the way of God revealed by Jesus, and repent if one did not, or to waste one's life plodding on the treadmill of moral deception, where evil is chosen to conquer evil. For John, what appeared good was not good—even if he "benefited" from it—if it was not in conformity with God's will as revealed by Jesus Christ. The John Leary who actually existed and whom people rightly remember for his goodness was not "the boy innocent" within a corrupt and corrupting world. This very good person rightly remembered was a human being of choice and repentance, of commitment and recommitment.

All his spiritual efforts, and there were many, were not however primarily focused on himself, on his own righteousness, on his own salvation, etc. His life was intensely ordered toward others. The prayers, the choices, the daily Masses and Communions, the repentance, the study, the retreats, etc., had one aim, namely, to make possible the deeds of Christ-like love, mercy, service and kindness here and now, in the particular concrete moment. John believed he could not genuinely serve people except by serving them in the way God revealed they should be served in the person of Jesus. But, in the world in which we actually live, such Christ-like love can only be given at the price of a voluntary, invisible martyrdom. Yet for John—and everyone who knew John knows this to be true—a cup of tea given in the spirit of Christ-like love was everything, but a banquet without that spirit was just passing time at the trough (1 COR 13). Whatever John did in terms of service for the imprisoned, for the hungry, for the homeless, for the unborn, for the illiterate, for the unloved, for the deceived; whatever he did to oppose without exception homicide and enmity in all their forms, from abortion to nuclear weapons, from capital punishment to military training, was the fruit of an effort to enflesh, to embody, to obey the Will of God as revealed by Jesus. For him this was the Right Way to serve people, as well as, the Right Way to love God (1 JN 20-21).

Now that John is dead, some may smugly ask, "What difference did it make in the end? Who cares today whether this guy tried to love as Christ loves? Who even remembers him beyond a few friends for whom he is an occasional thought?" "Face the facts," smirks the self-proclaimed realist, "common sense and simple observation verify that John Leary's daily and often painful struggle to choose to live in the Spirit of Christ-like Love has proved to be utterly irrelevant, utopian and devoid of any notable visible consequences. The self-reverential realist then points out those people who are "making a difference in this world" and who are not allowing the Will of God as revealed by Jesus to interfere with the successful implementation of their projects, programs and agendas.

John was of course aware of this perception of existence, this criticism of the Gospel. He rejected it as being without intellectual merit, spiritual meaning or hope. It was the shallow, self-absolving voice of the sin of success, where success is procured by giving it a priority over fidelity to the Will of God. For John, success outside the Will of God as revealed by Jesus was failure and failure within the Will of God was success. Good Friday and Easter Sunday were the great witnesses to this truth, as well as, the great warning to those who were not going to allow their agendas to get bogged down by the unrealisms of God's Will. John did not choose the Way of Christ because he did not know of any other options, nor did he chose it in ignorance of the objections raised against it. He chose it because there is only one Source of reality and one reality. Therefore, what is God's Will can never be unrealistic, impractical or without temporally and eternally significant good consequences—and Jesus revealed that Will.

"Icon" is the Greek word for image. A Christ-like icon is God's power and love in history because it invites people to a Christ-like life, which is God's power and love in history. When therefore one looks at John Timothy Leary, a twenty-four year old icon of the invisible Spirit of Jesus Christ, one sees the Truth of the Gospel proclaimed to others with love and the choice of the Gospel offered to others with supreme kindness. Through Jesus, John knew the Heart of God, the human heart and the heart of what matters:

> *Time is short. Eternity is long.*
> *Love as Christ loves,*
> *all else is dust in time and in eternity,*
> *for the true God is love.*

FUNERAL LITURGY FOR JOHN LEARY
SEPTEMBER 4, 1982
HOMILIST: EMMANUEL CHARLES MCCARTHY

PROLOGUE

To release a person or a community bound in a web of venomous falsehoods, that has imprisoned and malformed its mind and emotions since childhood, can be a near impossible task. In a cannibal society the theological truth of cannibalism is all but unassailable. So also is this the case with Christian mind-sets and theologies of justified homicidal violence and enmity. On a planet where 99% of Christians and Churches nurture from the cradle the moral acceptability of homicide and enmity for Christians, there is little room available for announcing the Good News of Christ's freeing and healing nonviolent love. However, as close to impossible as the task appears of extricating and restoring to spiritual health Christian minds and hearts ensnared and poisoned by homicide-justifying, enmity-approving fictions about Jesus and His Way, this is precisely the project that this small book undertakes. So let there be clarity! The secondary purpose of this book is to plead with the leadership of the Christian Churches to allow the Nonviolent Jesus of the Gospel and His Way of nonviolent love of friends and enemies to arise in the minds and hearts and lives of their communities. The primary purpose of this book is to beseech the laity of the various Christian Churches to accept Jesus as He is presented to them in the Gospel, that is, as personally nonviolent and as teaching a Way of nonviolent love as the Way of discipleship, as the Way of eternal life.

It is beyond the power of words to communicate the loss of delight, truth and peace that humanity has suffered because of the Churches' leaders chronic and obstinate refusal to teach what Jesus taught about homicidal violence and enmity. What experience of God would permeate Christianity and humanity today, what level of community would exist within humanity and among Christians at this moment if for the last 1700 years the Churches had taught and had struggled to live what Jesus taught and struggled to live in relationship to violence and enmity? In other words what would life be at this hour, and equally important, what would death be at this hour, if Christianity had religiously followed the Nonviolent Jesus of the Gospel and His Nonviolent Way? The Pythagorean Theorem would still be true and NaCl would still be salt if the Churches had professed and proclaimed the Nonviolent Jesus. But, how very, very, differently secular truth would have been applied, if the hundred of trillions upon hundred of trillions of moments which Christians have put into justifying and executing violence had been spent fathoming and following the Nonviolent Jesus.

Providentially, time has not yet ceased for me, for you or for humanity. Tomorrow is still a possibility. Today a truth can be proclaimed regardless of how many yesterdays failed to proclaim it. Every instant is an opportunity to bear witness to the truth and to correct a false witness from the past.

However, as Leon Festinger shows in his classic sociological study, *When Prophesy Fails* (1956), human beings can lie to themselves with sincerity, can convince themselves of what they even then know is not true.

> *[P]resented with evidence, unequivocal and undeniable evidence that his belief is wrong: What will happen? The individual will frequently emerge, not only unshaken, but even more convinced of the truth of his belief than ever before.*

Strange, indeed, is the temptation to untruth. Who can account for the ease, enthusiasm, earnestness and tenacity with which people embrace it?

If Biblically, truth is the self-communication of God to human beings, if philosophically truth is the conformity of the human mind to reality, from whence comes the motivation to choose untruth, to conform mind to non-reality, to illusion? Over the four millennia of human literacy much has been written as to why people propagate or accept known untruth, i.e., the lie. Fear, that pleasure will be missed or that pain will be encountered, has often been suggested as the Great Motivator that entices a person or a group to hold tight to blatant falsehoods. But, who really knows the source of the mystery that beguiles people to entrust their one and only life to what they know in their hearts is not so. All that can be said in faith is that to willingly profess as true what one knows to be untrue is to be in the service of "the Father of Lies in whom there is no truth at all and who is a murderer from the beginning" (JN 8:44).

Whether *All things flee thee for thou fleest Me*, will accomplish the liberating and therapeutic task for which it was created is now in hands other than the hands that penned it for Jesus, for the Church and for humanity.

To Teach What Jesus Taught: A Call to Accountability

God intervenes radically only in response to a radical attitude on the part of the believer—radical not in regard to political means but in regard to faith; and the believer who is radical in his faith has rejected all means other than those of faith. The appeal to and use of violence in Christian actions increase in exact proportion to the decrease in faith...Unbelief is the true root of the Christian championship of violence.

JACQUES ELLUL

The issue of whether Jesus teaches by word and deed a Way of Nonviolent Love of friends and enemies is settled. He does! All attempts today to justify violence from the life of Jesus or His teachings are devoid of spiritual and intellectual merit. That is not opinion, that is fact.

CALCULATED INATTENTIVENESS

Fortunately in our time spiritual leaders have all but ceased the farcical effort of trying to morally validate the violence of Christians by reference to Jesus and His teachings. Presently, the strategy of preference is calculated inattentiveness to the nonviolence of Jesus and the nonviolent nature of the love that He teaches to His disciples as divine and salvific. Christian Churches in our day do not, as in days past, try to explain away Jesus' teaching of Nonviolent Love by tortuously proving that He did not really mean what He said. No, in our day they just ignore it and replace it with some philosophical conceptualization of reality and its Source, which they then raise to an equivalent or superior status to the teaching of Jesus; e.g., "It is a God-given natural right to kill those who are trying to kill you. Killing other human beings is a tragic necessity in the present state of a fallen humanity with its immoral societies. To do what is natural or necessary cannot be sinful—on to homicide in good Christian conscience!" In this strategy Jesus' teaching on the subject does not get a hearing, except to be haughtily dismissed as simplistic idealism. He is allowed to enter the picture after the decision to kill has been made but only to be worshipped or perhaps to be called upon as a divine support person for the local team's homicide.

If we assume, as it is proper to do, that most religious leaders in the Catholic, Orthodox, Protestant and Evangelical Churches are not just CEOs running multi-million dollar corporations or subsidiaries thereof, but are men and women who believe in Jesus and want to teach what Jesus taught to the world as best they can—then why are they not doing it where homicidal violence and enmity are concerned? My judgment is that at root there are two reasons: either they do not know that Jesus teaches a Way of Nonviolent Love, or they know it but have no idea how to teach it in their communities without creating tormenting worlds of moral and spiritual chaos for their fellow Christians—and themselves.

Evasion by Seminaries

Since most seminaries do not offer a single course in the history, theology or spirituality of Christian Nonviolence, it is almost inevitable that most men and women being ordained from these seminaries will know little to nothing of the subject, will not have had it integrated into the rest of their formal theological education, e.g., with sacramentology, pneumatology and ecclesiology, etc., and will therefore not emphasize in their ministry what was not emphasized in their preparation for ministry. Based upon over 50 years of teaching Gospel nonviolence, I can assure my readers that the average bishop, minister and priest is as non-informed or misinformed on this subject as the average Christian. An occasional mention of Gandhi's or Martin Luther King, Jr.'s nonviolent civil disobedience within the context of a Peace and Justice course or a momentary tip of the hat to "Peace Churches" within the context of a Church History course or a student thesis here or there on Dorothy Day or A.J. Muste, etc., is the only contact with the subject that seminaries normally have available to their students.

The specific question of why seminaries throughout the world persist in their curricular evasion of the Nonviolent Jesus and His teaching of Nonviolent Love is a question that pleads for a thorough investigation but is beyond the scope of this publication. However, the consequence of this steadfastness in avoidance is that for a large majority of bishops, ministers and priests Jesus' nonviolence is a non-thought. This allows most of them to preach with their whole strength a Gospel that includes following Christ while simultaneously executing the heinous and unChrist-like acts that all wars demand of their participants. A priest told me several years ago that he had given a fellow priest who was dying a set of audiotapes of my retreat on Gospel Nonviolence. When after a week he returned to visit him, he asked him what he thought of the tapes. With visible emotion the dying priest replied, "Why didn't they tell me about this forty years ago?"

But what of those Christian religious leaders who are aware that Jesus taught a Way of Nonviolent Love of friends and enemies, yet still do not teach it? What about those pastors who know that Jesus firing a machine gun is not an authentic Christian icon (image) and that a follower of Jesus unleashing a barrage of bullets at human targets is an equally unauthentic Christian witness? What about those overseers of the spiritual and moral well-being of the various Christian communities who realize that in order to pick up the gun you have to put down the Gospel but who remain silent or diplomatically ambiguous on the issue?

Some twenty-five years ago a Catholic bishop said to me, "Just war? What just war? No such thing exists. But we must not tell this to the people." Now, at a distance, the easiest judgment to make on this man is that he is just a blatant hypocrite, posturing as an authoritative teacher of the Gospel when in fact he is intentionally withholding an important dimension of it. But, when seen close up he is a man of intelligence and of more than ordinary compassion. He simply does not see how he for his people—or a Pope and an Ecumenical Council for the entire Church—could teach that Christians cannot follow Jesus by participating in the military, without having nation after nation turn on its Christian population like enraged beasts. Lest it be thought that he was submitting a far-fetched argument to rationalize his own hypocrisy, I would here note the late biblical scholar John L. McKenzie's comment on the same subject:

> A Catholic bishop said to me, "Just war? What just war? No such thing exists. But we must not tell this to the people."...He simply did not see how he...could teach that Christians cannot follow Jesus by participating in the military, without having nation after nation turn on its Christian population like enraged beasts.

> *The statement of the renunciation of violence as a means of dealing with other people is clear enough. Christians have never questioned either that Jesus said it or that it admits no qualification. Christians have simply decided they cannot live according to these sayings of Jesus. To put it more accurately, they have decided that they do not wish to live according to these sayings...If the Roman Catholic Church were to decide to join the Mennonites in refusing violence, I doubt whether our harmonious relations with the government would endure the day after the decision.*

THE GRAND ILLUSION—THE CHRISTIAN STATE

It is illusion to believe that governments would not respond harshly to an institutional Christian withdrawal of allegiance to their militaries. All governments, democracies no less than dictatorships, require the power of homicide in order to exist and their militaries are what give them this power. All laws of a state are backed up by the organized violence of the state and will be enforced with lethal force if necessary. The renowned Protestant theologian-lawyer, Jacques Ellul says:

> *I have shown in detail that every state is founded on violence and cannot maintain itself save by and through violence. I refuse to make the classic distinction between violence and force. The lawyers have invented the idea that when the state applies constraint, even brutal constraint, it is exercising "Force"; that only individuals or nongovernmental groups use violence. This is a totally unjustified distinction. The state is established by violence. Invariably there is violence at the start. And the state is legitimized when the other states recognize it (I know that this is not the usual criterion of legitimacy, but it is the only real one!). Well then, when is a state recognized? When it has lasted for a tolerable length of time. During the state's early years the world is scandalized that it was established by violence, but presently the fact is accepted, and after a few years it is recognized as legitimate.*

Kill power is the ultimate power on which every government is based. Hence, the macabre incident during the 1992 Presidential campaign, when the white Rhodes Scholar-Governor returned to Arkansas to preside over the execution of a mentally retarded African-American man, makes total sense. No one is allowed to rise to a position of political power unless he or she proves to those who finance the ride up the political escalator that he or she is not squeamish about killing people, that he or she has the "right stuff." A non-negotiable "quality" one must exhibit for high office is the willingness to pull the trigger. As Tolstoy writes:

> *In spite of the unceasing efforts made by men in power to conceal this and to ascribe a different meaning to power, power is the application of a rope, a chain by which a person will be bound and dragged along, or of a whip, with which he will be flogged, or of a knife, or an ax with which they will cut off his hands, feet, ears, head—an application of these means or the threat they will be used. Thus it was in the time of Nero and of Genghis Khan and thus it is even now, in the most liberal of governments.*

The indispensable fuel for running the kingdoms of this world is violence. This is why Jesus rejected the temptation in the desert that offered him power over the kingdoms of the world. This is why the state is not an object of redemption in the New Testament. Power is the capacity to produce change. Jesus exercises many kinds of power. The power to heal, the power to forgive, the power to love enemies and the power of mercy are all forms of power and all produce change for the welfare of people in this world, as well as, in the next. Jesus and His cross are, in fact, called by St. Paul "the power of God and the wisdom of God" (1 COR 1:24). However, Jesus has no interest in the governmental power that Satan offers because governmental power is the power of homicidal violence. Jesus rejects becoming King of Israel or prime minister of a governmental political structure, and one wonders how so many of His followers over the centuries have, with clear Christian consciences, pursued, captured and exercised governmental power. However they did it, they did not do it in imitation of Christ.

> The indispensable fuel for running the kingdoms of this world is violence. This is why Jesus rejected the temptation in the desert that offered him power over the kingdoms of the world. This is why the state is not an object of redemption in the New Testament.

THE TEMPTATION OF POWER

In his final book, *The Civilization of Christianity*, the biblical scholar, Rev. John L. McKenzie, in order to illuminate the meaning of the temptation that offers to Jesus violent governmental political power, creates a dialogue in the desert between Jesus, called by his Hebrew name, Yeshu, and Satan called by his nickname, Old Nick. It reads in part as follows:

Nick: Yeshu, I have plans for mankind so big you could not understand them, smart as I think you are…[But] it takes time; it takes work and it takes good people; that is why I am here. I want you.

Yeshu: You do not want a simple village carpenter from Nazareth. Whoever came from Nazareth that amounted to anything? If you want a smart Jew, you will find plenty of them in Alexandria or even a few in Jerusalem.

Nick: Do not worry; I can give you anything you need except talent, and you have that from Adonai. Think of it, Yeshu; it is the biggest thing a man can get into, he can do more for more people, and it will last longer than anything else you could do. Yeshu, a man like you ought to think big; I can make it possible for you to do big… You will commit a sin by letting God-given talent rot in this rat hole of Palestine.

Yeshu: And I suppose it will also give me a chance to enrich myself and make the world a better place for me to live in?

Nick: I make opportunities, and it is for you to realize them. People who work for me have to work very hard, and many of them find that success is pleasure enough…

Yeshu: The late king Herod—did he work for you?

Nick: Not one of my outstanding employees—but yes, he did…But I expect far more from you than I got from Herod; he had a bit of a heavy hand—no finesse, shall we say? Augustus (there, Yeshu, was a man of whom I am proud) said that it was better to be Herod's sow than his son.

Yeshu: Did Herod's son and grandson work for you too?

Nick: Please do not mention those swine; I got rid of them. I demand a certain level of competence in my employees.

Yeshu: Suppose I did not want to do the kind of work for you which Herod and Augustus did—and I suppose Tiberius, the present Caesar, works for you too?

Nick: He either works for me or he is not Caesar.

CHRISTIAN VIOLENCE: UNBELIEF MADE FLESH

Presently, of course, in most Christian Churches a person(s) can remain in Full Communion, be considered faithful to Jesus and still be killing, helping to kill or planning how to more efficiently kill hundreds or thousands or even tens of thousands of his or her fellow communicants! But what if Jesus' teachings of Nonviolent Love of friends and enemies were taught by the Churches as an essential for membership? What would become of those hundreds of millions of Christians throughout the world from generals to privates who earn their living in the military? If homicide were forbidden to followers of Jesus, then could Christians play a role in assisting others to do an evil that they could not morally participate in themselves? If not, what then of the tens of millions of Christians who make their living in low-tech or high-tech munitions and arms factories or in the multi-billion dollar world of university homicide research, how would they survive? What would become of Christian politicians who, because of fidelity to the Lord and His Way, refused to pull the trigger? None of these questions represents a merely abstract moral dilemma unrelated to reality, once a Church or all the Churches would declare that following Jesus' Way of Nonviolent Love is a condition for Baptism and Full Communion. Some years ago a friend told me the response of a Protestant bishop after he listened to some of my materials on Gospel Nonviolence. "It is true," he said, "but I do not have the faith to subject my people to that."

The above-mentioned Protestant bishop sounds like an echo of the Catholic Grand Inquisitor in Dostoevsky's *Brothers Karamazov*. This literary character is fully aware of the teachings of Jesus; nevertheless, he keeps his fellow Christians from knowing them, because he loves the "little" people too much to permit them to be exposed to the unbearable burden of true freedom and true love that Jesus offers them. However, the good thing about this Protestant bishop's response is that he precisely names the location of the problem, namely, his own lack of faith. This is a notable step up from the silly justifications for Christian participation in homicidal violence that try to root themselves in a supposed lack of clarity about what Jesus taught on the subject. It is also a giant step up from the fear-induced utilitarianism of earthly self-interest, rhetorically ennobled as compassionate "realism"—"You just have to kill sometimes in this world to be a responsible Christian." This Protestant bishop's approach realizes that contemporary Scripture scholarship, as well as common sense, necessitates that it affirm that Jesus and His teachings are nonviolent. It then fabricates justifications for not "teaching them to observe all that I have commanded you" (MT 28:20). The general tenor of these rationalizations is as follows:

> *The only realistic way a Christian can respond responsibly to the tragedy of sin in the world, when confronted with a legal or an illegal horde of thugs, is to abandon Christ-God's Way of Nonviolent Love of friends and enemies and embrace that which Jesus teaches is the way of the Evil One—the wickedness of homicidal violence. The immorality of all societies necessitates that Jesus' Way of Nonviolent Love be abandoned by the Christian when called upon by his or her totally perishable immoral society to defend it by means of human slaughter against another, totally perishable immoral society. A Christian may morally do within a crowd what he or she is not morally permitted to do alone.*

Is Jesus neither compassionate nor realistic? Is the presupposition for this excuse for disobeying the Will of God as revealed by Jesus, the acceptance as true of the intellectually outrageous notion, that God, who "is love" (1 JN 4:8,16), and His Incarnate Word, "through whom all things were made" (JN 1:3) do not properly understand the essential nature of love and/or of reality?

To pray, "I believe Lord, help my unbelief" (MK 9:24) is a holy and acceptable Christian prayer for a time or for a lifetime for those struggling to be faithful to Jesus and His Way of Nonviolent Love. Certainly, many, if not most of the early Christian martyrs articulated this prayer in the face the organized, murderous barbarities of an overwhelmingly powerful Roman government. Such is probably the prayer of every Christian who seeks to be faithful during a Gethsemane moment in life. But, to tell fellow Christians that they may disobey the Lord and His teachings in the hour of a life and death crisis, on the basis of some subjective, speculative, fear-ladened, sin-drenched conjectures about reality and the possibilities it contains, is neither holy, nor proper, nor faithful, nor intelligent, nor loving, nor prudent, nor moral, nor good, nor right. With this quality of Christian moral thinking every martyr known could have avoided his or her fate. Indeed, martyrdom would be seen by the Church as a socially dissolute and impotent activity, rather than as sharing in the divine life, as placing divine yeast in the human dough, as the "seed of Christianity."

TO NOT TEACH WHAT JESUS TAUGHT IS EVANGELICAL STERILITY

So what is to be done? I really do not know how to minister to bishops, ministers and priests on this subject, but I know they must be ministered to. Their lack of knowledge is real and their fears are real. Yet the problem is also real. If Jesus taught a Way of Nonviolent Love of friends and enemies then those holding teaching authority in the Church, either directly by office or indirectly by delegation, would be under a divine mandate to teach what He taught on the subject of violence.

On numerous occasions I have been told by pastors of economically deprived congregations that teaching nonviolence in their Churches would be destructive, since the military is one of the few ways, if not the only way, for most of their young people to get out of poverty and get a trade. So, poor pastors and poor Churches can be as misleading about the nonviolent Jesus and His teaching of Nonviolent Love as rich popes and bishops. For almost a thousand years, protocol demanded that popes and bishops prostrate themselves before the Byzantine Emperor in the East. On Christmas Day AD 800, Pope Leo III, after crowning the illiterate Frankish King Charlemagne as Emperor of the Holy Roman Empire in the West, did the same. However, which is a more radical attack on the Lordship of Jesus Christ: the ceremonial gesture of subservient fawning, or the deed of refusing to proclaim the Way of Christ in order that the way of Caesar with its rewards may be followed with an untroubled conscience? Are accessories before the fact of such traitorous deeds, e.g., priests, preachers and pastors, in any better position than popes and bishops on their bellies before the Grand Pooh-Bah of the moment? Who knows for sure? All that is known is that Christian flunkies for the ever-violent Caesar, whether they be rich, poor or middle class, are *ipso facto* evangelically sterile, even if they are mouthing "Praise the Lord" all along their way from here to eternity and even if they are preaching to "standing room only" audiences.

> All that is known is that Christian flunkies for the ever-violent Caesar…are ipso facto evangelically sterile…even if they are mouthing "Praise the Lord" all along their way from here to eternity…and even if they are preaching to "standing room only" audiences.

THE ULTIMATE NORM OF CHRISTIAN LIFE

A Christian cannot have an underlying good intention when he or she knowingly chooses what is contrary to the Will of God as revealed by Jesus, that is, when he or she knowingly chooses what is normatively evil. One cannot do God's will by knowingly not doing God's will. One cannot do good by doing evil. One cannot proclaim the truth Jesus proclaimed by not proclaiming the truth that Jesus proclaimed. One cannot follow Jesus by not following Jesus. One cannot love as Christ loves by doing things that any sane person would find morally unthinkable for Jesus Himself to do. As one of the most profound Christian theologians of the twentieth century, Rev. Hans Von Balthazar writes:

> Christ is the concrete categorical imperative. He is the formally universal norm of ethical action, applicable to everyone...Christ's concrete existence—his life, suffering, death and ultimate bodily resurrection—surpasses all other systems of ethical norms. In the final analysis it is to this norm alone, which is itself the prototype of perfect obedience to God the Father, that the moral conduct of Christians has to answer.

Regardless of how many Christian signs and symbols one places around something that is not the will of God as revealed by Jesus, it cannot be raised thereby to the status of the will of God as revealed by Jesus. There are just some activities that are not Christ-like ways of doing. A house of prostitution can be filled with statues, icons, incense, bells, piped-in Gregorian chant, a theological library and a chapel but that does not make prostitution an act in conformity with the teachings of Jesus Christ. Nor, would the presence of a Christian chaplain in the house change anything if he or she led worship services and performed all the other duties expected of a chaplain but never raised the subject of the utter inconsistency between the teachings of Jesus and the profession of prostitution. Indeed, justified Christian prostitution could endure for a thousand years and it would still not be in conformity with the teachings of Jesus. The *autos-da-fé*, public rites at which Jews and heretics were burned at the stake, lasted from 1288 to 1826 as an officially approved Church activity. The longevity of a Christian practice does not validate this practice as an ultimate norm for the Christian life. The ultimate norm of Christian life has to be Jesus, His words and deeds—and if He is not the standard against which everything and all must be finally measured by the Christian, who or what is? Plato? Aristotle? Hugh Hefner? Cicero? Thomas Aquinas? Reinhold Niebuhr? The President? Wall Street? NBC? FOX?

> The *autos-da-fé*, public rites at which Jews and heretics were burned at the stake, lasted from 1288 to 1826 as an officially approved Church activity. The longevity of a Christian practice does not validate this practice as an ultimate norm for the Christian life.

TOADIES TO THE FATHER OF LIES

The dilemma of the gross incompatibility between Christ's teaching of Nonviolent Love and the Christian practice of justifying homicide is acute regardless of where one looks on this planet. Mutant spiritual offspring are given birth in ever increasing numbers the longer this incompatibility endures. If Jesus' clear and unambiguous teaching in the area of homicidal violence and enmity can be rendered nugatory, then it is theological and pastoral child's play to alter any other teaching of Jesus. But again, what is to be done? Faced with the realities of lack of knowledge and fear in the minds and hearts of pastors, I do not know. The entity that is "The Father of Lies who also is a murderer from the beginning" seems to have a death grip on the organizational Church and its leadership in this area. The best and the brightest have become his toadies.

TRUSTFUL FIDELITY CAN ACHIEVE THE IMPOSSIBLE

One thing I do know is this: people cannot dialogue about, act on, or be creative with ideas they have never heard. Perhaps step one would be for bishops, ministers and priests to immerse themselves in the history, theology and spirituality of Gospel nonviolence and then to candidly present this truth to their congregations with two understandings: first, that "We have failed miserably at this in the past, we are failing miserably at it in the present but let us work together to find our way back to fidelity in the future"; and second, that "The evil of violence is so coiled around the heart of the Church that we in our lifetime may never find our way back but will have to die in the hope that God in His Mercy will honor the fact that we have at least been truthful and that as Church we have searched for a way to return to fidelity." Of course with Jesus, the God of the Impossible, there is always the possibility that our efforts in unwavering obedience to Christ-God will be used by God to create an Exodus event or Resurrection experience—a saving phenomenon of superabundant fruitfulness that is directly tied to trustful fidelity but which no human thought process could have ever foreseen. The infinitely improbable happens regularly when Christians trustfully pray and act in conformity with the teachings of Jesus. But, Christians cannot pray and act on a teaching of Jesus that bishops, ministers and priests will not let them genuinely hear and encounter.

> Of course with Jesus, the God of the Impossible, there is always the possibility that our efforts in unwavering obedience to Christ-God will be used by God to create an Exodus or Resurrection event—a saving event of superabundant fruitfulness that is directly tied to trustful fidelity but which no human thought process could have anticipated.

THE ORDAINED TACTICS—IGNORE, MOCK, TRIVIALIZE

It is a fundamental proposition of hardball politics, secular and ecclesial, that the first line of defense against an unwanted truth is to prevent it from becoming part of the community's conversation. Such was the case with women's suffrage, such was the case with racism, such was the case with feminism and such is the case today in the Churches with the Nonviolent Jesus and His teachings of Nonviolent Love of friends and enemies. At this hour the Nonviolent Jesus and His Nonviolent Way, when they are allowed to enter into the conversation at all, are portrayed in a mockingly ridiculous fashion, just as women voting was so portrayed 150 years ago. This dismissive strategy renders a serious consideration of the subject a self-evident waste of time in the minds of everyday Christians. In reality no microphone is given to an unwanted truth because those who control the microphone fear that this truth may carry implications that would demand some serious changes (*metanoia*) on their part.

Referring to the carnage of the First World War at the beginning of the twentieth century Gandhi said, "I know I am walking on thin ice, but European Christianity does not understand the Asiatic Jesus." I also know that I am walking on thin ice but in reference to the carnage of the entire twentieth century I would say that mainline Christianity does not understand the Jesus of the Gospel who teaches a Way of Nonviolent Love of friends and enemies because bishops, ministers and priests have not taught what they were ordained to teach, that is, what Jesus Christ taught. An Anglican Bishop once answered Gandhi's inquiries as to why he did not explicitly educate his flock about Jesus' nonviolence by saying, "The people are not ready for it." Gandhi responded, "Are you sure it is the people who are not ready?" Ready or not, somehow bishops, ministers and priests must be told that they must not continue to evade this teaching of Jesus. Somehow they must be brought to see in faith that Jesus is trustworthy when He teaches His disciples a Way of Nonviolent Love of friends and enemies. Somehow they must be brought to see that they need not fear teaching the truth that Jesus taught, but rather, they need fear teaching as Jesus' truth what is not Jesus' truth.

> Ready or not, somehow bishops, ministers and priests must be brought to see in faith that Jesus is trustworthy when He teaches His disciples a Way of Nonviolent Love of friends and enemies.

THE ENFEEBLED FRUITS OF DISHONEST SHEPHERDING

During the twentieth century, the century of Cain, Christians killed more people in war—including more fellow Christians—than in all other centuries combined. This is proof positive that bishops, ministers, and priests—by refusing to teach what Jesus taught on the phenomenon of violence—have not served well those who have been entrusted to them and who trusted them to teach the complete truth about Jesus and His Way. The twenty-first century is now upon us. Unless bishops, ministers and priests can be reached on this issue of Jesus and His Way of Nonviolent Love, then Christianity can look forward to more of the same quality of ordained leadership in the twenty-first century that it has received in the twentieth century—and with precisely the same enfeebled fruits emanating from this dishonest shepherding. The blood on the hands of Church leaders,

> The blood on the hands of Church leaders, indeed on the hands of all the followers of Christ, should be their own—not the blood of others.

indeed on the hands of all the followers of Christ, should be their own—not the blood of others.

THE MORAL MANTRA

WWJD, "What would Jesus do?" has almost become a moral mantra among contemporary Christians. If Christians are to be followers of Jesus as their Lord and hence be faithful to His new and unique commandment, "I give you a new commandment: Love one another. As I have loved you, so you also should love one another" (JN 13:33-34), then to ask "WWJD" when a moral decision has to be made is just elementary spiritual sanity. The *Catechism of the Catholic Church* in §1970 says, "The entire law of the Gospel is contained in the *new commandment* of Jesus, to love one another as he loved us," and in §2822 states categorically, that Jesus' *new commandment* "summarizes all the others and expresses His entire will." John Paul II in his Encyclical on Christian morality, *Veritatis Splendor* proclaims:

> Following Christ is thus the essential and primordial foundation of Christian morality...Jesus asks us to follow him and to imitate him along the path of love, a love which gives itself completely to the brethren out of love for God: "This is my commandment, that you love one another as I have loved you" (JN 15:12). The word "as" requires imitation of Jesus...Jesus' way of acting and his words, his deeds and his precepts constitute the moral rule of Christian life.

WWJD is simply a short hand fidelity formula to help Christians obey His New Commandment and to help them discern how Jesus would love in a particular moral moment based on how God Incarnate loved while He walked this earth. WWJD, of course, also means, "What wouldn't Jesus do?" and this is a question equal in spiritual gravity to "What would Jesus do?" However neither the Christian nor the Christian Community can genuinely apply WWJD, in either its positive or prohibitionary form, if those responsible for teaching what Jesus taught, do not teach what Jesus taught, e.g., in relationship to homicidal violence and enmity. When bishops, ministers, priests and Churches bracket-out of their proclamation of the Gospel of Jesus' explicit, unequivocal teaching on revenge, retaliation, enmity, and violence, then WWJD becomes an unusable standard for Christians in these areas—except perhaps as a mechanism of nurtured ignorance by which evil is given an aura of sanctity. Note the inordinate amount of ink and air time the issue of whether or not Jesus would drive an SUV recently received. Whether Jesus would kill His

> When bishops, ministers, priests and Churches bracket out of their proclamation of the Gospel Jesus' explicit, unequivocal teaching by word and by deed on revenge, retaliation, enmity, and violence, then WWJD becomes an unusable standard for Christians in these areas—except perhaps as a mechanism of nurtured ignorance by which evil is given an aura of sanctity.

enemies does not receive a drop of ink or a wavelength of air time—even when war is raging or on the horizon. Could it be that this is precisely what the secular and ecclesiastical elites of the various Churches desire?

Bishops, ministers and priests are ordained in order to nurture in their communities growth in the Holy Spirit of Jesus Christ by honestly and completely telling the entire story of Jesus to those placed in their care. Jesus' story and Spirit then become part of the story and spirit of their communities and part of the story and spirit of each Christian in his or her community. If a person does not wish to truthfully tell the story of Jesus and nurture His Holy Spirit then why be ordained? Why give a community or individual Christians less than the entire story of Jesus to make their own? Are the allurements of a secure income, status, power and social acceptance so magnetic that they can seduce a Christian leader into falsifying a teaching of Jesus in order to obtain them or retain them?

The *Catechism of the Catholic Church* (§782) teaches that the Church "is marked by characteristics that clearly distinguish it from all other religious, ethnic, political or cultural groups found in history: Its law is the *new commandment* 'to love as Christ loved us'" (JN 13:34). This is the 'new' law of the Holy Spirit" (RM 8:2; GA 5:25). What is going on when Church leaders build and nurture Christian communities independent of Jesus' teachings of Nonviolent Love of friends and enemies? Should such men and women even be considered Church leaders? Do not Church leaders in the post-apostolic age bear the responsibility of seeing to it that their respective Churches "remain in the teaching of the apostles" (AC 2:42)? Should men or women, who are not 100% committed to leading a Christian community by, with, in and through fidelity to Jesus' *new commandment* as it specifically relates to the rejection of homicidal violence and enmity, ever be allowed in positions of Church leadership? If Jesus is nonviolent and lives a Way of Nonviolent Love of friends and enemies then that love that is "as I have loved" is Nonviolent Love. If a pastor cannot grasp this—which is so clearly communicated in the Gospels and which is enshrined forever in the indisputable and binding apostolic tradition of the Church—isn't he or she a real and present spiritual danger to the community and its life in the Spirit?

> [T]he Church "is marked by characteristics that clearly distinguish it from all other religious, ethnic, political or cultural groups found in history: Its law is the new commandment 'to love as Christ loved us'. This is the 'new' law of the Holy Spirit".

Ruling Religious Elites Selectively Shroud the Story

The most renowned moral theologian in the Catholic Church of the twentieth century, Rev. Bernard Häring, speaks of "the stubborn resistance of the ruling religious class to Christ's message and witness of nonviolence." He goes on to assert, "It is not possible to speak of Christ's sacrifice while ignoring the role of nonviolence." Yet, I remember Bishop Thomas Gumbleton of Detroit reflecting that he went through twenty-one years of Catholic education without ever being taught about Gospel nonviolence. I can make the same attestation down to the exact number of years. I am certain there are bishops, ministers and priests whose numbers go into the hundreds of thousands in the last century alone who would have to say the same thing, if asked. Is it not time to prepare seminarians to tell the whole story of Jesus? Is it not time to let congregations hear the whole story? Is there any spiritually sound Christian option except to tell the whole story of the Nonviolent Jesus and His Way of Nonviolent Love of friends and enemies? Precisely, who or what is at work when the leaders of a Christian community hear whispered to their souls, "Don't proclaim that Jesus is nonviolent and that His Way includes the Nonviolent Love of friends and enemies"?

Twentieth-century Christianity is what inevitably results when the whole story of Jesus is not told by all the Churches all the time. As sure as Christ died and rose from the dead, the twenty-first century Church will be a blood-red extension of the self-deceived and obstinate twentieth century church unless the whole story that Jesus left to be told is told by those who have been commissioned to tell it. It takes deep faith in Jesus to speak the truth about Jesus. It takes a deeper faith in Jesus to speak the truth that Jesus spoke. "Unbelief is the true root of the Christian championship of violence."

Quo Vadis, Domine?

Quo Vadis Domine is the name of my favorite church in Rome. It lies just outside the gates of my favorite place in Rome, the Callistus Catacombs. It is a tiny church, easily missed by tourists looking for "the grandeur that was Rome." It commemorates that time in the life of Christianity when St. Peter decides to remain in Rome, rather than go to another city and avoid persecution and death. While the historical environment of that time (54–68 AD) is well known, the precise historical details of Peter's choice are not. However, the spiritual drama of Peter's decision has been illuminated and immortalized by the Nobel Prize Laureate, Henryk Sienkiewicz, in his 1905 masterpiece *Quo Vadis*.

In the climactic moment of this novel Peter is leaving Rome with his friend, Nazarius, at the height of Nero's persecution of Christians. He meets the risen Jesus on the outskirts of the city. However, Jesus is walking into, not out of, Rome:

> *The traveling staff fell out of Peter's hand. His eyes were fixed immovably ahead. His lips were open, and his face reflected unbelievable surprise, immense joy, and rapturous exaltation.*
>
> *Suddenly he threw himself on his knees, his arms lifted upward and stretched to the light, and his lips cried out: "Christ! O Christ!" His head beat against the dust as if he were kissing the feet of someone only he could see.*
>
> *Then there was silence.*
>
> *"Quo vadis, Domine?" his voice asked at last, punctured by his sobbing. "Where are you going, Lord?"*
>
> *Nazarius heard no answer. But a voice of ineffable sweetness and abundant sorrow rang in Peter's ears, "When you abandon my people," he heard, "I must go to Rome to be crucified once more."*
>
> *The apostle lay still and silent with his face pressed into the dust. Nazarius thought he had either died or fainted, but he rose at last, picked up his pilgrim's staff, and turned again toward the seven hills.*
>
> *"Quo vadis, domine?" the boy asked like an echo of the apostle's cry.*
>
> *"To Rome," Peter murmured.*

CONSISTENCY

Common sense in people demands a consistency between word and deed before they take seriously a proclamation that asks a sacrifice from them. Imagine if after having taught, "Love your enemies," for three years, Jesus, instead of saying to Peter, "Put up your sword," had said, "Peter, get the other ear!" would people say of Him, "He teaches with authority"(LK 4:32)? If on the cross instead of praying, "Father forgive them for they know not what they do" Jesus cried out, "Father, have no mercy on those who have done this to me," would His teaching of "Love your enemies" possess any credibility?

Jesus was aware His teachings on the Way to Eternal Life would forever sound hollow if left unenfleshed. He had to walk through the furnace of His own truth before He could expect others to live what He proclaimed as the will of God. Verbal witness alone was sterile. "If he does not believe in his own truth enough to live it, why should I?" would be a reflex reaction to Jesus, or to anyone else, proclaiming the Gospel by words alone. As the philosopher Friedrich Nietzsche framed it: "You will never get me to believe in a redeemer, until you act redeemed."

In *Quo Vadis*, Peter visits Christians who are soon to be martyred. A Roman soldier, Vinicius, in love with a Christian woman, clandestinely places himself among the Christians in order to locate her. Peter speaks:

> [I]t's not enough to love just one's own kind; God died a man's death on the cross, he spilled his blood for all mankind, and even the pagans are turning toward him now... And it's not enough to love only those who love and treat you well. Christ forgave his executioners. He removed all blame from the Jews who turned him over to Roman justice to be crucified and from the Roman soldiers who nailed him to the cross.... "Only love is more powerful than hatred," the teacher said simply. "Only love can clean the world of evil."

By the time Peter finishes Vinicius is perplexed and disoriented:

> [T]hese ideas were a completely new way of looking at the world and totally rearranged everything known before. He sensed that if he were to follow the teaching, he would, for example, have to make a burnt offering of everything that had made him; he would have to destroy his thinking, crush all his perceptions, excise every habit, custom and tradition, erase his whole acquired character and the driving force of his current nature—burn it all to ashes, consign it to the winds, and fill the void with an entirely

different soul and a life on a wholly different plane. A philosophy that taught love for Parthians, Syrians, Greeks, Egyptians, Gauls and Britons seemed like lunacy; love and forgiveness to an enemy and kindness in the place of vengeance were simply sheer madness...What he heard seemed totally divorced from reality as he understood it, and yet it made his reality so insignificant, it was hardly worth a passing thought.

SANCTITY

Everyone has heard the arguments for following Jesus. However, there is only one argument that will be listened to—the argument that herein dwells the quintessence of sanctity, herein lies salvation. It is Jesus and only Jesus who is the incarnation of absolute Holiness. In all creation there is not a clearer manifestation of Holiness than Jesus. Jesus is Holiness. Sanctity is freely laying down of one's life, moment-to-moment, in order to love the Father and all of His children as Jesus loves the Father and all of His children. It is by following Jesus, it is in loving one another as Jesus loves us (JN 15:12; 13:34), that a person fulfills "the entire law of the Gospel" (NEW CATECHISM, SEC. 1970), that a person walks in the Way of sanctity, in the Way of salvation.

> Sanctity is freely laying down of one's life, moment-to-moment, in order to love the Father and all of His children as Jesus loves the Father and all of His children.

HEROISM

However, the way of sanctity is a heroic way because every step on this way is a step of love. Not a step of love as Caesar defines love, nor as Aristotle defines love, nor as Hugh Hefner defines love. It is love as Jesus defines love. It is love that has a cross not a sword at its core and as its means. It is a love that in the words of Vinicius is, "simply sheer madness." Yet, it is a love that renders every other love "so insignificant, it [is] hardly worth a passing thought."

Fr. Zossima, Dostoevsky's primary symbol in *The Brothers Karamazov* for what it means to be a Christian, says that Christ-like love "in action is a harsh and dreadful thing compared with love in dreams." To voluntarily enter the dynamic of Christ-like love for others, friends and enemies, is heroism in the superlative. It is, as the song says, being "willing to go into hell for a heavenly cause"—and to go there with Christ-like love as one's solitary weapon. It is risking responding to hurt, hate, cruelty, shame, calumny, violence and injustice exclusively with that love made visible by Jesus. It is bearing the "unbearable burden" of the cross of nonviolent, self-sacrificial Christ-like love every minute of every day because Love Itself has asked that it be done for the salvation of the world. To

> To voluntarily enter the dynamic of Christ-like love for others, friends and enemies, is heroism in the superlative....It is risking responding to hurt, hate, cruelty, shame, calumny, violence and injustice exclusively with that love made visible by Jesus.

commit one's life to this cross-centered love in a world soaked in evil takes boldness and courage. To act on this choice is to unite with the Holy, to imitate God, to literally participate in the life of the Divine.

Christ-like love can be very costly, but expensive or not, it is the power of God given to the Church. It has no more need of social status, coercive power, connections in high places, prestige, badges of distinction, money, intrigue or prerogative than a rose has a need to give a sermon to attract people. Humanity naturally gravitates to Christ-like love because humanity was made by Christ-like love and made for Christ-like love. Yet, heroic love is not auto-salvation; it does not depend on its own strength to face the satanic, as a nation would rely on its armaments to vanquish its enemies. Heroic Christ-like sanctity and love rest secure in the faith that regardless of how dreadful life may seem to be as a whole, or in a particular moment, God is love, almighty and present. Whether called upon or not, He is encompassing each one and all as a prodigal Father embraces a beloved son or daughter. Therefore, regardless of projected fearful outcomes, one can venture to love as Jesus loves, to be holy as Christ is holy because Love is with us now and always and forever and ever.

> Christ-like love can be very costly, but expensive or not, it is the power of God given to the Church....Heroic Christ-like sanctity and love rest secure in the faith that regardless of how dreadful life may seem to be as a whole, or in a particular moment, God is love, almighty and present.

Let us return for an instant to *Quo Vadis*. It was now only minutes before the Christians were to be herded into the arena of horror. Sobs, silence and desperation alternately punctuated the air. An anguished widow pleaded to God, "Give my son back to me, O Lord." A Christian father repeated and repeated, "The hangmen raped my little daughters and Christ let it happen." For another soon to die Christian, "the hair lifted on his head in terror" when he thought, "What if the Caesar of Rome was mightier than Jesus of Nazareth?" Peter quietly sat praying among the tormented faithful. Then he began speaking, so low at the outset that hardly anyone heard him:

> *I tell you in Christ's name you've nothing to fear! Life waits for you, not death. Joy without end, not torments. Song waits, not tears and moaning...."I tell you as God's apostle, widow, that your son won't die but will be born in glory to a new life, and you will be together. I tell you, father, whose innocent daughters they've soiled, they'll be as unblemished as the lilies of Hebron when you meet again. I say in Christ's name to all you mothers who'll be torn away from your orphaned children, all you who'll lose your fathers, all who cry for pity, all who'll witness the death of those they love, all who are sick at heart, unfortunate and fearful, and I say again to you who must die: You will wake as if from a dream into eternal light, and the Son of God will shine in your night."*

SECULARIZATION

Of all the dangers to the integrity of the Petrine ministry or the Episcopal ministry, the greatest is secularization (Latin: saecularis—worldly, temporal, as opposed to eternal). **By secularization is meant the adoption by the Church, its leadership and/or its laity, of the values, attitudes, beliefs, powers, needs and means of a secular society which values, attitudes, beliefs, powers, needs and means are hostile to or obfuscating of that Christ-like love that is the power of God given to the Church to lead people to Eternal Life.**

The secularization of the Church, its leadership and laity, is the axial betrayal that present-day leadership must confront and confess if the Church is to be renewed and revitalized. Secularization is a process that is not decades old, but rather centuries. It is no longer creeping through the Church, it is galloping. It also has become, due to literacy and mass media, more and more noticeable and scandalizing to more and more people—Christian and non-Christian.

The pretense can no longer be sustained that the "baptism" of secular methods of operation has served the Church well or even adequately. Can anyone look candidly at the Twentieth Century Church and maintain that the pastoral leadership of that Church is equal to the attacks that evil mounted against Christianity and humanity during the last hundred years? In 1916, as the Christian nations of Europe were savaging each other and justifying it as an acceptable and even noble pursuit for the followers of Jesus, Mahatma Gandhi remonstrated, "European Christianity does not understand the Asiatic Jesus."

> In 1916, as the Christian nations of Europe were savaging each other and justifying it as an acceptable and even noble pursuit... Gandhi remonstrated, "European Christianity does not understand the Asiatic Jesus."

The diabolical monstrosity between 1914 and 1918 that Church leaders in each nation ratified as conforming to the will of God as revealed by Jesus metastasizes into the religiously camouflaged satanic abomination of 1939 to 1945. Now that this Century of Cain is over, it is known, for example, that Christians killed more people in war in the Twentieth Century than they have in all the centuries since the time of Jesus. Christians also have destroyed each other in unprecedented numbers during the last century. Abortion rates among Christians in Europe and North America are sky high. A person, who claims that Jesus Christ is his favorite philosopher and who is simultaneously the foremost executioner of prisoners in his country, is elected President by a primarily Christian electorate. How much more evidence is needed to

> Now that this Century of Cain is over, it is know, fo example, that Christians killed more people in war in the Twentieth Century than they have in all the centuries since the time of Jesus.

verify that the long-term secularizing of the Church, beneath the veneer of personal or public piety, has been a spiritual and pastoral calamity?

Unless the past has been perfect, the future should be different from the past. Archbishop Charles Chaput writes, "Much of the western world may still appear to be Christian, but it is not—at least not in any real sense of the word 'Christian.'" No reasonable observer of the scene would disagree. But, who is responsible for this situation? It would be hoped that no Christian would become hostile or resentful toward those who raise the specter of entrenched secularism lurking beneath so much of what the Church's leadership and laity has done. Evasion is preposterous when salvation is at stake. Hebrew and Christian Scriptures are in accord: a sin left unnamed regenerates itself incessantly and with ever greater intensity. Denial only assures a future that mirrors the past. The "Ninth Hour" is upon the leadership of the Church. The cock crows. Jesus Christ is looking "straight at" (LK 22:61) those He has chosen (MK 3:13,14), those who have denied Him—for to deny His Way is to deny Him. His eyes are asking: "Are you, in all seriousness, ready to enter once again into the Way of the Nonviolent Messiah and bring those I have placed in your care with you?"

SURVIVAL

The taproot of the spiritually toxic problem of secularization is veiled but not entirely concealed. Worldly leaders are concerned with the survival of their societies or institutions. Secular leaders are denounced or deposed if they fail in promoting the survival of their group and its interest. With a few moments of thoughtfulness it can be perceived how fundamental the issue is that is created when the Church or its leadership is secularized.

If there is one thing the Church never has to worry about, it is the survival of the Church. Survival, which is a primary concern in the realm of the secular, is a non-concern in the realm of the Church. The Church survives, not by superb administration, financial acuity, clever PR gimmicks, coercion, violence, catering to elites, secrecy, anathemas nor by anything else human beings do to assure the survival of worldly institutions. The Church survives for one reason only—Christ guarantees its survival. Jesus Christ has never left the Church. He still lives in the Church and exercises His headship. There is never any need for anyone, anywhere or at anytime to be concerned about the Church's survival. In fact, a billion Christians fighting for the survival of the Church, would be an ignominious spiritual failure under the guise of a brilliant worldly success. It would be unbelief masquerading as heroic fidelity.

"My business is fidelity. God's business is success," explains Mother Theresa. This truth has to be deep in the heart of Jesus in Gethsemane, as well as, deep in the heart of those Christians that Peter speaks to on their way to the Circus Maximus. Likewise, it must reside deep in the heart of anyone who wishes to be a Christian—and most especially a Christian leader. Note, the saying is not, "My business is success, God's business is fidelity." The Church requires not one "pragmatic" sin, not one inch of departure from the way of Jesus, not one act that is not an act of Christ-like love in order to complete the mission Jesus committed to Her. The power the Church has been given to fulfill Her mission is the power of God, and that Jesus tells us is the power of love as He makes it visible

> "My business is fidelity. God's business is success," explains Mother Theresa...This truth must reside deep in the heart of anyone who wishes to be a Christian—and most especially a Christian leader...The power the Church has been given to fulfill Her mission is the power of God, and that Jesus tells us is the power of love...

in time and space. "One act of pure love," teaches St. John of the Cross, "is more valuable to the Church than all other acts combined." St. Paul would concur (1 COR 13). If a person wants access to a power superior to this, or to a power antagonistic to this then he or she should not be a Christian, let alone a Christian leader. If a Christian has succumbed to the temptation to employ the powers of the kingdoms of the world (LK 4:5-7; MT 4:8,9) then the "Ninth Hour" is upon him or her. If he or she will only have the courage of St. Peter and look into the Eyes that are looking "straight at" him or her, the Truth of the Nonviolent Jesus will be made clear.

THE NONVIOLENT FOLLOWER OF A NONVIOLENT LEADER

For a sincere follower of Jesus, the question always is "*Quo vadis, Domine?*"; recognizing full well that wherever Jesus is going, He is going there without the weapons of the kingdoms of the world: no swords, no guns, no halberds, no hate, no enmity. Unlike the founders of other religions, He is always armed solely with love, truth and absolute trust in the unfailing protection of the Father almighty. Only those who are interested in so following Jesus and hence in undertaking the anonymous martyrdom of a billion micro-acts of nonviolent Christ-like love toward both friends and enemies should have any interest in becoming Christians or Christian leaders. Such a commitment demands dying daily to the secularized self-understanding that has been nurtured and religiously legitimized over decades of life. However, this does not mean that a Christian is condemned to chronically live on the edge of sadness because he or she, like Jesus, has renounced the dominative power, gratuities and tacky glory that the kingdoms of the world offer. On the contrary this sacrifice of the secularly nurtured self on the nonviolent cross is made with magnanimity because it is required in order to love Christically—which, as noted earlier, is the *sine qua non* for proclaiming the Gospel with authority. However, proclaiming the Gospel with authority is how a follower of Jesus fulfills his or her most cherished goal, which is to co-operate with Him whose supreme desire is to ensure that all who must die "will wake as from a dream into eternal light, and the Son of God shine in their night" (JN 12:31; 1 TM 2:4; TI 2:11).

> However, proclaiming the Gospel with authority is how a follower of Jesus fulfills his or her most cherished goal, which is to co-operate with Him whose supreme desire is to insure that all who must die "will wake as from a dream into eternal light, and the Son of God shine in their night."

What a love! What a life! What a grace to be chosen for such a vocation!

Violent Monotheism: Truth or Falsehood

Judaism, Christianity, and Islam are monotheistic religions that teach a number of moral absolutes, rooted in an understanding of the nature and will of God, as revealed by their founders—Moses, Jesus, Mohammed. Monotheism organically calls forth a "whole heart, whole soul, whole mind, whole strength" commitment from the creature once the nature and will of the Creator is known.

In revelatory monotheism—regardless of whether God's revelation or Word is spoken through Jesus, Moses, Mohammed, Joseph Smith, Zoroaster, or through a designed order initiated in the first nanosecond of the Big Bang—it is of supreme importance to be sure that the Word attributed to God is, in reality, the Word of the Creator of the heavens and the earth. If these founders of faiths discern this Word incorrectly, then their followers logically end up making a "whole heart, whole soul, whole mind, whole strength" commitment to falsehood and unreality and therefore to idolatry, perhaps even to evil. Being wrong about this primal issue results in a person living his or her one and only life according to the spiritual delusions of another human being.

In Mark Twain's literary classic, *Huckleberry Finn,* Huck spends a great deal of time traveling down the Mississippi River with a black slave named Jim. They come to know each other quite well. Indeed, the quality of Jim's character, his kindness and generosity, impress and somewhat confuse Huck, since Jim is a slave. At one moment in their travels, Huck encounters a group of white men hunting escaped slaves, of whom Jim is one. Since childhood, his culture has indelibly hammered into Huck's mind and onto his conscience that any white person who protects a runaway slave will be sent to hell by God. What is Huck to do? He has come to know Jim as a human being rather than as a slave. However, he also has been taught what God's Will is, and that Huck Finn will be consigned to hell if he does not obey it. It is a terrible thing to fall for a word of God that is not the true word of God.

The God of Jesus, the God Jesus reveals, the one and only true God, is not a God who leads people in victories of homicidal violence over historical enemies*[SEE P3.2]. The God that Moses and that Mohammed reveal is a God who does do this. Moses and

Mohammed may not agree on all the details concerning this revelation of God, the when and where and for whom and against whom their God will sanction violence, but they generally agree on the fundamental notion, that the true God does sanction homicidal violence. So who has the correct vision of what kind of God God is and what God expects of people, Jesus or Moses and Mohammed?

Cannot Serve Two Masters

It is a matter of logic: Either Jesus, or Mohammed and Moses are proclaiming a false revelation about God on an issue of primal importance. Either Jesus, or Mohammed and Moses are teaching as the will of God something that is not the will of God. The clarity of the revelations of each of the three is beyond dispute. Equally beyond dispute is the fact that the revelations of Moses and Mohammed are contrary to the revelation of Jesus on this matter.

The one says that there is nothing of God or God's will or God's way in homicidal violence; the other two say that homicidal violence can be consistent with God, His will, and His way. One says homicidal violence is objectively evil. The others say it can be objectively good. Whose image of God is consistent with the Reality? Whose is erroneous on a grand scale? Whose "revelation" is, in fact, revelation? Whose is just an illusionary, humanly-generated idea of the Deity?

In a polytheistic religion, there is no incongruity in asserting that one god is violent and permits, even wills, homicidal violence by people against people under certain conditions, e.g., to pursue pleasure or justice, and that another god is nonviolent and wills nonviolence unto death. In polytheism, gods might support or oppose incest, just as gods might support or oppose violence.

However, to assert in monotheism that God is both violent and nonviolent is to declare that God is violent—that is the necessary logical conclusion. It is analogous to an individual saying "I am nonviolent but..." The "but" is the place where violence is chosen and is justified. Nonviolence means there is no "but." Divine Nonviolence means that in the nature, will, and way of God there is no "but." Hence, for any

---

*"All the Gospels agree that Jesus refused armed defense. Whether he said what Matthew quoted is really irrelevant ('Put up your sword. He who lives by the sword perishes by the sword' (MT 26:52). It is a nice quotation, but we do not need it to establish that Jesus was totally opposed to the use of violence for any purpose and therefore I see no necessity to argue this uncontested truth." —Rev. John L. McKenzie, former president of The Society of Biblical Literature and Exegesis, former president of the Catholic Biblical Association. Taken from *The Civilization of Christianity*, pages 137-138.

morality based on serving God by doing His will on earth as it is done in heaven, it makes all the difference in heaven and on earth whether there is a "but" in the reality and will of the Holy One. In monotheism there cannot be two ultimate moral Masters, nor can a person serve two contradictory Divine truths. In the moment of choice he or she must follow one and abandon the other—a person cannot serve both a Nonviolent God and a violent God.

> However, to assert in monotheism that God is both violent and nonviolent is to declare that God is violent. It is analogous to the person who says, "I am nonviolent but..." The "but" is the place where violence is chosen and is justified. Nonviolence means there is no "but."

THE MARTYR

The crowning service a person can perform for his or her Divine Master is to be a martyr in obedience to his or her Master's will. The English word "martyr" is derived etymologically from the Greek word *"martys"* which means witness. A martyr, then, is a witness even unto his or her own death to the true God and His Will. A person can be a martyr on behalf of a God of violence or on behalf of a God of nonviolence. But one cannot serve as a witness for both. To die while killing another human being, believing it to be God's Will, is martyrdom in submission to a certain kind of God. To die while refusing to kill another because homicide is contrary to the Will of God is also martyrdom, but martyrdom in obedience to another kind of God.

By logical necessity, one of these forms of martyrdom is objectively not martyrdom at all, but is instead, a waste of life on behalf of an idolatrous illusion. It is pseudo-martyrdom, subjective good intentions in the service of objective untruth and the unholy. The other of these forms of martyrdom is objectively truth and sanctity incarnate. Martyrdom is the triumph of life over death. Pseudo-martyrdom is the triumph of death over life. Which is one and which is the other depends on the kind of God God in fact is.

Something of towering temporal and eternal magnitude is at stake here. Those who try to conceal this issue, or muddle it, or avoid it, or denigrate its significance perform no service for God or for humanity. Moreover, Moses and Mohammed and Jesus are straight-forward in their respective revelations concerning God and His Will *vis-à-vis* violence. They are crystalline—and they radically disagree. The theological, spiritual, moral, and practical importance of this incongruity cannot be overstressed, because God is the heart of the matter regardless of what the matter is. An erroneous apprehension of His Reality and Will would have

> Something of towering temporal and eternal magnitude is at stake here. Those who try to conceal this issue...perform no service for God or for humanity... An erroneous apprehension of His Reality and Will would have consequences so catastrophic that they would reverberate through the galaxies to the threshold of eternity—and possibly beyond.

consequences so catastrophic that they would reverberate through the galaxies to the threshold of eternity—and possibly beyond.

THE GOSPEL

The Gospel proclaims that Jesus is not only a great teacher, the Prophet, the Messiah and the Suffering Servant, but is also the Lord, the Alpha and the Omega, the pre-existent Word through whom all things were made, the definitive revelation of God, the self-revelation of God, the incarnation of God, God! It is also Gospel truth that in all of Jesus' suffering, as in all of His life and ministry, He refuses to defend himself or others with violence, let alone use violence to punish others, pursue His cause, promote His self-interest, or seek retribution.

> It is also Gospel truth that in all of Jesus' suffering, as in all of his life and ministry, He refuses to defend himself or others with violence let alone use homicidal violence to punish others, pursue his cause, promote his self-interest or to seek retribution.

The previously cited eminent biblical scholar, Rev. John L. McKenzie, states: "No reader of the New Testament, simple or sophisticated, can retain any doubt of Jesus' position toward violence directed to persons, individual or collective, organized or free enterprise: he rejected it totally." Why is Jesus nonviolent? The answer to this axial question of Christic morality is precisely stated in the words of the most renowned Catholic moral theologian of the twentieth century, Rev. Bernard Häring: "Jesus is nonviolent because God is nonviolent." God acts as God is: "I and the Father are one" (JN 10:30); "Whoever has seen Me has seen the Father" (JN 14:9); "Christ Jesus is the image of the invisible God" (COL 1:15; 2 COR 4:4).

I am certain that Moses and Mohammed, because of their zeal for the Holy One and His Will, would have taught that God is nonviolent and therefore His ways are ways of nonviolence, if they had seen God and His Will to be nonviolent. But they did not! Did they not see it because it is not true, or did they not see it for some other reason? This is perhaps the most critical spiritual question that humanity and all forms of monotheism must resolve. Either Jesus' revelation is drop-dead wrong, or Moses and Mohammed are purveyors of gross error regarding God and His Will. Who is right? Who is wrong?

WHEN

If God is the kind of God who approves the use of homicidal violence against bad people, or even against good people, if the cause is thought good enough (collateral damage, human sacrifice, etc.)—if God, in other words, is a violent God—then a death for a death, an eye for an eye, a tooth for a tooth, collateral damage for collateral damage, is morally possible, and may even be required. If one believes that God endorses homicidal violence, then the only question left for violent monotheism is when He endorses it. Theologies, sophisticated and simple-minded, complementary and contradictory, that designate the when, abound.

But if God is nonviolent, then returning death for death, collateral damage for collateral damage, is morally impossible. If God never smiles on human slaughter, if God never smites the enemy, if true monotheism is nonviolent monotheism, then the issue of when never arises, and theologies of when need not be written—as they were never written during the first three hundred and fifty years of Christianity. If God is as Jesus reveals and reflects Him—nonviolent, loving and caring for all—then homicidal violence is forbidden, regardless of whether or not it is defined by human beings as legal or illegal, romantic or sordid, just or unjust, legitimate or illegitimate, necessary or unnecessary, revolutionary or establishmentarian. If God is nonviolent, then homicidal violence is as absent as incest from the moral will of the Divinity, since God, His Will, and His Way are absolutely one, absolutely simple, absolutely without division.

> If God is nonviolent, then homicidal violence is as absent as incest from the moral will of the Divinity, since God, His Will and His Way are absolutely one, absolutely simple, absolutely without division.

THE ENEMY

Does the omniscient and omnipotent God place anyone on this planet with the right to kill another person? Can the enemy of a state, tribe, religion, economic system or person objectively be the enemy of God? Can it ever be the objective will of God to kill the enemy of a state, tribe, religion, economic system or person? For the kind of God who is violent and therefore has a moral will which contains the possibility of justified violence, the answer is "Yes." For the kind of God revealed by the Nonviolent Jesus, for the Nonviolent God, who communicates by word and deed a love of enemies even unto one's own death, the answer is "No." In such a Divinity the enemy of a state, religion, etc., is never the enemy of God but is always a daughter or son of Abba—a daughter or son who is to be loved as "God made flesh" reveals that she or he should be loved—now and always.

In the world of violent monotheism, regardless of the institutional or theological architecture it assumes, it is inevitable that one person's dream will be another person's nightmare, that one person's collateral damage will be another person's beloved daughter or son or spouse or parent or friend, that one person's freedom fighter will be another person's terrorist, that one person's military hero will be another person's mass murderer, that one person's God will be another person's fiend. In the world of nonviolent monotheism such humanly contrived divisions and linguistic delineations are literally non-realities and non-thoughts. Because the Nonviolent

> In the world of violent monotheism...it is inevitable that one person's dream will be another person's nightmare, that one person's collateral damage will be another person's beloved daughter or son or spouse or parent or friend, that one person's freedom fighter will be another person's terrorist, that one person's military hero will be another person's mass murderer, that one person's God will be another person's fiend.

God made visible in Jesus and with whom Jesus is one (JN 10:30; JN 14:9), i.e., Abba, "makes His sun rise on the bad and the good, and causes His rain to fall on the just and the unjust" (MT 5:45), He can never be experienced as any human being's Nightmare. Therefore, He can never be conscripted to justify the creation of nightmares for any of His sons and daughters.

WORSHIP

Do all the monotheistic religions worship the true God? Most Jews and Muslims believe that the worship of Jesus as God is objectively a serious religious error and is displeasing to God. To worship Jesus as the incarnate God is to commit the cardinal theological sin of Judaism—foreign worship, and of Islam—idolatry. "It is the formal recognition and worship as God of an entity that is in fact not God," as Rabbi David Berger, states.

Now, suppose a monotheist believes that God approves of, or even demands, that His creatures practice incest—what would follow from this for a Jew, Muslim, or Christian? If a Jew, Muslim, or Christian were to pray with him, would they be praying with someone who believes in the same God that they do? Could a Jew, Muslim, or Christian pray with this man without denying his or her own truth, faith, and God? Could a Jew, Muslim, or Christian bow down and worship a God who was the kind of God who justifies or requires incest? Would they be worshiping as God an entity that in fact was not God? Human beings, created in the image and likeness of God, strive to imitate the Divinity they worship—for in the imitation of the Holy One lies the Way of holiness. Is incest on this Way? Is violence on this Way? Worship of the unholy is idolatry. Imitation of the unholy is evil.

Concerning God, is the only truth necessary to avoid idolatrous worship acceptance that God is One—i.e., that there is only one God? Concerning the worship of God, is it acceptable to worship in any spirit—provided only that it is the One God who is being worshipped? Jesus gives Christians concrete direction here. While not condemning all past efforts of human beings to fulfill their innate desire to worship God, He states: "But the hour will come—in fact it is here already—when true worshippers will worship the Father in spirit and truth; that is the kind of worshipper the Father wants. God is spirit, and those who worship must worship in spirit and truth" (JN 4:23,24). The Spirit Jesus is speaking of here is His Spirit, the Spirit of God, the Spirit of the Holy, the Holy Spirit, the Spirit with whom He is consubstantial.

> While not condemning all past efforts of human beings to fulfill their innate desire to worship God, He states: "But the hour will come—in fact it is here already—when true worshippers will worship the Father in spirit and truth; that is the kind of worshipper the Father wants. God is spirit, and those who worship must worship in spirit and truth" (JN 4:23,24).

After Jesus, is not authentic worship for the Christian worship in the Nonviolent Spirit and the Nonviolent Truth of the Nonviolent Jesus? After Jesus, can a Christian pray:

> *Destructive Daughter of Babel*
> *A blessing on the man who treats you*
> *As you have treated us,*
> *A blessing on him who takes and dashes*
> *Your babies against the rock!*
>
> Psalm 137:8,9

or after Jesus, can a Christian:

> *...slay the idolaters, wherever he finds them.*
> *Arrest them, besiege them, and*
> *lie in ambush everywhere for them.*
>
> Koran, Sura ix:5

After Jesus, can a Christian pray against enemies? After Jesus, can a Christian pray for victories of homicidal violence over historical enemies? After Jesus, can Christians pray for justice implemented by homicidal violence? After Jesus, can a Christian pray for revenge? After Jesus, can a Christian pray for an eye for an eye, for collateral damage for collateral damage? After Jesus, are such prayers by Christians a burlesque of prayer? For a believer in or for a follower of Jesus, such prayers are *non sequiturs*—are they not?

OTHER DIVINE EXPECTATIONS

To avoid any confusion of mind, it should be candidly stated that God expects more of people than engaging in violence or not engaging in violence. However, other expectations of God, based on the kind of God God is and His revelation, are beyond the scope of this essay, which is concerned solely and specifically with whether monotheism is violent or nonviolent. Judaism, Christianity and/or Islam might see mercy as the supreme attribute of the Deity. This would mean that God would expect that people created in His image and likeness would make a supreme effort to be merciful. Whether God is violent or nonviolent would be considered in relation to the extent that this attribute reveals (or denies) the true nature of Divine Mercy. Can Divine Mercy ever come from the barrel of a gun or can it never come from the barrel of a gun? Can or cannot the God of Mercy ever be glorified by homicidal violence? The fundamental Divine expectation here is mercy, but in order for it to be a moral good it must be ordered to the Nature and Will of the one true God—whatever He may be, violent or nonviolent. Mercy-killing, whether the killing is directed toward self or others, could be morally acceptable if God is a violent God. If he is not, mercy-killing is always forbidden.

INSTITUTIONAL CHRISTIANITY

Up to this moment, institutional Christianity in its Catholic, Orthodox, Protestant or Evangelical manifestations has been mentioned very little. The reason is that where homicidal violence is concerned, as the non-Christian world well knows, Christianity's history is one of complacent betrayal, its theologies are dismal tracts of doublespeak and its leaders have been and continue to be obdurately obscurantist. It is disquieting for a Christian author to have to acknowledge that institutional Christianity is the incarnational denial of its Founder's teaching about God, God's Will and God's Way on such a momentous phenomenon as homicidal violence.

Since the fourth century, Christian leadership has turned the Nonviolent Jesus and His teachings upside down, in order that the God of institutional Christianity could take His place alongside the other warrior Gods of monotheism, who approve, require, permit, and sometimes even assist their faithful in homicidal victories. Christian rulers—secular and ecclesial—accomplished this by the creation of the Christian Just War Theory.

More generally, the method for standing the Nonviolent God, made visible in Jesus, on His head can be called the Christian Just Homicidal Violence Theory when it is expanded to include not simply the radical un-Christ-like activities of war, but also the equally radical un-Christ-like activities of capital punishment, or other homicidal acts committed in the name of personal self-interest and self-defense, such as violent revolution and abortion. Thus, over the last 1700 years, almost every species of violence has been religiously legitimized in the name of the God of institutional Christianity. This theology of God-based, justified violence has permitted the institutional Churches of Christianity to obtain by violence, and to maintain by violence, vast amounts of wealth, in order to worship their God and serve His interests—and possibly, the interest others, including their own.

Today, and for the past seventeen centuries, institutional Christianity operationally has offered, and continues to offer, to humanity a God who ratifies what Jesus unambiguously rejected—homicidal violence. It dares to teach what Jesus never taught by word or deed, Justified Homicidal Violence Theories, and it teaches them even in the face of the fact that Jesus explicitly commissioned His Church "to teach them to obey all that I have commanded you" (MT 28:20).

Over these seventeen centuries, Christianity has more than matched Judaism and Islam in holy homicides, in so-called justified homicide, in "God-is-with-us" religious rhetoric on behalf of the home team's homicide. Whether the God that institutional Christianity claims to be following is the God that it is following when it operates out of the ethos, ethic, theology, spirituality, energy, and spirit of violent monotheism is a non-question in Catholic, Orthodox, Protestant, and Evangelical Churches. Violent monotheism is simply the taken-for-granted truth, the unexamined conclusive presumption of these institutions. Perhaps the manner of life adopted and invested in by Rome, Constantinople, Canterbury, Geneva, and all subdivisions and affiliates thereof does not permit them to ask those questions that would reveal the discordance between their violent monotheism and Jesus' nonviolent monotheism.

> Over these seventeen centuries, Christianity has more than matched Judaism and Islam in holy homicides, in so-called justified homicide, in "God-is-with-us" religious rhetoric on behalf of the home team's homicide.

DISTRUSTING JESUS

So, today, structures built and sustained by violent monotheism are all that humanity possesses as the features and fruits of institutional monotheism. The God of the Nonviolent Jesus, the God who is the Nonviolent Jesus has no structure for human association built and sustained according to His Nonviolent Design. Nonviolent monotheism remains unincarnated in the mainline and evangelical churches of Christianity—even the struggle to incarnate it is chronically minimalist.

It is as if these institutions want the person of Jesus, but want Him without His revolutionary truth concerning the kind of God God is and what God expects. It is as if they desire Jesus, but without His God because, like Jews and Muslims, these ecclesiastical institutions do not believe Jesus knows what He is talking about on the matter of the relationship of Divinity to violence. Christian institutions, their leaders and members, simply do not trust that Jesus knows God's Plan for conquering the spirit of Cain that roams through time, relentlessly seeking people and groups of people to possess and souls to devour.

How Jesus can be God, yet not know God's Plan; or how the teaching of the Source of Reality can be considered unrealistic or ineffective, I shall leave for others to explicate. But since Christians and Christian leaders think Jesus' teachings on the rejection of

> But since Christians and Christian leaders think Jesus' teachings on the rejection of violence are fatuous, fanciful, utopian, idealist, silly, impractical, and an embarrassment, this effectively guarantees that Christian leaders and their followers will never attempt to implement them.

violence are fatuous, fanciful, utopian, idealist, silly, impractical, and an embarrassment, this effectively guarantees that Christian leaders and their followers will never attempt to implement them. This in turn assures that structures built on and sustained by nonviolent monotheism will never arise and give witness to the power and wisdom of the invisible God of whom the Nonviolent Jesus Christ is the visible image (COL 1:15).

HOPPING CHRISTIANS

A primal truth and a foundational falsehood are in direct and irreconcilable conflict here. Each seeks from humanity that level of allegiance due to God alone. Maybe it is time for people of all religions and, most especially, for the religious aristocracy in each religious institution, to take to heart that moment on Mt. Carmel (1 KG 18:18FF) when Elijah gathers the Israelites and cries out to them: "How long do you mean to hop, first on one leg and then on the other? If Yahweh is God follow him; if Baal, follow him."

Christians, and most especially Christian leaders, you must become spiritually serious. If you believe that Jesus is wrong about God and His Way, do not follow Him—follow Moses or Mohammed or some other person or philosophy that teaches a violent monotheism. But if you believe that Jesus is correct about what kind of God God is and what He expects of people, then follow Him without apology and with zeal.

> If you believe that Jesus is wrong about God and His Way, do not follow Him—follow Moses or Mohammed or some other person or philosophy that teaches a violent monotheism. But if you believe that Jesus is correct about what kind of God God is and what He expects of people, then follow Him without apology and with zeal.

Be adults with *bona fide* integrity! If the Nonviolent Jesus is mistaken about the nature of God and the will of God, then He is self-evidently not who the Gospel says He is: the Christ, the Lord, the Word, etc. If, however, He is accurate in His revelation about the nature and will of God, then embrace Him as your Lord, Savior, and Teacher, and unreservedly affirm His Way of Nonviolent Love of friends and enemies as the will of the All Holy One, Abba. For the sake of humanity, and for the sake of your own integrity, stop hopping between truth and falsehood.

"X" OR NOT "X"

Nonviolent monotheism or violent monotheism: Which is the truth about God? Which is the falsehood about God? Between two meaningful propositions, "X" and not "X," there is no middle ground. If one is true, the other is false. To say this should not offend a rational person who believes there is only one God, regardless of his or her denominational association. Elijah does not say and could never say, "If you cannot believe in Yahweh and follow him, at least believe in Baal and follow him."

In the end, there is no ecumenically delicate way to finesse this stark choice between violent and nonviolent monotheism, as there is no ecumenically dainty way to water down the radical, inherent disaccord in dogma between Christianity, which proclaims Jesus is God, and Judaism and Islam which say that Jesus is not God. The plain fact is that while Christianity teaches that Jesus is to be worshipped, Judaism and Islam say that worship of him is idolatry. Should Christians deny the divinity of Jesus and cease worshipping Him in order not to offend the religious sensibilities of Jews and Muslims? Should Christians expect Jews and Muslims to proclaim that Jesus is God and worship Him in order to humor their religious sensitivities?

Or, should Jews and Muslims and Christians simply agree to teach that Moses and Mohammed are also God as Jesus is God? Of course not!

The foundation document of Christianity, the New Testament, clearly presents Jesus as Lord, *Logos*, God from all eternity, through whom all things were made. The foundation documents of Judaism and Islam, the Hebrew Scriptures and the Koran, do not present Moses or Mohammed as God. So also, these foundation documents do not present Moses and Mohammed as having the same understanding of God and God's will in relation to violence and enmity as does Jesus. Someone is right and someone is wrong as to whether the worship of Jesus is idolatry. Likewise, someone is right and someone is wrong as to whether God, His Will and His Way are nonviolent.

To those who wish to be excessively politically correct in matters religious, it must be pointed out that chronic evasion of the hard questions of religious consciousness is a solemn offense against truth, reason, integrity, meaning, and God. As the Dalai Lama notes in his *Ethics for the New Millennium*, "[A]s we advance along the path of one tradition or another, we are compelled at some point to acknowledge fundamental differences."

The central issue being raised in this essay is not, I repeat NOT, institutional affiliation. The issue is truth—Divine truth and truth about the Divine; true worship and worship of the true God. It is quite possible for a Jew and Muslim to believe in and follow a Nonviolent God, although to do so they would have to part company with explicit teachings of Moses or Mohammed. Likewise, it is possible for a Christian to believe in and follow a violent warrior God. However, to do so he or she would have to part company with the explicit and consistent teachings of Jesus.

An individual's particular religious affiliation is not the problem here. What kind of God God is, and what God expects of human beings with regard to violence is the sole concern, and the soul's concern: "X" or not "X".

Serve the Truth.

He Does Not Break the Bruised Reed: Capital Punishment and Christian Mercilessness

*A man looks pleadingly at you
with a last appeal in his eyes,
and you kill him.*

"It is God, who is 'rich in mercy,' whom Jesus Christ has revealed to us as Father." With these words Pope John Paul II begins what I believe to be the most eternally significant event of his pontificate, namely, the publication of the Encyclical, *Dives in Misericordia*, "Rich in Mercy." Toward the end of this encyclical the Successor of Peter proclaims that "mercy [is] the most stupendous attribute of the Creator and the Redeemer." Hence, the true God, as opposed to idols conjured up in the human psyche, is a God of Holy, Infinite and Everlasting mercy. This is good, good, good news for every human being. In fact, it is the best news any human being could hope for or imagine.

WALDORF ASTORIA

Mercy, of course, need only be given where mercy is needed. Someone consuming a $135.00 lunch at the Waldorf Astoria is in no need of the mercy of food, although he or she may be in need of some other corporal manifestation of Divine Mercy. It is the Lazarus who dies every nine seconds from starvation in this world, the undernourished child whose brain is being irrevocably damaged, and the elderly person reduced to eating dog food who are in need of mercy made visible in bread. Likewise the only people who require the mercy of forgiveness are those who need forgiveness, that is, those who have intentionally harmed us. If someone gives us a two-week, all-expenses paid vacation we do not say, "I forgive you." Either we mercifully forgive those who have hurt us or we do not forgive at all. "It is precisely because sin exists in the world," writes John Paul II, "that God, who is love (1 JN 4:8), cannot reveal Himself otherwise than as mercy" (EMPHASIS IN THE ORIGINAL). Amidst all the Christian elocutions flowing from pulpit, radio, television and audio/video tape, amidst all the high and low Christian theologizing issuing from books, journals, newspapers and the internet, it is possible for the straightforward commands of Jesus to get lost. Jesus' commission to His disciples in the last paragraph of the Gospel of Matthew could not be clearer: "Go you therefore and make disciples of all nations, baptizing them in the name of the Father and of the Son and of the Holy Spirit and teach them to obey all that I have commanded you" (MT 28:19-20). The explicit conversion command that Jesus teaches also could not be more understandable: "I want mercy, not sacrifice" (MT 9:13). Obfuscations and distortions can be concocted to assure that the obvious is never seen or to guarantee that what is of primary concern for Jesus is reduced to an incidental concern for the billions to whom He has given the gift of faith. However, "I want mercy, not sacrifice," and "[T]each them to obey all that I have commanded you" perpetually stands in judgment on such political-intellectual maneuvers. Those who profess faith in Jesus may discount, ignore, modify or rationalize away His teaching in order to advance their interests. However, His words are forever there, inviting them back to the truth of Truth Incarnate, reminding them of the purpose for which the gift of faith has been bestowed upon them.

CHRIST'S MESSIANIC PROGRAM

If Jesus is as St. Paul says, "the visible image of the invisible God" (COL 1:15), if the God Jesus proclaims is "rich in mercy" (EPH 2:4), if "the Father and I are one" (JN 10:30), if "he or she who sees Me sees the Father" (JN 14:9), then what else could Jesus command other than, "I want mercy, not sacrifice," since the Father is "rich in mercy." Mercilessness, regardless of the quality of logic, the cleverness of euphemism or the impressiveness of ritual by which it conceals and perpetuates itself, is never of God and is never a part of the economy of salvation. It is mercy that initiates and consummates the process of salvation in Christ. This is why Pope John Paul II writes in *"Dives in Misericordia,"* "Christ's messianic program, the program of mercy, becomes the program of His people, the program of the Church." This means Christ-like mercy must be the program of each baptized person without exception and without any recesses. "The Church lives an authentic life when she professes and proclaims mercy," declares the Pope. Hence, the individual Christian of whatever Church—Catholic,

Orthodox, Protestant or Evangelical—lives an authentic life when she or he professes and proclaims by thought, word and deed Christlike mercy.

Advocate vs. Accuser

The Advocate, the Paraclete, the Public Defender that God in His mercy sends to this world to act on behalf of human beings is the Spirit of the Father who is rich in mercy, is the Spirit of the Son who is one with the Father, is the Spirit of the Holy, is the Spirit of Mercy. Satan, the Accuser, the Adversary of God and humanity, is *ipso facto* the spirit of mercilessness, the spirit of all that is anti-Christ. Mercilessness is from hell. Indeed, hell is a perpetual state of being confirmed in the merciless: "I was hungry and you did not give me to eat, I was thirsty and you did not give me to drink, I was naked and you did not clothe me, I was in prison and you did not visit me;" etc., (MT 25:31-46). This teaching of Jesus is the standard of judgment at the end of time: mercy or mercilessness? It does not require a doctorate from Harvard Divinity School to get this straight. There is something so profoundly different between an act of mercy and an act of mercilessness in time, that they fashion opposite outcomes in eternity.

> The Advocate...that God in His mercy sends to this world to act on behalf of human beings is the Spirit of the Father who is rich in mercy...the Accuser, the Adversary of God and humanity, is *ipso facto* the spirit of mercilessness.

Radical Evil

Forget the anthropomorphic imagery of devils with pitchforks, etc. Fixating on images that try to describe what is beyond individual and communal human experience, and hence beyond description, just serves to undermine the gravity of a life and death mystery with eternal implications. Because of truths we can only get a glimpse of through the revelation of Jesus, we know that indifference to the relievable suffering of another human being—mercilessness—is radical evil (MT 25:46). We also know by this same revelation that responding to the relievable suffering of another human being—mercy—results in entrance into "the Kingdom prepared for you since the foundation of the world" (MT 25:34).

> Because of truths we can only get a glimpse of through the revelation of Jesus...we know that indifference to the relievable suffering of another human being—mercilessness—is radical evil.

Provided, a person first has faith in Jesus as her or his Lord, God and Savior, this makes sense. Jesus reveals to us that God is a Father/Mother/Parent who is rich in mercy. Reason may be able to tell us God exists but only revelation can tell us God is a Parent rich in mercy. John Paul II in his Encyclical says, "Making the Father present as love and mercy is, in Christ's own consciousness, the fundamental touchstone of His mission as the Messiah." Faith in the self-revelation of God in Jesus is preeminent

> A God is who Father of each person expects human beings to relate to each other…as brothers and sisters endeavoring to assist each other in being merciful as Christ is merciful…in being helpers of one another on The Way of Mercy that leads to everlasting life for one and all.

because until one knows what kind of God God is, one cannot know what God expects of those He created. Jesus teaches that God who is rich in mercy expects those who wish to be in union with the Divine also be rich in mercy. A God is who Father of each person expects human beings to relate to each other not as capitalists to communists, not as Americans to Iraqis, not as have's to have-not's, not as Croats to Serbs, not as the righteous to the sinners, not as Pilate to Jesus, but as brothers and sisters endeavoring to assist each other in being merciful as Christ is merciful, in being merciful as their mutual Father in heaven is merciful, in being helpers of one another on The Way of Mercy that leads to everlasting life for one and all.

Renaming Mercilessness

In *Dives in Misericordia* John Paul II emphatically states that, "Mercy constitutes the fundamental content of the messianic message of Christ and the constitutive power of His mission." Now if mercy is the essential teaching and power of Jesus' mission, if mercy is His conversion demand, if mercy is the standard of judgment at the end of the world, if mercy is the most stupendous attribute of the Creator and Redeemer, is it conceivable that a Christian, someone who truly has faith in Jesus as their Lord, God and Savior, would set aside mercy even if he or she could gain the whole world or some paltry piece thereof? Would it not be unwise or incongruous for a believer in Christ to even entertain such a thought? Would it not be tragic unseriousness to engage in un-Christ-like mercilessness and then try to pacify one's soul and fool God by the crafty renaming of mercilessness as "mercy"? "If our hopes in Christ are limited to this life only, we are the most pitiable of people," writes St. Paul (1 COR 15:19). For the Christian to live in time as if eternity did not exist is senseless. A fact of life is, that even if mercy does a person no earthly good, it is of infinite value. For a Christian to choose mercilessness rather than mercy, in order to gain the totally perishable, is spiritual recklessness.

> "Mercy constitutes the fundamental content of the messianic message of Christ and the constitutive power of His mission." Now…is it conceivable that a Christian, someone who truly has faith in Jesus as their Lord, God and Savior, would set aside mercy even if he or she could gain the whole world…?

Philosophy or God's Will

State laws authorizing the homicidal violence of the death penalty, under which Christians reasonably destroy others in clear conscience, can be accredited or discredited depending on one's use of reason. What philosophy builds up, philosophy can tear down. As one of the most renowned Catholic Biblical Scholars of the

Twentieth Century, the late Rev. John L. McKenzie, noted on many occasions, the Church has no commission from Jesus to teach philosophy. This means that the place of reason in the Christian life is to figure out how to implement the teachings of Jesus, not to figure out how to modify them, ignore them, dismiss them, undermine them or abandon them. Now if Jesus teaches His followers, "I want mercy, not sacrifice," if Jesus teaches His followers, "Be merciful as your Heavenly Father is merciful," if as Pope John Paul II says, "Mercy constitutes the fundamental content of the Messianic Message of Christ and the constitutive power of His mission," then for what purpose should reason be employed by the Christian and by the Church? To rationalize mercilessness into mercy? To legitimatize the substitution of some philosophy of justified mercilessness, devised by a fellow lump of clay, for the revealed teachings of Our Lord? St. Paul's warning to the Church in Rome is pertinent here: "The more they call themselves philosophers, the more stupid they grew, until they exchanged the glory of the immortal God for a worthless imitation" (RM 1:22,23).

What cannot be denied is that in each instance of that form of homicidal violence called capital punishment the spirit of mercilessness reigns, albeit under the disguise of mercy in such gestures of pseudo-compassion as a tasty "last meal." This is only mercilessness with manners. The truth is that the spirit that enters history through Cain and does its most horrific work on Calvary is the same spirit that enters the state death houses, envelopes the guillotines, fills the gas chambers, and laughs cacophonously at God while another infinitely loved son or daughter of the Father is tormented and destroyed. Is this spirit the same spirit that acts through non-legalized killers when they take the lives of others?

You bet it is! It is the perverted and perverting spirit of mercilessness, manifest as homicidal violence, that is at the root of all this destruction, legal or illegal, reasonable or unreasonable, sordid or romantic. John Paul II wrote in his Encyclical, Rich in Mercy, that, "[T]he genuine face of mercy has to be ever revealed anew." Is the Face of the Father, who is rich in mercy, revealed today by those Christians, whether they be presidents, governors, legislators, judges, wardens, guards or citizens, who promote, operate or profit from the various state death chambers? Is it magnified by those bishops, pastors, priests and ministers who teach their people that as followers of Jesus they can engage in state-sponsored homicidal activities?

PRAISE THE LORD AND...

The blood on Jesus' hands is His own. Capital punishment is not what Jesus taught, it is what He suffered. Crucifying, gassing, beheading, hanging, shooting, electrocuting and poisoning people are not deeds of Christlike mercy. The God who is rich in mercy is never glorified by homicidal violence. "Praise the Lord and pass the ammunition," "Praise the Lord and fire-up Old Sparky," "Praise the Lord and turn on the gas," "Praise the Lord and release the poison," "Praise the Lord and start the suction machine" are blasphemous falsehoods if Jesus is Lord. Their source is the "Father of lies who is a murderer from the beginning" and not the "Father who is rich in mercy." These are the works and words of the Adversary of mercy, the Accuser of Christ, masquerading as a Divine support person for homicide. Indeed, whatever the Anti-Christ may be, its hallmark will be mercilessness—more than likely an exquisitely rational and an acutely practical mercilessness gilded with a spellbinding veneer of pseudo-holiness and intellectual sophistication.

LIFE THAT OUTLASTS TIME

The death penalty for Christians is not primarily a matter of governmental politics. It is a matter of accepting or rejecting the morality taught by the Son of God as the Will of God. It is a matter that affects life which outlasts time. If Jesus is only a philosopher, then rejecting the risks of mercy in favor of power, prestige, pleasure, nationalism, religionism, comfort, or some political philosophy, etc., is a rational option. But, if Jesus is the definitive revelation of God and God's will to humanity, then rejecting the risks of mercy is spiritual suicide. Here again perhaps, St. Paul is pertinent when he warns the Church in Corinth with these words: "As Scripture says, 'I shall destroy the wisdom of the wise and bring to nothing the learning of the learned. Where are the philosophers now'" (1 COR 1:19-20)? Where are the philosophers and politicians, preachers and practitioners of justified mercilessness now?

All are sacred, but no one is sinless. No one is going to come to her or his last breath praying, "God, have justice on me!" But, if it is mercy we desire from God in the afterlife, is it not mercy we should offer to others in this life?

Is the meaning of Jesus' parable (MT 18:23-35), about the debtor who is forgiven by the king and who then will not forgive someone who is in debt to him, really so nebulous? Surely, when the king asks the forgiven person who refuses to forgive, "Should you not have had mercy on your fellow servant as I have had mercy on you?", the place of mercy in life and in death, in time and in eternity is being highlighted in neon by Jesus. "Forgive us our trespasses as we forgive those who trespass against us" is either meaningless babble into limitless emptiness or it is a request that God judge us as we have judged others. "Blessed are the merciful for they shall obtain mercy" (MT 5:7) is Jesus' guarantee that mercy is the medicine for healing the soul diseased by personal sinfulness. And, how ruinous of the immortal soul does He say the choice of mercilessness is (MT 25:45 46; LK 16:19)? Take a moment and ponder the depth of disintegration that takes place in a being created in the image and likeness of a God who is rich in mercy when:

> *a man looks pleadingly at you*
> *with a last appeal in his eyes,*
> *and you kill him.*

WWJD

Christians must cease endorsing and participating in capital punishment because it is blatantly incompatible with following the Nonviolent Jesus of the Gospels and His Way of nonviolent merciful love of friends and enemies. Christians must discontinue advocating and justifying capital punishment because it is in direct violation of Jesus' "new commandment" to "love one another as I have loved you" (JN 13:34) which the Catechism of the Catholic Church (§1970) says "contains the entire law of the Gospel," and "summarizes all the other [commandments] and expresses His entire will" (§2822). As a person cannot imagine Jesus burning heretics at the stake, he or she equally cannot imagine Him gassing, shooting, guillotining, electrocuting, poisoning or crucifying any human being for any reason. What Christians cannot see Christ doing, they are not morally permitted to do. Christians must halt all active support of capital punishment because by their support they bear false witness to other Christians and to the non-Christian world, and thereby become obstacles to people coming to Jesus and knowing the one and only true God. By bearing false witness such Christians, who were chosen to be instruments of the merciful healing power of Jesus Christ, become instead agents of the pandemic of organized mercilessness that is spreading throughout global humanity.

Finally, Christians regardless of rank, status, class or occupation must abandon capital punishment because they were created from Mercy for Mercy and in Jesus they have been granted the gift of knowing that the Way to Mercy beyond time is by the Way of Mercy in time. Regardless of what other faiths or

> **Christians…must abandon capital punishment because they were created from Mercy for Mercy and in Jesus they have been granted the gift of knowing that the Way to Mercy beyond time is by the Way of Mercy in time.**

philosophies may say, Christians are commanded by Jesus to ever reveal the Face of Mercy to humanity. This they can accomplish only by following the Way of Jesus, the Nonviolent Suffering Servant of Isaiah, who in His mercy "does not break the bruised reed" (IS 42:3).

And now, my reader, let me conclude by asking you a question that only God will hear you answer. In your heart of hearts what do you desire? Do you want to "break the bruised reed" or do you want to be as merciful as Jesus? Before answering, just pause for a moment and consider the words of one of the holiest and most learned Christians in the 20th Century, St. Edith Stein, herself a victim of capital punishment and of Christian mercilessness:

> *"It is mercy that makes us one with God."*

Calling Down Fire:
Lost Sheep and Lost Shepherds

> BAGHDAD—A militant Islamic website showed footage yesterday of the beheading of an American man, which it claimed was in retaliation for the Abu Ghraib prison-abuse scandal that exploded nearly two weeks ago.
>
> The footage shows a bearded man in an orange prison jumpsuit identifying himself on camera as Nick Berg, a 26-year-old civilian contractor from West Chester, Pennsylvania. He said he was the son of Michael and Susan Berg, and the brother of David and Sarah.
>
> Moments later, five men, their faces concealed with headscarves and black ski masks, are seen pulling Berg to the side, then thrusting a large knife into his neck. There is a spine-chilling mix of sounds, with Berg screaming as the men shout: "Allahu Akbar!" or "God is great!" (BOSTON GLOBE, 5/12/04)

Is there not something wrong in the Church when Christians, on both sides of a battle line, are receiving the Body of Christ in Communion at 9 a.m. in preparation for going out to kill each other at 11 a.m.? The fact, that this practice has been in the Church since the Constantinian revision of Christianity in the Fourth Century and continues to be acceptable to this very hour, underlines both the seriousness and urgency of the issue. So, is this Eucharistic custom a proper use, a misuse or a sacrilegious abuse of the Sacrament that Jesus instituted on the night before He was killed by the ruling religious politicos and state functionaries in Jerusalem two thousand years ago?

Remember, Jesus went to His death explicitly and unequivocally rejecting violence, loving His enemies, praying for His persecutors and without a trace of revenge, retaliation or retribution. In His teachings, person and death He is super-abundantly merciful to those for whom justice would have insisted upon lethal justice. Is not the remembrance of these Gospel truths about Our Lord's sacrifice on Golgotha not intimately and irrevocably tied to His "Do this in remembrance of Me" command at the Last Supper? On top of this, it is at the First Eucharistic celebration that Jesus mandates for His disciples His unique and new commandment: "Love one another as I have loved you." (JN 13:34) In light of all this, how is it spiritually, theologically or pastorally legitimate for Christians who are planning to kill other Christians—or non-Christians—to participate in the Holy Eucharist, Holy Communion?

HOLY COMMUNION IN THE SERVICE OF HOMICIDE AND ENMITY

Today, in the Catholic Church, with the introduction of laypersons as extraordinary ministers of the Eucharist, a new and giant step has been taken down the 1700 year old road of putting Holy Communion at the service of homicidal violence and enmity and the spirit that orchestrates them. I think the best way to apprise my readers of this new homicide-justifying Eucharistic front is to quote briefly from an article which is written by a Catholic U. S. Army Captain and which appears in an August 2003 issue of a national Catholic magazine. The title of the article is "Calling for Fire." The subtitle is "A Knight Serving God and Country in Iraq."

> *As a field artillery officer in the U.S. Army, there have been many times that I have had to call for fire. This occurred most recently last spring during Operation Iraqi Freedom and an attack by the 3rd Brigade of the 101st Airborne Division on the city of Al Hillah, in south central Iraq. For me, the mission meant putting well-placed artillery rounds into Al Hillah and controlling the fires of more than 40 artillery pieces in support of the advancing infantry.*
>
> *Prior to leaving Fort Campbell, KY last February, I attended a one-day training session to be an extra-ordinary minister of the Eucharist or EME. We learned how to conduct prayer services and Communion services (in the absence of a priest).*
>
> *At the first Mass I attended in Iraq, I stood with my fellow leaders, soldiers, a few photojournalists and the celebrity journalist Geraldo Rivera…Following dismissal, the chaplain asked if there were any EMEs at Mass. I raised my hand…He impressed upon me that my duties included performing the Catholic Communion service in the absence of a priest. With that, he gave me guidance on what I would need. Before I left for Kuwait, my brother (a priest), gave me a pyx (for carrying the consecrated Host)…The priest (military chaplain) gave me the most important gift of all. He placed in my hands Hosts that had been consecrated at the Mass and said, "Go…God will be your strength out there."*
>
> *The first occasion I had to conduct a service was after the battle of Karbala. My artillery battalion was there in support of another unit. In the morning, I realized it was a Sunday, the first Sunday I had the chance to conduct a service. What I did not realize*

was the number of people, both Catholics and non-Catholics, who would show up. The Lord's Prayer brought beaming smiles to all those present. Catholics came forward to receive Holy Communion while others sat and prayed quietly… Throughout the rest of Lent I continued to do what I could to make Sunday seem like more than just another workday. In Baghdad, a priest from another brigade came to celebrate Mass on Easter…He replenished my supply of Hosts and sent me on my way.

Since then I have had the opportunity to perform a service for my brigade and/or battalion every Sunday and on Ascension Thursday…I was inspired to write this one night as I contemplated what I could do to make Pentecost a more meaningful celebration. I remembered that at Pentecost we call on the fire of the Holy Spirit. I realized that next Sunday I would "call for fire" in a whole new way.

EUCHARISTIC FRATRICIDE

If this account does not send shivers through the souls of all Catholic, Orthodox and Protestant bishops who read it, then they better pinch themselves to see if they have any spiritual life left in them. A soldier running around a battlefield killing people with consecrated Hosts in his pocket and knapsack or having consecrated Hosts waiting for him back in his tent, so that when he is finished killing people he is able to conduct Communion Services for his fellow killers, is not what the Eucharist is about. This is the Eucharist and Communion being employed to divinize those very spirits that the Lord came to earth to vanquish. It is the spirit of Cain being cloaked in divine approval. It is fratricide being given Christ's blessing. It is Jesus Christ, body and blood, soul and divinity, word and deed being conscripted in order to religiously legitimize the extreme antithesis of what He is, did and taught. It is the cacophonous false witness of a nationalistic Christianity that subordinates the explicit and unequivocal teachings of Jesus on violence and enmity to nation-state interests, as defined by the ruling class of the moment. It is Christian pietistic fervor stripped of Jesus' fundamental teachings on violence, enmity and retaliation. It is Holy Communion as presented to the world by Franz Josef Rarkowski, the Catholic Military Bishop of Germany, in his 1944 Lenten Pastoral, where he exhorts his flock to receive Communion in order to have what it takes to go out and kill for Hitler and the nation: "They (the military chaplains) will distribute the Bread of Life among you, and I am certain that the power of the Lord will come over you and will give you the strength to give your best as soldiers of the German Army for Führer, Volk and Vaterland."

UNENLIGHTENED SHEPHERDING

But, let me be transparently clear, lest an unwanted and unintended misconception creeps in here and misdirects attention from the central concern of this essay.

In no way am I criticizing or judging the young army captain who was commissioned by the Church as an extraordinary minister of the Eucharist. Nor, is there the slightest thought or desire to criticize or judge any military person who received Communion from him or from anyone else on the battlefield. Those responsible in this matter are solely the bishops of the Church—each individually and all collectively. They and only they can formally permit enmity-filled, lethally hostile groups of Christians, embarked on programs of victory through homicidal violence, to receive Communion. If they did not ecclesiastically approve, justify and encourage it, this young army captain and his fellow killers of fellow human beings, including fellow Christians, could not participate in the Agapé Meal on the killing fields or in anticipation of premeditated human bloodletting. The lay military man or woman giving Communion or receiving Communion before, during or after intentional participation in the homicidal violence of war is not the person being called to account here. The issue is exclusively the bishops of the Catholic, Orthodox and Protestant Churches and their willingness to allow this Sacrament, the Holy Mystery of the Lord's Supper, to be used in a way that gives divine endorsement to a spirit whose lair is the world of perpetual horror called hell.

Non-Empathic Shepherding

"Beyond the fear and exhaustion is a sea of horror that surrounds the soldier and assails his every sense," writes former Ranger, Paratrooper and West Point instructor, Lt. Colonel Dave Grossman, in his book, *On Killing*. He continues:

> Hear the pitiful screams of the wounded and dying. Smell the butcher-house smells of feces, blood, burned flesh and rotting decay, which combine into the awful stench of death. Feel the shudder of the ground as the very earth groans at the abuse of artillery and explosives, and feel the last shiver of life and the flow of warm blood as friends die in your arms.

William Manchester in his Pulitzer Prize nominated book, *Goodbye, Darkness: A Memoir of the Pacific War*, opens the door to truth a little, so that reality beyond the hermetically sealed room of blinding war propaganda may be seen:

> You tripped over strings of viscera fifteen feet long, over bodies which had been cut in half at the waist. Legs and arms, and heads bearing only necks, lay fifty feet from the closest torsos. As night fell the beachhead reeked with the stench of burning flesh.

Of course we need only look at the daily newspaper to realize that war is not what the government's professional falsifiers present it as: An Iraqi woman sitting in a van with her two daughters sees both their heads blown off without any warning (Boston Globe); an Iraqi father, standing a few feet from his 33 year old daughter who has just received her Ph.D., sees her heart literally pushed out of her body by a missile that comes through the window of their flat but does not explode (London Mirror). Is anything described by Grossman, Manchester or the two newspaper stories not from the spirit that resides in hell? Is anything described not the ordinary, daily stuff of war? General William Tecumseh Sherman sums it all up with brutal succinctness:

> *I am sick and tired of war. Its glory is all moonshine. It is only those who have neither fired a shot nor heard the shrieks and groans of the wounded who cry aloud for blood, for vengeance, for desolation. War is hell.*

Did Christ come so His followers could raise "holy" hell on earth with clear consciences? Did Jesus institute the Eucharist so His followers could derive from it the strength of mind and soul to go out and kill other followers of His—or to kill non-followers of His?

MOONSHINE SHEPHERDING

I assume that what I am about to say will be considered a cultural breach of good manners by Christian bishops and those who think bishops should not be held publicly accountable by the Christian community for their public acts within the Christian community. But, sometimes there is no way to communicate a truth to those who live by a false perception and an erroneous interpretation of reality, a perception and an interpretation that are destroying people body and soul, other than by risking being forever labeled strident. Be that as it may, I and many, many other Christians and non-Christians are "sick and tired" of watching bishops, oh-so-cunningly, spiritually valorize the horror that war brings into existence, by teaching that what Christian men and women do for their side in war is somehow in compliance with the Will and the Way of God as revealed by Jesus Christ. I have watched for over 60 years Catholic, Orthodox and Protestant bishops ceaselessly exchange the Glory of God, made visible in the nonviolent Jesus Christ, for the moonshine of nationalistic military glory. Worse I have watched bishop after bishop, almost without exception, work diligently to make militaristic moonshine more palatable to the sheep of their flocks by artificially lacing it with the saccharine lie that this is a way of life and death in conformity with the Way of life and death of "our Sweet Jesus."

It has been said by many over many centuries of Church history that "the road to hell is paved with miters." How any one would know this is beyond me, since the final judgment takes place and Gehenna subsists in realms of existence beyond time and space. But, what can be said with moral and intellectual certainty is that over the last 1700 years of Church history "the road to that manifestation of hell which is called war is paved with miters." Indeed bishops of every ilk have queued up in "holy" support of just about every side of every war fought in the West over the last millennium and a half. Is it any wonder that I and many, many others are "sick and tired" of watching this pitiable, contrived, morally feeble and long-playing episcopal charade of justifying unspeakable evil in the name of Jesus?

If this infidelity were "merely" on the level of the oaths that men in some Churches have to swear, in direct contradiction of Jesus' explicit teaching against oath taking, before they are permitted to be ordained bishops, it would be a serious but not soul-sickening matter. However, utilizing the episcopal office to administer continuous doses of the theologically sweetened moonshine of war to those Christians whose spiritual life has been entrusted by Christ to one's care is altogether on a different scale of "I will not obey." Moonshine is a powerful drug that undermines right-mindedness. Sweet-tempered moonshine is poison, because palatability guarantees lethally excessive consumption. When bishops become the spiritual confectioners for war, by justifying in the name of Jesus homicidal violence and enmity, then being "sick and tired" of what they are about should be the automatic and minimum Christian response.

IMMATURE SHEPHERDING

Unfortunately for the Church and for humanity, most Christians of most Churches will find the article, CALLING FOR FIRE spiritually edifying. Likewise, most Christian bishops will see nothing wrong with a man with consecrated Hosts running around a battlefield killing people. Nor, will either see anything amiss with going from killing enemy human beings to conducting Communion services and receiving Holy Communion. The episcopacy and laity of practically all Churches will experience no problem with any of this, because from the time they themselves were lambs their shepherds were pumping artificially flavored, spiritually-sugared martial moonshine into them through every channel available.

There really is nothing much more to say. The whole situation is sorrowfully clear. However, there is zero chance, barring some extraordinary act of divine intervention, that the bishops of any of the mainline Churches of Christianity any place in the world will change their minds and hearts and wills and behaviors on this matter of militarized Eucharists. Too addictive is spiritually sugarcoated military moonshine and too enticing and enslaving are its totally perishable fruits. There is no way on earth that the bishops of the Christian Churches are going to be able to perceive that they and their predecessors have exchanged the Glory of the Cross for the moonshine of the Cross turned upside-down, the sword. There is no way, short of a miracle, that bishops and most members of most Churches are going to grasp that the nonviolent love of friends and enemies that Jesus embodies and teaches is vocational and not merely political, tactical or philosophical; that it comes simultaneously to the

Christian with Christ's call to be His chosen disciple; that it is an irremovable dimension of His command to "Follow Me."

JESUS OR ELIJAH

However, as someone who believes in miracles, let me conclude with a Gospel passage that Scripture scholars tell us is intentionally constructed to echo and to repudiate as God's will and spirit a story about Elijah found in 2 KINGS 1:10-14. In this Old Testament story Elijah kills his enemies on two occasions by the invocation, "Let fire come down from heaven and destroy you." In the Gospel (LK 9:51-56) two of the Apostles, two of the first bishops in the lineage of Apostolic Succession, James and John, are indignant when a Samaritan village does not allow Jesus, a Jew, to stay there for a rest. And so, overcome by that spirit that resides in hell but relentlessly endeavors to take up residence in the human heart, they say to Jesus, "Lord, do you want us to call down fire from heaven and burn them up?" But, Jesus "turning, rebuked them and said, 'You do not know what spirit it is you are made of. The Son of Man came not to destroy people's lives but to save them.'"

The Nonviolent Trinity

"He is the image of the invisible God."

COL 1:15

It is believed by some that God can be known by observing the world. The material universe could not have created itself. Something cannot come from nothing, so the argument goes. Therefore, God must exist. There are some philosophical objections to this process of thought but let us for the moment accept as true that God's existence can be deduced from a reasoned analysis of an experience of a minuscule portion of the universe.

Beyond Reason to Revelation and Faith

However, even if creation can tell us that God is, what it cannot tell us is that God is love, that God is savior, that God is Father/Mother/Parent. For this awareness, revelation is necessary. A rational interpretation of the world with its horror, pain, madness, war, greed and victimization could reasonably lead a person to conclude that God is indifferent to human beings. If there is belief in a God of unconditional love and perpetual forgiveness, a saving God, then the belief is based on something other than what mere reason can establish. Such an understanding of the Source of all is a matter of faith, that is, faith in something other than human reason.

> ...even if creation can tell us that God is, what it cannot tell us is that God is love, that God is savior, that God is Father/Mother/Parent. For this awareness, revelation is necessary.

From where, however, does such a faith come? What is its origin? Why would one think it is true? For the Christian this faith comes through Jesus Christ. But, immediately it may be asked why a person should have faith in what Jesus teaches about God? Why is His knowledge of God superior to anyone else's knowledge of God? The straightforward answer to these question is that Jesus Christ can tell humanity the truth about God because of who Jesus Christ is. Jesus Christ is God "made flesh" (JN 1:1-14).

When Christians of apostolic times profess that Jesus is the Son of God, the Word of God and The Lord and begin to worship Him, while simultaneously continuing to worship the Father of Jesus as God, those who do not share the Christians Faith ask them to explain themselves. The response these apostolic Christians give to their inquirers is that Christ Jesus "is the image of the invisible God" (COL 1:15). In other Books of the New Testament the same reality is proclaimed in different language, e.g., "I and the Father are one" (JN 10:30), or "Whoever has seen Me has seen the Father" (JN 14:9). In the person of Jesus an infallible authority on God enters history and with Him a new, revolutionary understanding of God penetrates history. The new understanding demands that a new name for God be found in history—Trinity!

> In the person of Jesus an infallible authority on God enters history and with Him a new, revolutionary understanding of God penetrates history.

THE PERFECT ICON OF GOD

The early Christian community experiences Jesus as the perfect image and complete revelation of the Father. It recognizes that for the Son to be truly "the image of the invisible God," He must possess the divine attributes of the Father. This is precisely what the Church teaches. There is nothing of the perfection of the Father that is lacking in the Son. The Son is "true God from true God." To use the language of the theologians, there is no ontological gradation between the Father and the Son. There are no degrees of divinity between them. The Son is the consubstantial image of the Father. The Son does not simply participate in God; the Son is God.

It is because God places in human history a perfect icon of Himself, the Son, that Jesus is the Way to the Father. Jesus reveals the Father. His Messianic mission is to reveal the true God as Father/Mother/Parent. The Son is the definitive revelation of the Father. To see Jesus, that is to see Jesus in His words and deeds, is to see the Father (JN 14:9) for God acts in the way God is. As St. Gregory of Nyssa writes, "There is no contradiction at all between the will of the Father and the will of the Son. The Lord 'is the image of the invisible God,' immediately and inseparably united to the Father whose will He obeys in every moment." The will of the Son never varies from the will of the Father and hence the work of the Son, which is the fruit of His own willing, reveals nothing less than the will of the Father.

> It is because God places in human history a perfect icon of Himself, the Son, that Jesus is the Way to the Father.

GOD IS ONE

The New Testament is the written testimony about Jesus' words and deeds. It faithfully hands on what Jesus Christ, while living among people, did and taught for their salvation. It is the ultimate record of His words and works, and hence of His will and the will of the Father.

Now in the New Testament Jesus teaches by words and deeds a Way of nonviolent love of friends and enemies. This is incontestable. As the renowned Biblical scholar, the late Rev. John L. McKenzie says, "If we cannot know from the New Testament that Jesus rejects violence, we can know nothing of his person or message. It is the clearest of teachings....Jesus authorizes no one to substitute violence for love." But, as previously noted, the work of the Son is the will of the Father. Jesus is like us in all things except sin. He wills the Way of nonviolent love of friends and enemies as a response to evil, even lethal evil, because God wills the Way of nonviolent love of friends and enemies as a response to evil—even lethal evil. Jesus lives this will of the Father with only those faculties which all human beings have at their disposal. Jesus is nonviolent because God is nonviolent and because He desires His disciples to be nonviolent as God and He are nonviolent. Again, God acts as God is. The invisible God chooses to become visible in the incarnation of Jesus

> "If we cannot know from the New Testament that Jesus rejects violence, we can know nothing of his person or message. It is the clearest of teachings.... Jesus authorizes no one to substitute violence for love."

so that human beings, who are made in the image and likeness of God (GN 1:26), can choose to be nonviolent as God is nonviolent, can choose to imitate God by imitating His Incarnate Word, Jesus.

The Holy Spirit is, of course, the Holy Spirit of Jesus Christ (ROM 8:9). The Holy Spirit is active in Jesus and Jesus is consubstantial with the Holy Spirit. Since Jesus is nonviolent and since His Father is nonviolent, the Holy Spirit must be nonviolent since the Holy Spirit proceeds from the Father and the Son. Because the Nonviolent Son and Nonviolent Spirit are consubstantial with the Nonviolent Father, that is, because God is one, the gift that the Holy Spirit bestows on the believer is the gift of the Life of the Nonviolent God. Communion with the Nonviolent Spirit of Christ is communion with the Nonviolent God—The Nonviolent Trinity.

VIOLENT MONOTHEISM—VESTING A LIE

What is apparent from the New Testament is that Jesus rejects the lie of violent monotheism as emphatically as he rejects the lie of polytheism. God, who is to be loved whole heart, whole soul, whole mind, whole strength, is God whose image is the nonviolent Christ Jesus. Yet, somehow on July 16, 1945, the name of the God of Nonviolent Love is given as the code name

> What is apparent from the New Testament is that Jesus rejects the lie of violent monotheism as emphatically as he rejects the lie of polytheism.

for the testing of an instrument designed to produce unbound human carnage—the first atomic bomb. How is this possible? How is it possible that the Trinity of nonviolent love is the name assigned to a weapon's test whose purpose is to secure victory by mass homicide? To code name the first atomic bomb test "Trinity" is the extreme of

Orwellian doublespeak. It could not be more deceitful or absurd if the first A-Bomb were code-named "Jesus"! How could intelligent people even consider such an erroneous designation?

The answer is obvious. Seventeen hundred years before the pseudo-Trinity of violence explodes in the New Mexico desert, the pseudo-Trinity of violence explodes in the heart of Christianity. Seventeen centuries ago, Christianity begins to imbibe in violent monotheism, a monotheism whose God, contrary to the teaching of Jesus, leads people in the homicidal conquering of historical enemies. The spirits of violence, retaliation, greed, deceitfulness, oppression, destruction, terror and cruelty, all of which are utterly necessary to conduct war and all of which are utterly contrary to the Spirit of the Trinity, begin to be operationally justified as spirits compatible with the Spirit of the invisible God whose image is Christ Jesus. Christianity gradually becomes another in the line of religions employing God to validate its own violence and the violence of those who cater to its interests.

> The spirits of violence, retaliation, greed, deceitfulness, oppression, destruction, terror and cruelty, all of which are utterly necessary to conduct war are utterly contrary to the Spirit of the Trinity...

BETRAYAL OF THE NONVIOLENT TRINITY

Lest it be thought that I am exaggerating the betrayal of the Nonviolent Trinity as imaged by Jesus Christ consider the contemporary spiritual debacle of Catholic Croatia and Orthodox Serbia, of Protestant and Catholic Ireland, of Hutu and Tutsi Catholic Rwanda. Here are groups of Christians chronically and obsessively absorbed in homicidal hate of each other. However, practically everyone in each of these societies starts each day by making the sign of the cross or by saying in some manner that he or she worships the Father, the Son and the Holy Spirit. For most Catholics, Orthodox, Protestants and Evangelicals then, "God" does not incarnationally mean God as imaged by the Nonviolent Jesus Christ. On the contrary, for most Christians, Trinity means a violent monotheism that enables their homicidal activities to be placed under divine sponsorship. This has been the case in almost every place on earth where Christianity—in any of its forms—has taken hold over the last 1700 years. In the last seventeen centuries no sociologically identifiable unit of people has killed more human beings in war than the group that answers to the name Christian—the group that professes belief in the Trinity. Is it not then understandable why the scientists and military personnel in the New Mexico desert in 1945

> For most [Christians], "God" does not incarnationally mean God as imaged by the Nonviolent Jesus Christ. On the contrary, for most Christians, Trinity means a violent monotheism that enables their homicidal activities to be placed under divine sponsorship.

6.4 | THE NONVIOLENT TRINITY

did not consider it blasphemous to name an instrument of mega-violence after what they perceived to be Christianity's God—the Violent Trinity?

If humanity's image of God is distorted, humanity's image of itself and of the world will be distorted. To worship and to love whole heart, soul, mind and strength a God of violent monotheism, who condones, justifies and even encourages homicidal violence, is to ensure humanity a continuing history of divinely approved, self-righteous homicide with all the nauseating vomitus it ceaselessly disgorges. Violent monotheism is not only a false presentation of God, if Christ Jesus "is the image of the invisible God," it is also a major motivator to homicide in the human situation. To divinize homicidal violence is to promote homicidal violence because what is thought to be the will of God, people are encouraged to do—and to do with great zeal.

Divine Conscription as Spiritual Fraud

"God is on our side" has been the rallying cry for incalculable human slaughter. Year after year, century after century, God has been drafted to go to war by practically every state and revolutionary military operation, by practically every nation and tribe. However, before Divine conscription is possible, the religious elites of the various societies have to assure the political and economic elites, as well as, the "nobodies" who must kill and be killed, that God is indeed quite open to being drafted! But if Christ Jesus "is the image of the invisible God," then God has permanent conscientious objector status. The Nonviolent Trinity can never be honestly conscripted to legitimatize, motivate or spiritually underpin homicidal violence for any earthly or heavenly reason—and the religious leadership of the Churches have no commission to teach otherwise.

> The Nonviolent Trinity can never be honestly conscripted to legitimatize, motivate or spiritually underpin homicidal violence for any earthly or heavenly reason—and the religious leadership of the Churches have no commission to teach otherwise.

Violent monotheism is killing humanity. It is corrupting all of human existence—especially religion. The only antidote to this planetary spiritual plague is for Christians and Churches to commence to communicate gently, persistently and publicly that the nonviolent Jesus is the true image of the invisible God, and then to try to live out personally and socially the network of implications that flow from this great truth of nonviolent monotheism.

Worshipping and Following the True Image of God

God is the heart of the matter, no matter what the matter is. The question of God is inevitably present in all the other questions that stimulate and haunt the human mind. All humanity and all human beings are faced with a choice. Will the best and the brightest, as well as, the least and the dullest continue down the disastrous and destructive path of worshipping and following images of God created from their own fearful, sin-drenched and finite consciousness, or will humanity accept, worship and follow God as revealed in the image of the nonviolent Jesus Christ?

People, however, cannot choose an option they have never heard. Unless the true image of God as revealed by Jesus is gracefully presented to humanity, humanity will continue in its sorrowful and self-torturous enslavement to false images of the Holy. Silence on this matter serves only the status quo, serves only violent monotheism. There is an indispensable requirement, placed on those whole believe, to unashamedly and unhesitatingly proclaim the Good News of The Nonviolent God of Love, The Nonviolent Trinity of Love. The active, committed witness of Christians and Churches, who believe that the nonviolent Jesus "is the image of the invisible God," is obligatory, if all forms of violent monotheism are to become as unthinkable to the human spirit as child sacrifice now is.

> Unless the true image of God as revealed by Jesus is gracefully presented to humanity, humanity will continue in its sorrowful and self-torturous enslavement to false images of the Holy.

If you accept this task of Trinitarian faith, this labor of Nonviolent Christic love, you will be making a monumental contribution to genuine peace on the earth. You will also be doing what Christ chose you to do. You will be living unto eternal life what you pray when you say, "Glory be to the Father and to the Son and to the Holy Spirit, now and always and forever and ever. Amen."

Patronizing God

For over fifty years throughout the world I have been teaching Christians and Non-Christians about the Nonviolent Jesus of the Gospel and His Way of nonviolent love of friends and enemies. Most of the time in most places the reaction has been one of incredulity. In practically every case every sophomore in high school, every refined moral theologian, every bishop, priest and minister, every Christian in pulpit and in pew has risen to his or her feet to inform me that Jesus' teachings on nonviolent love are impractical, unrealistic, idealistic, childish, fanciful—or all of the above.

In this regard I recall a French woman who rejected the notion of a Nonviolent Jesus by offering that, "Jesus may be God but He is not stupid!" Now while this woman's phraseology may be more entertaining than that of most who reject or ignore the Nonviolent Jesus of the Gospels, it is an accurate encapsulation of what most Christians think about Jesus' teaching of nonviolent love of friends and enemies. They justify their dismissal of such an "irrational" teaching with rationales like the following:

> *Let's be realistic. In the real world no one in his or her right mind is going to give up the protection of violence. It would be crazy. It is a jungle out there. I am a nonviolent person, but if someone tries to take something away from me that I love, that I need or that is mine, I am not going to turn the other cheek or give him my tunic when he takes my cloak. I am going to give him a punch in the mouth, a kick in the groin, time in prison or a bullet in the chest—otherwise I'd become a doormat for the world. Survival is the first law of nature and no one survives in this world without the use of violence. No nation could last a week if it followed Jesus' teaching of nonviolent love of friends and enemies. That is why no Christian politician, regardless of how many Christians populate a nation, ever runs on the platform of the Sermon on the Mount. A nonviolent politician in the model of the Nonviolent Jesus would be unelectable even if a state were 100% Christian! Jesus may be God but He is not stupid—and neither are we, His disciples, supporters, and promoters!"*

REJECTION OF VIOLENCE AND ENMITY

At no place in the Gospel does Jesus come into such acute conflict with the prevailing idea of God and God's will as when He confronts homicidal violence and enmity.

The dichotomy, between what people believe God and God's will to be in regard to violence and enmity and what Jesus says they are, could not be greater—then or now. The rejection of violence and of enmity is an inextricable part of the Gospel as proclaimed by Jesus in word and deed. It is also a major theme in the life of original Christianity. As one of the most renowned Catholic Biblical scholars of the Twentieth Century, Rev. John L. McKenzie, says, "If we cannot know from the New Testament that Jesus rejected violence, we can know nothing of his person or message. It is the clearest of teachings."

> The rejection of violence and of enmity is an inextricable part of the Gospel as proclaimed by Jesus in word and deed.

Jesus' understanding of what kind of God God is and what God expects of us is radically out of harmony with people's religious consciousness at the time of His birth, as well as at the time of the two-thousandth anniversary celebration of His birth. In his seminal work on the subject of the Jewishness of Jesus entitled *Jesus of Nazareth* (1921), the famous Hebrew Biblical scholar Joseph Klausner, writes:

> *There was yet another element in Jesus' idea of God, which Judaism could not accept. Jesus tells his disciples to love their enemies, as well as their friends since their Father in heaven makes his sun rise on the evil and on the good and sends his rain upon the righteous and the ungodly...With this Jesus introduces something new into the idea of God... But his teaching has not proved possible. Therefore he left the course of ordinary life untouched, wicked, cruel, pagan and his exalted ethical idea has been relegated to a book, or at most becomes a possession of monastics and recluses who live apart from the paths of ordinary life...As a sole and self-sufficient national code of teaching Judaism could by no means agree with it...and such has been the case with Christianity from the time of Constantine to this present day...Pharisaic Judaism was too mature; its purpose too fixed to change. Its leaders were fighting for their national existence and grappling with foreign oppressors and with semi-foreigners that sought to crush it, and with a decadent idolatry that sought to absorb it. In such days of stress and affliction they were themselves far removed and would remove also their fellow Jews from the dangerous fantasies (of Jesus), an extremism which most of the race could not endure. They saw at the outset what the end would be (of following Jesus)...How could Judaism accede to such an ethical ideal?*

Today, can it not be said that the leaders and laity of the Catholic, Protestant, Orthodox and Evangelical Churches are too mature, too fixed in their purposes to teach and to follow Jesus' Way of nonviolent love of friends and enemies as a sole and self-sufficient code for living? In these days of stress and affliction—when each Church is fighting for its own particular identity and survival, when each Church is grappling with decadent idolatries that are trying to influence it and when each Church must be perpetually vigilant for enemies who wish to undermine its political power and to confiscate its wealth—are not the rulers of each Church under a moral imperative to remove themselves and their fellow Christians far from the dangerous fantasies of Jesus which, if followed, would guarantee the destruction of the Church? How could Church leaders accede to such an ethical idea, to a way of nonviolence? Does not reasonableness mandate that no Church give a "microphone" to the Nonviolent Jesus and His Way of nonviolent love of friends and enemies—lest Christians actually begin to follow this fatuous program of self-destructive behavior?

Simultaneous Adoration and Rejection

It has long been known in Christianity that adoration of Jesus (Praise the Lord!) is much less costly than imitation of Jesus. Yet, is not each Christian obliged to ask what he or she is doing when he or she says, "I adore You, O Lord, but I am not going to follow you in your clear-cut stance toward homicidal violence and enmity?" If the One being adored has explicitly commanded a form of behavior, what does it mean spiritually to discredit a Divine Imperative issuing from the adored One? What does it mean to believe in Jesus as the Messiah, the Christ, the Son of the Living God and not believe Him? What does it mean to consume the Nonviolent Lamb of God in Holy Communion with no intention of trying to become like the Lamb who is consumed? What does it mean to have faith in Jesus as Lord and Savior while at the same time justifying the premeditative, chronic and obstinate refusal to do what He commands: Love your enemies (MT 5:43; LK 6:27); Love one another as I have loved you (JN 13:34, 15:12); Put away your sword (MT 26:52); etc.? What does it mean to be a teacher in the Church and intentionally choose not to teach what Jesus taught? Finally, what does it mean, when immediately before His ascension into heaven Jesus speaks directly and exclusively to His Church's leaders and says this:

> *"Go ye therefore and make disciples of all nations, baptizing them in the name of the Father and of the Son and of the Holy Spirit, and teach them to obey all that I have commanded you."?* (MT 28:19-20)

One Is Known Only by Words and Deeds

The only way in this world that any person can be known—and that includes Jesus—is by his or her words and deeds. Separate a person from her or his words and deeds and there is nothing of the person to experience, to know or to have faith in. The only Jesus Christ that exists is the Jesus Christ of the words and deeds found in the

Gospel. Separate Jesus from His words and deeds, and all that is left is a non-existent, humanly created, imaginary character named Jesus. For example, the Jesus of the Gospels is Jewish, regardless of how many Irishmen think, say or wish He were Irish! Any presentation of Jesus as an Irishman from Dublin rather than as a Jew from Nazareth is a presentation of a Jesus who is no more a person of historical existence than is Mickey Mouse. So, also, any presentation of Jesus as someone other than a person who teaches and lives unto death a Way of nonviolent love of friends and enemies is a presentation of a character of the imagination, rather than a person of history. An Irish historical Jesus is a non-Jesus Christ historically. A Jesus using or endorsing homicidal violence and enmity in the name of self-interest, self-defense or social responsibility is also a non-Jesus Christ historically. Pope John Paul II writes in his encyclical, *Redemptoris Missio* (1990), "One cannot separate Jesus from the Christ or speak of a 'Jesus of history' who would differ from the 'Christ of faith'...Christ is none other than Jesus of Nazareth." The only Jesus there is to adore, praise, worship, proclaim, consume, imitate, trust and have faith in is the Nonviolent Jesus who lived and taught a Way of nonviolent love of friends and enemies by His words and deeds in history.

SPIRITUAL SCHIZOPHRENIA—PRAISE GOD AND PASS THE AMMO

Most Christians are members of Churches that praise Jesus while simultaneously dismissing His Way of nonviolent love of friends and enemies. This spiritual schizophrenia of worshiping the Nonviolent Jesus of the Gospel while morally endorsing the way of homicidal violence and enmity is so pervasive in the Churches of Christianity and in the Evangelical movement that it is experienced as spiritual sanity and theological acuity. Most nationalistic or ethnic Christians proudly and matter-of-factly say of their Christian ancestors: "Our forefathers, they lied, they killed, they plundered but...they kept the faith!" There is possibly no more mammoth spiritual incongruity, no more anti-Gospel spiritual ejaculation, no more distorted presentation of Jesus and His Gospel than the title of the popular Christian Hymn, "Praise the Lord and Pass the Ammunition!" How is it possible for Christians, whether Catholic, Orthodox or Protestant, whether rulers or ruled to endure living with such a searing contradiction at the center of their faith and life?

Church Teaching Reflects Paucity of Faith in Jesus

After all, Jesus did not die of old age. He died by homicidal violence and He died giving a very clear and consistent response to it—a response in continuity with what He had been teaching as God's will for the prior three years of His public life—a response in discontinuity with what the Churches have been operationally teaching as God's Will for the last 1700 years.

Perhaps an analogy could be clarifying. If General George Patton commands his troops to turn right for victory and instead they salute him and then defy him by intentionally turning left, can it be honestly maintained they have faith in him? If Jesus commands, "Love your enemies," "Put away your sword," and His followers fall down and worship Him and then defy Him by hating and destroying enemies and justifying it, can it honestly be maintained that they have faith in Him? For most people it is difficult to fathom how one can be saved by faith in Jesus when one does not have faith in Jesus. Patton's way ceases to be the way of people who have faith in him when they turn left. All the salutes in the world cannot compensate for what is transparently non-faith. Jesus' Way ceases to be the way of people who have faith in Him when they turn to justifying their enmity and homicidal violence. A legion of "Praise the Lord" exaltations cannot compensate for what is transparently non-faith.

> For most people it is difficult to fathom how one can be saved by faith in Jesus when one does not have faith in Jesus....Jesus' Way ceases to be the way of people who have faith in Him when they turn to justifying their enmity and homicidal violence.

To lose faith in Patton's way is *ipso facto* to lose faith in Patton. So, also, to lose faith in Jesus' Way is *ipso facto* to lose faith in Jesus. To abandon Patton's way is synonymous with saying, "General Patton, I don't think you know what you are talking about. General Patton, I don't trust you. General Patton, I will not follow you." To abandon Jesus' Way is likewise the equivalent of saying, "Jesus, you don't know what you are talking about. Jesus, I don't trust you. Jesus, I will not follow You."

The Aberrational Transition from Cross to Sword

Christians have turned the cross of nonviolent love upside down thus making it into a sword of holy homicide. But, Christians and Churches are not cognizant that they have inverted and perverted the nonviolent cross of Christ. Mahatma Gandhi notes that the only people in the world who do not see Jesus as nonviolent are Christians. How is this possible? One technique, which Churches employ to avoid seeing what they do not want to see, to avoid seeing what they cannot bear to see, is the process of nurturing children and adults into a taken-for-granted understanding of the Gospel that

> Mahatma Gandhi notes that the only people in the world who do not see Jesus as nonviolent are Christians.

allows them to believe that patronizing Jesus is a valid substitute for obeying Jesus. Whether, it is the French woman rendering silly the Nonviolent Jesus and His way of nonviolent love of friends and enemies, or the self-reverential Christian moral theologian telling Christians how many rocks they may justly possess to throw at each other, or the patriotic leadership of a Church threatening excommunication if Christians refuse to kill when the politicians of their state call upon them to kill, the operational spiritual reality is the same. It is the communal humoring of Jesus by words that praise Him to the high heavens, while communally discrediting Him by morally affirming deeds that unambiguously proclaim, "I will not be caught dead following Your ridiculous Way of nonviolent love." When practically all the Churches of Christianity reach an implicit ecumenical agreement that this is acceptable Christian practice, then the young and newly arrived are placed outside the possibility of perceiving the Nonviolent Jesus. What one has no idea of, one cannot act in conformity with.

Anti-Evangelization in the Extreme

The Christian who sets aside Jesus' "clearest teachings," that is, His teachings on the rejection of violence and enmity, while at the same time calling Him "Lord," not only brings into disrepute these teachings, but also instantly tarnishes the credibility of all the teachings of Jesus, indeed, of Jesus Himself. This practice—of individually and collectively contradicting and correcting Jesus on His teaching on how God desires His followers to deal with violence and enmity—is the single most significant factor in the Church's inability to evangelize contemporary literate people. No amount of money nor state of the art public relations technique can camouflage the Divinity-denial implicit in this contradicting and correcting behavior. To proclaim that Someone is the Pre-existent Word of God through whom all things were made and then in the next breath to pooh-pooh His teachings of nonviolent love of friends and enemies as naïvely simplistic or nonsensical is anti-evangelization in the extreme. Who wants to be part of a religious community that cannot distinguish a cross morality from a sword morality? Who wants to be part of a religious group that equates taking up the sword with taking up the cross? Who wants to be part of a Church that invests so much of its intellectual and monetary resources in efforts to convince itself and the world that the sword is the cross? And finally, who wants to adore or commit himself or herself to a God who does not know what He is talking about?

Liturgical Pampering of the Holy One Is Not Enough

When Jesus proclaims at the close of the Sermon on the Mount, "It is not those who say, 'Lord, Lord,' who enter the Kingdom of Heaven, but those who do the will of my Father who enter the Kingdom of Heaven"(MT 7:21), He is saying, "Patronizing God is not enough." The liturgical pampering of the Holy One while ignoring, distorting and belittling His will is not the Way to salvation taught by Jesus, the ultimate revealer of the Will of God to humanity. Christianity is not only a liturgical and conceptual religion but also is an incarnational religion.

> Christianity is not only a liturgical and conceptual religion but also is an incarnational religion....meant to be lived, incarnated, made carnal, enfleshed.

Gospel truth is meant to be conceptualized and celebrated but it is not meant just to be conceptualized and celebrated. It is also meant to be lived, incarnated, made carnal, enfleshed. The most used verb by Jesus in the Gospel is "do." In the case of Christianity the Message and the Messenger are one and the same. Jesus is the Word of God "made flesh." To denigrate the Message as simple-minded tripe for First Century Galilean rubes is to denigrate the Messenger. To show contempt for the Message is to stigmatize the Messenger. Faith in Jesus demands faith in His Way. The truth of this dimension of the Gospel can be articulated by the lyrics from the old song, Love and Marriage: "You can't have one without the other." The song goes on to insist, "Try! Try! Try to separate them, it's an illusion." Jesus and His Way of nonviolent love of friends and enemies cannot be severed from each other. It is self-deception to convince oneself that a Christian or a Church can brush-off His Way of nonviolent love without brushing Him off. The Nonviolent Jesus and His Way of nonviolent love are two sides of the same eternally redeeming Coin. "You can't have one without the other." You cannot have the Coin of redemption with only one side.

Clerical and Academic Disdain for the Nonviolent Jesus

I have observed for over three decades an ecumenical panorama of Church leaders, circumlocutory academic moralists and bombastic Evangelical preachers condescendingly assume a posture of bemused intellectual and spiritual superiority when directly confronted with the Gospel truth of the Nonviolent Jesus and His Way of nonviolent love. With the wave of an "authoritative" hand, they dismiss the Nonviolent Way of Jesus with "know-it-all" one-liners like, "I haven't time for that nonsense," or "That's irrelevant sectarianism," or "That's just a lot of fundamentalist theological drivel," or, as one cleric disdainfully remarked when he was read a passage that Thomas Merton authored on Gospel nonviolence, "Merton lives in the woods. I live in the real world." In the upper echelons of the Churches of Christianity Gospel Nonviolence remains the unexamined teaching of Jesus; indeed, it is the unmentioned and the unmentionable teaching of Jesus. Not surprisingly then, at the lower levels of the Churches of Christianity, it is the untaught teaching of Jesus. The powerful in each of the Churches, as well as in the Evangelical Movement, Marian Movement, Charismatic Movement, etc., struggle assiduously to guarantee that Gospel nonviolence will never be intelligently presented to Christians, that Gospel nonviolence will always be perceived by Christians as a ludicrous or fanatical moral option. No "microphone" is given to it in the Churches unless for some unexpected reason Church leadership absolutely has to permit the ordinary means of communication in the Church to be made available to it. However, after such rare moments occur, everything is done to minimize, derogate and blacken the nonviolent Message while, of course, sparing no amount of energy and money to aggrandize, salute and cheer the Messenger.

TRUE PRAISE OF GOD IS ABANDONMENT TO NONVIOLENT LOVE

Patronizing God is a cosmic absurdity at which right-mindedness would have a belly-laugh if it were not for the horrid consequences that such religious inanity has brought upon the Churches and through the Churches has brought upon the rest of humanity. True praise of God can never be a patronizing activity. "Praise the Lord and Put Away Your Swords," "Praise the Lord and Love Your Enemies," "Praise the Lord and Love as Jesus Loves," these are songs of authentic praise, yet to be composed. These are the hymns of Christian sanity, sanctity and fidelity. These are songs of praise that without exception communicate an unspoken but self-evident secondary theme: "Jesus, I trust in You." However, the patronizing of Jesus that attempts to pass itself off as praise, also communicates an unspoken but self-evident secondary theme: "Jesus, I do not trust in You."

The decision facing the Christian and the Christian Churches is clear-cut: to patronize the Lord or to praise the Lord; to abandon oneself to the Nonviolent Jesus and His Way of nonviolent love or to abandon the Nonviolent Jesus and His Way of nonviolent love. The Christian and the Churches must either use praise as a patronizing decoy for faithlessness, religious self-deception and "justified" disobedience or else they must enter into praise as the atmosphere of Divine-human synergy that empowers them to obediently live by faith the Way of the Cross of nonviolent love. These are the alternatives and they are exclusive alternatives. A Christian "cannot serve two masters" (MT 6:24).

Now, it is time to choose! Now is the moment of judgment. The choice is before us: to praise God or to patronize God. Praising Jesus will shine such Uncreated Light on the Gospel that truths about God, about human beings, about nature, about evil, never before seen, will be illumined for the salvation of the world. Patronizing Jesus will only continue the fearfull darkness in which the Churches of the Constantinian tradition of Christianity live. It will amount to no more than the spiritual equivalent of "whistling in the dark." It will do nothing to enlighten, by the Nonviolent Uncreated Light (JN 1:1-14) that has come into the world, a humanity being ceaselessly butchered by its own hand. The crisis is present—now, today, this hour, this moment.

> Praising Jesus will shine such Uncreated Light on the Gospel that truths about God, about human beings, about nature, about evil, never before seen, will be illumined for the salvation of the world.

Let us pray!

PRAYER: All praise to our Lord, God and Savior, the Nonviolent Jesus Christ and His Way of nonviolent love of friends and enemies, now and always and forever and ever.

RESPONSE: Amen.

What say you, my reader? Amen?

Will the Reformed Church Be a Peace Church?

In this world the Church is always required to reach an equilibrium between integration with culture and identification with culture. The two temptations to implementing this requirement properly are the temptation of withdrawal and the temptation of secularization. Except for an occasional small group, the temptation of withdrawal is a non-temptation for the Church today. Secularization—the adoption by the Church of secular powers, values, attitudes, beliefs, behaviors, systems and spirits that are contrary to the teaching of Jesus—is the most serious and enticing temptation facing the Church at this time. Indeed, succumbing to the temptation of secularization is the most grievous sin of the historical Church and the most overlooked and ignored. A brief review of some fundamentals is perhaps in order before confronting the most noxious manifestation of secularization that plagues the churches to this very hour.

> Secularization is the most serious and enticing temptation facing the Church at this time.

THE HEAD OF THE CHURCH

There is only one Head of the Church and that is the Nonviolent Jesus Christ. There is no successor of Jesus Christ in the Church because Jesus Christ has never left the Church. The Nonviolent Jesus Christ was, is and always will be the supreme authority in the Church. The center of gravity in the Church is the enduring life of Christ in the Church, not any particular ministry. It is He who guarantees the survival of the Church, not clever administration, wealth or secular power. Therefore, it is the Church's relationship to the Nonviolent Jesus that is the non-negotiable, essential factor in determining what the Church's ends are and what means the Church may use to accomplish these ends. It is this relation that illuminates whether an activity of the Church is a spiritually healthy integration into culture or a disobedient excursion into the dead-end of secularization.

The Great Commission Jesus gives His Church is:

> *Go, therefore, make disciples of all the nations; baptize them in the name of the Father and of the Son and of the Holy Spirit, and teach them to observe all the commands I gave you. And know that I am with you always; yes, to the end of time* (MT 28:19,20).

MEANS AND ENDS

The Church then, to use St. Augustine's phraseology, is to be an extension of the life and mission of Jesus in time and space. Self-evidently, for the Church to be this, it must use Christ-like means if it expects to be faithful to and fulfill its Christic commission. Un-Christ-like means cannot produce Christ-like ends. Hence, secularization, the employment by the Church of secular means and/or ends that are incompatible with the means and/or ends of Christ, is a spiritual catastrophe of the highest order when it occurs—regardless of the earthly benefits that may accrue to the Church by the use of such means.

> [S]ecularization...is a spiritual catastrophe of the highest order when it occurs—regardless of the earthly benefits that may accrue to the Church by the use of such means.

Now it is true, that the pope is not the Church, nor are the cardinals, bishops, priests, ministers, deacons, elders, overseers or superintendents the Church. These positions are ministries within the Church, no more or no less important than any other ministry in the Church. As the saying goes, "We are the Church." True enough. But, this theological fact carries with it obligations of the most serious temporal and eternal significance. Since we are the Church, each and everyone of us is explicitly called by our relationship to its Nonviolent Head, the ever-present Jesus Christ, to live according to His way and means in order to bring about the ends for which He created the Church. Therefore it is not just popes, cardinals, bishops, priests, ministers, etc., who are subject to the temptation of secularization. It is each and every Christian and the entire Church that can be seduced by powers, values, attitudes, beliefs, systems and spirits that are incommensurate with the life, spirit, teaching and mission of the Nonviolent Jesus Christ.

> Since we are the Church, each and everyone of us is explicitly called by our relationship to its nonviolent head, the ever-present Jesus Christ, to live according to His way and means in order to bring about the ends for which He created the Church.

SECULARIZATION OF THE CHURCH

Secular society almost universally endorses exacting one's "pound of flesh" under the rubric of justice and imposing one's will by means of causing pain to another. However, as has been previously noted, the ends of secular society are not the same as the ends of that society called the Church and therefore the means cannot be the same. The end for which the Church exists is to help people become saints, that is, to help bring people into the fullness of life, into an eternally graced union with God through the Nonviolent Jesus. Therefore, a legal or illegal lynching-party is never a witness to Christ, even if it is praying the rosary or singing the St. Francis Prayer of Peace, even if all its participants are baptized and it is led by a cadre of ecclesiastics in full canonicals.

> The end for which the Church exists is to help people become saints, that is, to help bring people into the fullness of life, into an eternally graced union with God through the Nonviolent Jesus.

Violence, dominative power, i.e., the infliction of suffering and/or death on other human beings in order to achieve an end, is the *sine qua non* of all secular societies, all states. As Carl J. Friedrich, Eaton Professor of the Science of Government at Harvard University, writes in the concluding paragraph of his book, *The Pathology of Politics*, "Our analysis has, I hope, shown that politics needs all these dubious practices; it cannot be managed without violence, betrayal, corruption, secrecy and propaganda." Or, as Tolstoy, speaking about dominative power communicates, less prosaically but perhaps far more acutely:

> "[P]olitics needs all these dubious practices; it cannot be managed without violence, betrayal, corruption, secrecy and propaganda."

> [T]he acceptance of Christianity without the abandonment of power is a satire on, and a perversion of, Christianity. The sanctification of political power by Christianity is blasphemy; it is the negation of Christianity. After fifteen hundred years of this blasphemous alliance of pseudo-Christianity with the State, it needs a strong effort to free oneself from all the complex sophistries by which, always and everywhere (to please the authorities), the sanctity and righteousness of State-power, and the possibility of its being Christian, has been pleaded...

> Let us take the history of that government which first formed an alliance with Christianity. A robbers' nest existed at Rome. It grew by robbery, violence, murders, and it subdued nations. These robbers and their descendants, led by their chieftains (whom they sometimes called Caesar, sometimes Augustus), robbed and tormented nations to satisfy their desires. One of the descendants of these robber-chiefs, Constantine (a reader of books and a man satiated by an evil life), preferred certain Christian dogmas to those of the old creeds...So he decreed that this religion should be introduced among those that were under his power.

> No one said to him: "The kings exercise authority among the nations, but among you it shall not be so. Do not murder, do not commit adultery, do not lay up riches, judge not, condemn not, resist not him that is evil."

> But they said to him: "You wish to be called a Christian and to continue to be the chieftain of the robbers—to kill, burn, fight, lust, execute, and live in luxury? That can all be arranged." And they arranged a Christianity for him, and arranged it very smoothly, better, even than, could have been expected...

> But more even than that: they sanctify his robber-chieftainship, and say that it proceeds from God, and they anoint him with holy oil...[T]his same religion has existed for fifteen hundred years, and other robber-chiefs have adopted it, and they have all been lubricated with holy oil, and they were all, all ordained by God...

And as soon as one of the anointed robber-chiefs wishes his own and another folk to begin slaying each other, the priests immediately prepare some holy water, sprinkle a cross, take the cross and bless the robber-chief in his work of slaughtering, hanging, and destroying...

True religion may exist anywhere except where it is evidently false, i.e., violent; it cannot be a State religion.

True religion may exist in all the so-called sects and heresies, only it surely cannot exist where it is joined to a State using violence.

There are of course innumerable methods and forms of inflicting suffering and death beyond those Friedrich and Tolstoy enumerate. However, a baptized Christian or a church using dominative power no more make it an activity in conformity with the will of God as revealed by the Nonviolent Jesus than a priest blessing soldiers before a battle makes their homicidal violence Christ-like.

BARTERING AWAY JESUS' LEGACY

The acceptance by the Church of the use of dominative power by her members and for her own purposes is the primary form of secularization that has bedeviled Christianity since the Fourth Century. At that time the Church—perhaps more accurately the Church's leaders—bartered away for dominative power, and for the riches and secular prestige that accompany it, the Divine Truth entrusted to her by Jesus and the Apostles, i.e., His Way of nonviolent love of friends and enemies. Thus, she became a holy ornament, a cultic decoration, a religious legitimizor of the Roman Empire much like her pagan predecessors. In other words the Church, by succumbing to the temptation to secularization, began the process of becoming a religious domination system in support of secular domination systems—liberal and conservative, democratic and dictatorial. These ecclesiastical domination systems, over the centuries, took on a variety of shapes: papal, episcopal, and congregational, Catholic, Orthodox and Protestant. Indeed much of the division and acrimony among the Churches of Christianity today resulted from murderous "theological" fights over which domination system was the holy domination system. However, what they all ecumenically agreed upon was that they could do violence and inflict suffering or death on other human beings to get the job done—whatever the job was—and still be faithful to Jesus.

Consider this excerpt from Authority in the Church by one of the most renowned Biblical scholars of the Twentieth Century, Rev. John L. McKenzie:

The offer of power over the kingdoms of the world is placed third (and presumably in the climactic position) by Matthew (4:8-10), second by Luke (4:5-9). Jesus rejects the offer with a quotation from Deuteronomy (6:13) in which it is commanded that worship be given to Yahweh alone. Certainly the story means that secular power is not to be acquired at the price of the worship of Satan; but do we grasp the import of the story fully if we think that the only thing wrong with the offer of secular power is that it came from Satan? In the New Testament, "the world" in the pejorative sense is the realm of the power and the authority of Satan; the reign of God is opposed to this power, and the struggle between the two reigns is constant and deadly. St. Ignatius Loyola made this the theme of the meditation on Two Standards in the "Spiritual Exercises." Like most Christian interpreters from early times, St. Ignatius did not question the implicit assertion in the temptation narrative that secular power is Satan's to give. The offer is not rejected because Satan is unable to deliver what he promises; it is rejected because secular power is altogether inept for the mission of Jesus, indeed because the use of secular power is hostile to His mission.

WHICH POWER SAVES?

Philosophically, "power" is the capacity to make things happen, the capacity to produce change. There are many forms of power available to human beings and to human communities. Knowledge is power, it makes things happen, it produces change; as does love, curiosity, hope or care. Violence, dominative power, also produces change but since it is a form of power rejected by Jesus in word and deed, right up to the moment of His death on the Cross, it cannot produce any change in the Church that is consistent with the Church's mission. So we must be clear on how dangerous and destructive the secularization of power in the Church is. To the extent that a Christian Community has given in to the temptation of secularization, it is not only to that degree incapable of carrying out the mission of Jesus, it is to that degree incarnating a hostile force that is working against the mission of Jesus under the auspices of the name of Jesus. Secularization in the Church is complete when secular powers, values, beliefs, etc., which are overtly contrary to the teachings of Jesus become so ingrained in the *modus operandi* of the Church that they are without question taken for granted to be Jesus' teachings, even though Jesus' own words and deeds contradict them.

> To the extent that a Christian Community has given in to the temptation of secularization…it is to that degree incarnating a hostile force that is working against the mission of Jesus…

BROADWAY

"We are the Church." We have a Head. We have a mission of Christ-centered, nonviolent love and service to friends and enemies that is intended to result in eternal salvation for all humanity. We have a choice: to be or not to be what we are. "We as Church" can choose to continue down the broadway of secularization where homicidal violence, retaliation, revenge, enmity, retribution, shaming,

> "We are the Church." We have a Head. We have a mission of Christ-centered, nonviolent love and service to friends and enemies that is intended to result in eternal salvation for all humanity.

dominative power, vindictiveness and cruelty exist logically, legally, honorably and piously. But, before "We as Church" go this way let us just stop for a moment and ponder the implications of the words of the Biblical scholar I previously mentioned, the late Rev. John L. McKenzie:

> *One can conceive of two dangers to the unity and the integrity of the Church: anarchy and the secularization of power. Of the two, Jesus spoke very little about the danger of anarchy; he spoke frequently and earnestly about the danger of the secularization of power...Jesus left no instructions on how the Church should be governed. I think this is a legitimate conclusion; he left instructions on how the Church is not to be governed, and that is according to the model of secular power. As long as this corrupting influence is excluded, he seemed to have little interest in how the leaders of the Church were to exercise their leadership...*
>
> *He commissioned the Church to find new forms and structure for an entirely new idea of human association—a community of love. In an organization capable of indefinite expansion in time and space, it is more vital that it have unity of spirit, achieved by the indwelling personal Spirit, than that it have rigid forms incapable of adaptation to cultural changes and the movement of history. The Church could not fulfill this commission unless Jesus also endowed it with the resources to find new forms. He did endow it with these resources in the ideal of loving service [diakonia], a new and revolutionary form of authority which Christians could see in his own personal life and mission. Apart from this, there is the incalculable resource of the Spirit dwelling in the members of the one body of Christ. These resources can be inhibited by the greatest danger pointed out by Jesus: the creeping secularization of authority.*

ETERNITY, SANCTITY, CHURCH

We are the Church and we have a choice to make, as well as a temptation to overcome, because a secularized, violence-justifying flock directing the Church is not a dram's worth of improvement on a secularized, violence-justifying shepherd running the Church. Neither can help the individual person nor all humanity reach its essential vocation of eternal participation in the life of God who is love (1 JN 4:8,16) as revealed by the Nonviolent Jesus Christ. So while it should not have to be said to Church leaders, it urgently needs to be said to Church leaders or to "wannabe Church leaders," that what cannot foster and support this primal vocation of one and all becoming a saint has no legitimate place in the Church which has the Nonviolent Jesus as its Head. Specifically this means that every scintilla of justified violence and enmity must be exorcised from the Church, because violence and enmity are hostile to the Holy Spirit of Christic sanctity and are therefore enemies of eternal salvation.

To See God Face to Face

Recently I was driving to the Basilica of Saints Peter and Paul in Rome. As I turned onto what I believed to be *Viale SS. Pietro e Paolo*, I glanced up at the street sign and it read, "Gandhi!" I looked back to the road, then looked up at the street sign again. This time it read, "*Viale SS. Pietro e Paolo!*"

After spending time at the Basilica, I walked to the beginning of *Viale SS. Peitro e Paolo* and there it was! Two street signs were on the same pole at slightly different angles: one informing its readers they were about to enter *Viale SS. Pietro e Paolo*, the other telling readers they were about to enter *Piazza Gandhi*. It turned out that *Viale SS. Pietro e Paolo* crossed and overlapped *Piazza Gandhi*. All of this brought a sense of relief, knowing that I was not hallucinating a Gandhi street sign in Rome! Upon reflection a thought came to consciousness that I had never before analyzed. I realized how symbolically appropriate it was that these two signs be together, that these two places be intersecting, that these three people be perceived in one glance.

St. Peter and St. Paul are the major figures in the first generation of Christianity. St. Peter is indisputably the leader of the Apostles and the earliest Church. St. Paul is the Apostle of the Gentiles. Both are called personally by Christ to their respective missions. Both, after arduous spiritual labor, die as martyrs in Rome and enter into an eternal union with God.

Mohandas Gandhi is born of Hindu parents on October 2, 1869 in India, where he spends most of his life. He is ordinarily called *Mahatma* (Great Soul) in the East and West. Like St. Peter he is married. For spiritual reasons, during the second half of his life, he lives under a voluntary vow of celibacy like St. Paul. Gandhi is never baptized and is never a member of any Christian Church. He remains a Hindu all his life. On January 30, 1948 he is assassinated by N.V. Godse, a conservative Hindu fanatic, who believes Gandhi is corrupting Hinduism.

Do these lives genuinely intersect as *Piazza Gandhi* and *Viale SS. Pietro e Paolo* do or do they only touch tangentially? Is there a reality in these three human existences that could honestly be considered a vital common denominator?

ST. PETER AND ST. PAUL

Peter and Paul are obviously united. In their personalities, tastes, levels of literacy and occupations they have little in common. But, the Spirit that abides in one is the Spirit that abides in the other and that Spirit is the Holy Spirit of Jesus Christ. Because of this Spirit, Peter and Paul are closer to each other than each is to his own breath. So in determining whether the crossing and overlapping of the Street and the Piazza is a valid spiritual symbol, the issue is whether Mahatma Gandhi is authentically united with St. Peter and with St. Paul by the Holy Spirit of Jesus Christ.

MAHATMA GANDHI

Gandhi was better versed than most people in the Bible and in the history of Christianity. His first conceptual contact with the Christian Scriptures took place in 1889 when he met a Christian in a vegetarian boarding house in England while studying to be a lawyer. This man gave him a Bible and extracted from him a promise that he would read it. Gandhi in his autobiography, *My Experiments with Truth*, recollected that he "plodded through" the Old Testament, "but the New Testament produced a different impression, especially the Sermon on the Mount which went straight to my heart." He later recounted, "The gentle figure of Christ, so patient, so kind, so loving, so full of forgiveness that he taught his followers not to retaliate when abused or struck, but to turn the other cheek—it was a beautiful example of the perfect man."

> "The gentle figure of Christ," he [Gandhi] later recounted, "so patient, so kind, so loving, so full of forgiveness that he taught his followers not to retaliate when abused or struck, but to turn the other cheek—it was a beautiful example of the perfect man."

THE KINGDOM OF GOD IS WITHIN YOU

He finished his study of law in England and proceeded to South Africa in 1893 where he established a lucrative practice. During these years he often had discussions with Christians of various ilks. Some impressed him; some depressed him; all wished to convert him. In 1894 he received from a Mr. Coates, a Quaker, Tolstoy's *The Kingdom of God is Within You*. It "overwhelmed me," he reported. "It left an abiding impression on me. Before the independent thinking, profound morality and the truthfulness of this book, all the books given me by Mr. Coates seemed to pale into insignificance." *The Kingdom of God is Within You* was Tolstoy's *magnum opus* on the nonviolent Jesus and His Sermon on the Mount. It was a profound turning point in Gandhi's life which he publicly acknowledged for the rest of his days. As Raghavan Iyer wrote in his classic, *The Moral and Political Thought of Mahatma Gandhi*:

> ...Tolstoy's *The Kingdom of God Is Within You*.... "overwhelmed me," [Gandhi] reported. "It left an abiding impression on me....it was a profound turning point in Gandhi's life...

> *His early hesitancies about nonviolence were overcome by reading Tolstoy's "The Kingdom of God Is Within You" and he became a firm believer in Ahimsa (nonviolence).*

"It was the New Testament which really awakened me to the rightness and value of passive resistance," explained Gandhi.

> When I read in the Sermon on the Mount such passages as 'Resist not him that is evil; but whosoever smiteth thee on thy right cheek, turn to him the other also,' and 'Love your enemies and pray for them that persecute you, that ye may be sons of your Father in Heaven,' I was simply overjoyed and found my own opinion confirmed where I least expected it. The Bhagavad Gita deepened the impression, and Tolstoy's The Kingdom of God Is Within You gave it permanent form.

A Follower of Jesus

In 1915 Mahatma Gandhi returned to India. Over the next thirty-three years he, like St. Peter and St. Paul, tried to live and teach the way of nonviolent love of friends and enemies as proclaimed by Jesus in the Sermon on the Mount. In fact, he even went so far as to declare, "If I had to face only the Sermon on the Mount and my own interpretation of it, I should not hesitate to say: 'Oh yes, I am a Christian!' But I know that at the present moment if I said any such thing I would lay myself open to the gravest misinterpretation." Yet, despite his concerns about

> [Gandhi remarked], "If I had to face only the Sermon on the Mount and my own interpretation of it, I should not hesitate to say: 'Oh yes, I am a Christian!'"

how people, e.g., politicians, journalists, professional religionists, might misuse his reverence for and unity with Christ, he continued to publicly declare the depths of his relationship with Jesus. After a 1931 trip to Rome he wrote:

> There is nowhere, in the little world I have seen, anything to compare with the wonderful frescoes in the Sistine Chapel or the marvelous sculpture in the Vatican. Apart from the incomparable Michaelangelo's paintings in the Chapel, there is a statue of Jesus on the Cross which is capable of moving the stoniest heart....[W]hat would not I have given to be able to bow my head before the living image at the Vatican of Christ Crucified.... The image of Jesus Christ which I saw in the Vatican at Rome is before my eyes at all times....Living Christ means a living Cross, without it life is a living death.

Certainly we have arrived at a juncture where the lives of SS. Pietro e Paolo and Gandhi intersect. The precise place where they unite is the Cross of Nonviolent Love at the heart of the Sermon on the Mount, which is incarnated on Golgotha.

How profoundly Gandhi experiences his union with Jesus can be seen when he proclaims, "Jesus is nonviolence par excellence." Remember, nonviolence is the defining word, symbol and reality of Gandhi's life. The Indian word that he employs, which is translated into English as nonviolence, is *Ahimsa*. It is a word, like *agapé* in the New Testament, which simultaneously describes the nature of God, the essential nature of each human being and the Spirit in which people should always relate to each other and to all of God's creation. He explains it thusly:

> *Ahimsa requires deliberate self-suffering, not a deliberate injuring of the supposed wrong-doer...In its positive form, Ahimsa means the largest love, the greatest charity. If I am a follower of Ahimsa, I must love my enemy or a stranger to me as I would my wrong-doing father or son....Ahimsa is love in the Pauline sense and something more than the love defined by St. Paul, although I know St. Paul's beautiful definition is good enough for all practical purposes.*

Can there be any doubt that the very same Spirit that guides the lives of Saints Peter and Paul until their martyrdom, saturates the life of Mahatma Gandhi until January 30, 1948?

JOHN PAUL II AND GANDHI

On February 1, 1986, Pope John Paul II made the cremation site of Mahatma Gandhi at Rajghat his first stop in India. He opened his remarks that day by noting that, "It is entirely fitting that this pilgrimage should begin here, at Rajghat, dedicated to the memory of the illustrious Mahatma Gandhi, the Father of the Nation and apostle of nonviolence. The figure of Mahatma Gandhi and the meaning of his life's work have penetrated the consciousness of humanity." John Paul then went onto note that, "Two days ago marked the thirty-eighth anniversary of his death. He who lived by nonviolence appeared to be defeated by violence. Yet, his teachings and the example of his life live on in the minds and hearts of millions of men and women....The heritage of Mahatma Gandhi speaks to us still. And, today, as a pilgrim of peace, I have come to pay homage to Mahatma Gandhi, hero of humanity." As if this were not enough, as if he wanted to insure that his words would be as unambiguous as humanly possible, the Successor of St. Peter declared that, "From this place which is forever bound to the memory of this extraordinary man, I wish to express to the people of India and of the world my profound conviction that the peace and justice of which contemporary society has such great need will only be achieved along the path which was the core of his teaching."

> [Pope John Paul II] declared that, "From this place which is forever bound to the memory of this extraordinary man, I wish to express to the people of India and of the world my profound conviction that the peace and justice of which contemporary society has such great need will only be achieved along the path which was the core of his teaching."

It would be hard to overestimate the enormity of the spiritual and religious implications of what the Vicar of Christ said that day. Recognizing that this is the Pope speaking before the world's media about a universally known spiritual leader whose entire personal and public identity is grounded in nonviolent love as God's will and who says that Jesus is the ultimate manifestation of this nonviolent love should shock Christians in general and Catholics in particular into pondering why the Vicar of Peter should publicly so endorse and so identify with this man. The New York Times and most other newspapers around the globe reported the next day that the official Vatican spokesman, Joaquin Navarro Valls said that John Paul's praise for Gandhi was extraordinary: "I haven't heard the Pope saying such things in relation to anyone, living or dead."

REALPOLITIK AND THE SERMON ON THE MOUNT

There are in the Church the people of realpolitik. They are the ones who, with an indulgent smile toward those they consider naïve, say "The Church will live by the Sermon on the Mount the day after the United States elects a President with the Sermon on the Mount as his platform." Perhaps they are right. In mainline and Evangelical Churches in order to be baptized or to receive communion worthily or to be ordained deacon, minister, pastor, priest or bishop, a person is not required to try to live according to the Sermon on the Mount. Indeed, despite all the stellar talents that exist within the College of Cardinals in the Catholic Church, it can be fairly asked, "Where is the 'Gandhi' among them? Where is the one who is known for a lifetime of teaching that the Jesus, who Christians are to follow, is 'nonviolence *par excellence*'? Where is the one of whom it is said, '*The Sermon on the Mount* is the *Magna Carta* of his life?'" The same questions could be asked about most Church leaders of most Churches for most of Christian history. In fact, today and for many centuries past, no one looks at the Church, whether it be the Church of Rome, the Church of Constantinople, or the Church of Canterbury, and exclaims, "There is the communal incarnation of the Sermon on the Mount. There the Sermon on the Mount is taken seriously." It is as if Church leadership and membership have simply decided to veil the Sermon by praising it sumptuously in word while religiously ignoring it in deed. It is as if innumerable Christian worlds have been erected without any reference to it and now these worlds, out of fear of undermining their status, *modus operandi* or credibility, must abandon the Sermon operationally by claiming it to be utopian and unrealistic, a mere non-binding counsel of perfection for a spiritual elite who do not have to deal with the "real" world.

> [N]o one looks at the Church of Rome, the Church of Constantinople or the Church of Canterbury, and exclaims..."There the Sermon on the Mount is taken seriously."

THE MASTER QUESTION

So, perhaps the believers in ecclesial realpolitik are accurate in their assessment. Gandhi thinks so when he notes that, "Much of what passes as Christianity is a negation of the Sermon on the Mount." But, if they are correct, one of the questions that must be asked is whether Church structures, which do not permit leadership to live according to the Sermon on the Mount, should be structures in the Church? Or alternatively, if Church structures do permit leadership ministries to abide by Jesus' teachings in the Sermon on the Mount, then should not people be selected to work in these structures who possess the spiritual acumen and creativity to so operate? There is a moment in his life when Mahatma Gandhi asks an Anglican bishop why he does not teach his people about the nonviolent Jesus and His nonviolent Way. The bishop responds that, "The people are not ready for it." Gandhi then asks, "Are you sure it is the people who are not ready?" The master question to be posed to those who wish the Church to operate on secular assumptions about reality and power, on non-Sermon on the Mount and non-Calvary understandings of existence is this: What is it, that the institutional Church needs to do in order to fully accomplish the mission assigned to Her by Christ, that cannot be done by fidelity to Jesus' teachings of nonviolent love of friends and enemies as proclaimed in the Sermon on the Mount and in the "Sermon" from Golgotha?

> The master question...is this: What is it, that the institutional Church needs to do in order to fully accomplish the mission assigned to Her by Christ, that cannot be done by fidelity to Jesus' teachings of nonviolent love of friends and enemies.

THE MEDIUM AND THE MESSAGE

It has long been accepted by those who study the communication of values that, "the medium is the message." Dissonance between content and the means of communicating it subverts content. For an anti-pornography association to raise money by selling pornography not only invalidates its anti-pornography message but also affirms a pro-pornography position. Without a great deal of dissimulation, rationalization, cunning, logical razzle-dazzle and propaganda recruiting and retaining members for such an organization from among anti-pornography advocates would be impossible.

The structures, the means and the media through which a content is made accessible must communicate the truth of that content as clearly as the rhetoric. If they do not, then the structures, means and media become a self-evident denial of the very truth they are meant to convey. Said starkly, the Sermon on the Mount cannot be taught nor can Jesus be proclaimed effectively by structures, means and methods of operation that are deprecatory, dismissive or hostile to His Sermon on the Mount. Would Christianity even exist at this hour if the Medium of Golgotha did not match the Message on the Mount? Is Jesus or the Jesus-event even conceivable unless the Medium is the Message? Consistency between medium and message is an undeniable and irrevocable dimension of the Divine Plan made visible by Jesus' words and deeds. For Church leadership then, the establishment and maintenance of a consistency between the ends for which the Church exists and the means chosen to achieve these ends is a paramount pastoral and moral obligation because of the immensity of what is at stake: fidelity to Jesus and eternal salvation.

THE COROLLARY

The solemn corollary of the previously posed "master question" is this: "What is it that can be done by fidelity to Jesus' teachings of nonviolent love of friends and enemies as proclaimed in the Sermon on the Mount and in the "Sermon" from Golgotha?" Are there unimaginable miracles lying dormant in these Sermons? Is there, within fidelity to these Sermons, a hidden power that can conquer evil, destroy death, illuminate a wisdom more fundamental than human conjecture, banish all that makes the universe ceaselessly groan for redemption? Do these sermons contain the mustard seed of power that can empty tombs and make dry bones come to life?

> **Are there unimaginable miracles lying dormant in these Sermons?**

There is an axial self-disclosure in the opening of Gandhi's autobiography that is pertinent here. Strangely, or maybe not so strangely, it is seldom referred to, even by those who are familiar with his life and writings. The passage exposes the overriding desire that directs Gandhi's life, indeed, it is the pivotal text for making sense of his life:

> *What I want to achieve—what I have been striving and pining to achieve these thirty years—is self-realization, to see God face to face. I live and move and have my being in pursuit of this goal. All that I do in way of speaking and writing and all my ventures in the political field are directed to this same end.*

It adds infinite gravity to Gandhi's decision to unconditionally walk in the way of the nonviolent Jesus and His Sermon on the Mount once it is recognized that he primarily chose this path not because it would liberate India from the British, not because it was easy or hard, not because it was culturally or religiously acceptable, but simply because he saw it to be the way to eternal union with God.

OPUS DEI

Gandhi's choice is in accord with the teaching of Jesus, who reveals an intimate connection between the Sermon on the Mount and salvation when, at the conclusion of the Sermon, He states, "It is not those who say, 'Lord, Lord' who will enter the Kingdom of Heaven but those who do the will of my Father in heaven" (MT 7:21). It is the will of the Father that Jesus is making known in His Sermon on the mount. It is the Father's will that he is living on Golgotha. For those who have "minds to understand," Jesus is declaring that the work of God, *opus Dei*, cannot be accomplished by adopting and "baptizing" the mentalities and mechanizations of the world of realpolitik. To the contrary, He is explicitly announcing that the Sermon on the Mount, which is "made flesh" on Golgotha, is the *opus Dei* unto eternal salvation. SS. Pietro e Paolo and Mahatma Gandhi concur. Their crossing and overlapping lives serve, now and forever, as resplendent and corroborating signs. These signs point to the

Way of Jesus as the Way to the Kingdom of Heaven, as the Way to accomplish all that needs to be accomplished to conquer evil, to empty tombs and to see God in an eternal face to face.

Follow the Nonviolent Jesus OR Follow the Nonexistent Jesus

The follower of the nonviolent Jesus must be committed to proclaiming by word and deed, in season and out of season, that the only Jesus there is or ever was to believe in, to follow, to pray to, to worship is the nonviolent Jesus of the Gospel. Such Christians have to be resolutely dedicated to bringing this Gospel truth and its network of implications to all the Churches of Christianity. The most immediate and self-evident of these implications is that nonviolent love and authentic discipleship are always and forever bound to each other. Said another way: if any Church or Christian proclaims that the Jesus of the New Testament can be followed by intentionally destroying other human beings that Church or person is either a liar or else that the Church or person is deceived and is living according to a grotesque falsehood. Helping Churches and individual Christians caught in this deadly perversion of Gospel truth is a mandatory mission for any Christian who has accepted the grace full Gospel Truth that reveals the Son of God as Nonviolent Love Incarnate.

The follower of the nonviolent Jesus is engaged in this task because love of and fidelity to Christ "compels" (2 COR 5:14) it. Where God morally expects more from a person, silence is sinful. A person is not permitted to stand by and say nothing while someone teaches that arsenic is cough medicine. It would be intolerable for a Church or a Christian to look on in silence as the minds of those chosen by Jesus to be His disciples are being poisoned by counterfeit proclamations about the Christ and His Way.

Human integrity alone would insist that if a person, e.g., Jesus, lives and dies on behalf of a truth, e.g., the nonviolent love of friends and enemies as the Way of God, this truth should be acknowledged as his truth, whether people agree with him or not. So at one level Christians committed to proclaiming the nonviolent Jesus and His nonviolent way are simply individuals or groups of people possessing the decency and integrity to give the man Jesus what is fairly due Him, an honest presentation of the truth He taught, lived and died doing.

PEACE AND SALVATION

However, the almost imperceptible number of Christians, who pledge allegiance to the nonviolent Jesus, exists for purposes far, far beyond this. The renowned Biblical

Scholar, the late Rev. John L. McKenzie writes in his Dictionary of the Bible that, "Peace in the New Testament becomes very nearly synonymous with salvation." The God of Christianity is "the God of Peace" (RM 16:20; 1 TH 5:23; PH 4:9) "made visible in Christ Jesus." (COL 1:15) Therefore, the Christian who is selected for the imitation of Christ-God (JN 13:34) is by that fact alone called to the life of God, "to a life of peace." (1 COR 7:15). Hence, Jesus in the Beatitudes designates the "peacemakers" as "sons and daughters of God" (MT 5:9) because they share in and impart to others the very Life, the Shalom, of their Divine Parent. It is then, in and only in communion with the God of Peace, which is established by and only by imitation of and obedience to the Prince of Peace and His Way of Peace, that the Church and the Christian receive the grace of true peace and are thereby enabled to be agents to all humanity of that peace which is "nearly synonymous with salvation."

PEACE: THE SELF-COMMUNICATION OF GOD

In the New Testament peace is the Self-communication of the God of Peace through, with and in His Word, the Prince of Peace, Jesus. Communication is an exchange, limited by a person's capacity to receive it, which creates a community or communion between the transmitter and the recipient. Self-communication is the highest form of communication since the communicator himself or herself is given to the recipient—the giver and the gift are one. However, in all communication, the effectiveness with which a communicator can enter into another person's existence is inhibited or enhanced by the receiver's abilities. A deaf person cannot hear the clearest oral communication. A blind person cannot grasp what is written in perfect penmanship. A mind and a heart closed to the nonviolent mind and nonviolent heart of the Nonviolent Prince of Peace can neither hear nor see nor understand the Nonviolent Word of God—regardless of how precisely, simply, creatively or powerfully the Word is presented.

PEACE: THE END AND THE MEANS TO THE END

This is where, that presently minuscule number of Christians proclaiming the nonviolent Jesus enters in. They are spiritual and intellectual magnifying glasses for their fellow violence-justifying Christians and for the rest of humanity. Their mission is two-fold. First, they desire to be instruments for the free Self-communication of the God of Peace in the Nonviolent Jesus Christ to the Churches, to individual Christians and to the world. Second, they desire to awaken the Churches, other Christians individually and the world to Jesus' teaching, that nonviolent love of friends and enemies unto death is the Way to that peace which is "nearly synonymous with salvation," to that peace which is the Self-communication of God. The methodologies, by which they can offer this service of magnifying for others the good news of the God of Nonviolent Love made visible in Jesus Christ, are as countless as minds are creative—but the Spirit in which they are offered is One, namely the Nonviolent Holy

Spirit of the Nonviolent Jesus. In order to open the eyes of the Churches so they can see the Nonviolent Word, in order to open the ears of Christians so they can hear the Nonviolent Word, and in order to open the minds of all human beings so they can understand the Nonviolent Word of God, the nonviolent Christian missionary should accept as her or his own A.J. Muste's insight that, "Peace is not the end, peace is the way." In 1936 this great apostle of Gospel nonviolence writes:

Begin by assuming that, in some degree, in some situations, you must forswear the way of love, of truth, must accept the method of domination, deceit, violence—and on that road there is no stopping place. Take the way of war and there is war—not only between nations, classes, individuals—but war, division and consequent frustration within your own soul. Thus, it seems to me that we have to say that peace is indivisible. "Peace is indivisible," not only in the geographical and diplomatic sense, but in the sense that the way of peace is really a seamless garment that must cover the whole of life and must be applied in all its relationships. Every pseudo and partial pacifism breaks down.

One must first do what has to be done with one's self in order to be able to accept the Self-communication of the Nonviolent Holy Spirit of Peace, before he or she will be in a position to transmit to others the Nonviolent Word of Peace. In this world the Word effectively rides on the breath of the Spirit. It seems to me therefore that every Christian committed to Gospel nonviolence must, if "Peace is indivisible," say, "Amen," to the declaration of faith of the Quaker, James Nayler, which he made while dying as the result of being robbed and beaten in 1660 A.D.

There is a Spirit which I feel that delights to do no evil, nor to avenge any wrong, but delights to endure all things, in hope to enjoy its own in the end. Its hope is to outlive all wrath and contention, and to weary out all exaltation and cruelty, or whatever is of a nature contrary to itself. It sees to the end of all temptations. As it bears no evil in itself, so it conceives none in thought to any other. If it be betrayed, it bears it, for its ground and spring is the mercies and forgiveness of God. Its crown is meekness. Its life is everlasting love unfeigned; it takes its kingdom with entreaty and not with contention, and keeps it by lowliness of mind. In God alone it can rejoice, though none else regard it.

Peace is the gift of the God of Peace and is the task of the assemblies and individuals who are disciples of the Prince of Peace. The task cannot be accomplished without embracing the gift of the Nonviolent Holy Spirit of Peace. Acceptance of the gift cannot be achieved without removing whatever barriers have to be removed in order to receive the Communication. Does this mean that the Christian is prohibited from confronting evil in the world until he or she has arrived at an unshakable rock of tranquility from which he or she can never be moved? Absolutely not! It means only that when Churches and Christians lose touch with the peace of Christ, which is part and parcel of Jesus' understanding of God and God's Way, that they do what must be done to get out of the un-Christ-like, un-Holy spirit in which they are operating. Churches and Christians must never allow themselves to accept the falsehood that evil can be overcome by an un-Christ-like spirit motivating thoughts, words or deeds.

Repentance and Praxis, Praxis and Repentance

In other words for the nonviolent Christian missionary to be all that she or he can be in bringing the Churches of Christianity back to the Nonviolent Jesus and His teaching of Nonviolent love of friends and enemies as the Way "to that peace that the world cannot give," she or he must go to war internally and unceasingly against each and every spirit that does not proceed from the Nonviolent Holy Spirit of the Nonviolent Jesus Christ. To refuse to enter into this war of the spirits or to fight it without bona fide earnestness is to guarantee that all efforts to re-convert the Churches to the Nonviolent Jesus and His Nonviolent Way will be defective, and hence largely ineffective. Seriousness of purpose dictates seriousness in acquiring and applying those means that are essential in order to achieve the purpose. To by-pass this internal war in order to fight a more public war on behalf of Gospel nonviolence is to become an incarnational witness against one's own truth. Both wars must be fought simultaneously and with equal vigor. Praxis and repentance, repentance and praxis are one and the same reality for those who wish to proclaim the Nonviolent Jesus and His Nonviolent Way to God and Peace.

"Follow Me!" "Come Back to Me!"

Said pointedly: for a Christian or a Church to follow Jesus only in terms of external behavior—or worse only in terms of telling others to follow Jesus in their external behavior—is *de facto* not to follow the Nonviolent Jesus who lives, but is instead to follow the nonexistent Jesus who never was. If people are going down the road of violence and enmity, Jesus is never in front of them leading them on. It makes no difference whether the road of violence and enmity is an interstate highway of high-tech mass murder or a secret back alley of revenge-drenched mental images. No one can be following the Jesus of the Gospels on such a road because He never takes such a way. It is impossible to follow a person down a road on which he never walks. Jesus' position geographically in relationship to all roads of violence, whether they are concretized in thought, word or deed, is that He stands at their entrance crying out to those who have embarked upon them: "Turn around! Come back to Me!"

Only God can conquer evil and death in any or all of their manifestations. The God of Peace in the Nonviolent Jesus communicates Himself to humanity in order to do just this and thereby gift humanity with that peace, "that passes all understanding." The nonviolent Christian missionary must be as open and faithful to this graceful Divine Self-communication when raising the issue of others not hearing the Nonviolent Word of God, as she or he expects others to be in accepting the Nonviolent Word of God. This is not meant as a law of good salesmanship, nor as a warning to avoid the charge of pharisaism. This is a necessary orientation of the mind, heart and will without which the Nonviolent Word of God in all its power cannot reach others through us.

FIDELITY NEEDED, NOT A CROWD

It is a Biblical truism that God does not need numbers, God needs only fidelity. From Abraham to Jesus it can be seen that the fidelity of the one or the few is more important to the realization of God's Plan than all the king's horses and all the king's men. Which of us passing by the stinking, little rat-infested hill called Golgotha on the first Good Friday two thousand years ago and seeing the naked, brutalized, suffocating Jesus of Nazareth would have said, "There is a man more powerful than Tiberius Caesar? There is a man who will move the world beyond anything that Tiberius could ever dream!" Not one of us would have thought such thoughts. Not one of us would have looked at the poor soul on the cross, gasping for breath in order to be able to say, "Father, forgive them for they know not what they do," and reflected to himself or herself, "There is power that will leave Caesar in the dust!" Yet, today, two thousand years after that first Good Friday, Tiberius Caesar is but a footnote in history and all time is measured by that poor soul, struggling to love his enemies and to overcome evil with good until his last agonized death rattle. Freely given fidelity in thought, word and deed, in mind and heart, in desire and behavior, in little matters and great to God's will and way as revealed by the Nonviolent Jesus is all God wants and all God needs to renew the face of the earth beyond anything that any human being can envision.

PACIFISM: AN IMPRECISE CHRISTIAN TERM

However, it is necessary to be clear about what is God's will and God's way as revealed by Jesus before incarnational fidelity can be given to it. Now, pacifism is a word that first enters into a modern language about the year 1880 in France. The Oxford English Dictionary first cites it in the 1910 edition. The word is of questionable Christian validity today. It does not define or describe what the nonviolent Way of Jesus is. In practice it can be an outright interference to hearing all that Jesus does say about nonviolent love in the Gospels. Pacifism is the rejection of war based on either philosophical or revelatory grounds. Gospel nonviolence is the conformity of mind and heart, soul and body, desire and behavior specifically to the person of the Nonviolent Jesus and His Way of nonviolent love of friends and enemies. Such conformity self-evidently makes participation in war morally impermissible and in this sense the Christian is a pacifist. But, the Christian is commissioned by vocation to go so far beyond simply not participating in war, that the word, pacifism, can be gravely misleading to the normal person trying to discern what the will of God is as revealed by the Nonviolent Jesus.

Christians who only reject the homicidal violence of war, but let us say, endorse the homicidal violence of capital punishment are not following the revelation of God's Way in Jesus. They are simply living according to a philosophical position of selective homicide, based on some human perspective and some rationale about who should live and who should be killed. I raise the distinction between pacifism and Gospel nonviolence at this point in order to reflect with clarity on the mass murder spree in which the United States government was previously involved in Iraq and how the nonviolent follower of the Nonviolent Jesus must respond. I raise it to help insure that our incarnational fidelity will be given to the Nonviolent Jesus and not to some nonexistent Jesus.

COMING BACK FROM MORAL DWARFISM

Let us begin by having the uprightness to do what Albert Camus asked, namely to call murder "murder," when we see it. I call Gulf War II murder because I am a disciple of Jesus Christ and according to the Way of morality announced by Him in the Gospel, it is murder. However, even by the most contorted application of the traditional standards of that utterly irrelevant spiritual sleeping pill called the Christian Just War Theory, this business in Iraq is blatant murder. This walk on the dark side, that has been organized by the U.S. and British political and economic elites, is not Frazier vs. Ali. It is Al Capone and his machine gun-toting thugs blowing away a third grade class. It is murder by all traditional institutional Church standards—and murder does not become anything less than murder just because it is mass murder or legalized.

Those who directly support murder are *ipso facto* complicit in murder. Jesus Christ, Son of God, would have pleaded with those of His disciples who were in Iraq to "put up their weapons, obtain conscientious objector status, come home and repent." Jesus Christ, Son of God, would say to those of His disciples who were at home and who were accrediting this human slaughter: "Stop it! Stop encouraging and motivating my disciples and your brothers and sisters in Christ to kill those whom I dearly love! Stop listening to those professional Christian leaders among you who are telling you to do and to support what you know darn right well I would never do and never support. Stop listening to them. Stop supporting them. Stop! Instead, read, re-read and re-read again and again and again My words. Then come back to Me with all your heart."

THE EVIL PERSON?

For the sake of spiritual clarity and authentic Christic love, the distinction between evil and sin must be considered at this point in the discussion of the nonviolent disciple's response to the murder operation in Iraq. Evil takes place when a person does something contrary to the will of God. Sin takes place when a person with full knowledge freely consents to do evil. If a person gives another person arsenic instead of cough medicine, an evil has occurred and the terrible consequences of evil will unfold. However, if the person did not know he or she was giving arsenic instead of cough medicine, then no sin has been committed, since he or she did not have knowledge that what was on the spoon was arsenic and therefore could not have had the intention to choose evil. None of us knows how free any person is at any moment to consent or to withhold consent to evil. None of us ever knows how much knowledge or lack of knowledge of the truth of the matter any person has at any moment. Therefore, none of us, no one of us, is in a position to morally judge whether another is a sinner. Indeed to morally judge another human being a sinner would be contrary to the explicit teaching of Jesus (MT 7:1; LK 6:37; RM 2:1-2).

However, it is necessary to judge whether an act *per se* is evil or not, whether or not an act *per se* is contrary to the objective will of God as revealed by the definitive Word of God, Jesus, the Christ. The American and British homicide program in Iraq is objectively murder for anyone for whom Jesus and His teachings represent the will of God. Whether a single American or British Christian politician or soldier, patriot or preacher who supported the murder in Iraq has sinned only God knows. The Christian precept, that reads, "Hate the sin but love the sinner" is not quite correct. It should read: "Hate the evil but love, as the Nonviolent Christ would love, the person who is doing it." This distinction between evil and sin and the psychological, emotional, cognitive and spiritual orientation it invites are at the very heart of the internal practice of Christic nonviolent love, from which the external practice of nonviolent love organically must flow. Without this absolutely required distinction, the person and the evil he or she is doing are symbiotically meshed into one reality in consciousness and conscience, namely, into that entity that is called "the evil person."

Once this gigantic spiritual, psychological, emotional step is taken, it is only a half step to killing evil by killing evil people. Those who are committed to the nonviolent Jesus of the Gospel must not only never take the half step, they must assiduously avoid taking that gigantic first step, even if it means they must sacrifice all their earthly alliances and effectiveness. The disciple of the Nonviolent Jesus must, if necessary, wage a Battle of Armageddon internally, in order to steadfastly keep before his or her eyes the Gospel truth that the person doing an evil is an infinitely valued, eternally loved son or daughter of God. For once this Gospel truth is lost from consciousness and replaced by the "evil person" concept, a road has been entered upon on which as A. J. Muste says, "there is no stopping place."

Nothing herein said is meant in the slightest to suggest that the follower of the Nonviolent Jesus and His nonviolent Way should ignore evil or kowtow to it. On the contrary, since Jesus' entire life is one passionate battle after another against evil, the nonviolent disciple's entire life must be one passionate battle after another against evil. But again, since only God can conquer evil, the battle must be conducted with zeal according to the Battle Plan given to us by His Son, His Word, Jesus—even if it kills us to limit ourselves to this Battle Plan.

A Time of Temptation

We have read the words of the U.S. sergeant in Iraq (NY Times: 3-29-03):

> *"We had a great day. We killed a lot of people...We dropped a lot of civilians but what do you do?...I am sorry, but the chick was in the way."*

We have seen the pictures: decapitated infants, maimed little girls, children screeching uncontrollably from burns, parents out of their minds with horror and grief.

We have heard the Goebbelsesque propaganda:

> *"Saddam threw the U.N. inspectors out on trumped up charges that the U.S. was using them for espionage; Saddam has weapons of mass destruction that are an imminent threat to the U.S. and the world".*

We have witnessed mega-corporate mass media nightly lie by commission and omission and use its power to drum up the emotions of barbarous patriotism on behalf of murder.

We were outraged and incensed by the unrelenting spread of the anti-Christic spirits of evil released by that war, not just in Iraq but here in the U.S.?

The evil of raw violence, devoid of even moral pretense, seems to sit in the driver's seat and boldly dares anyone to try to interfere with its agenda. Churches, theologians and preachers have already begun the propaganda process by which they plan to baptize Orwellian Christianity. The theologies and homilies Christianizing the new National Security State are upon us. We may perhaps feel impotent and irrelevant, frightened and intimidated before the capacity of a relatively small coterie of men, with long histories of homicidal violence behind them, to bring so much evil into so many Churches and so many lives.

This then is a moment of temptation for us who struggle to be good faith disciples of the Nonviolent Jesus. Do we continue to follow the Nonviolent Jesus or do we dump

Him in order to follow one or another of the nonexistent Jesuses? Will we allow our commitment to love of enemy and to overcome evil with good to be ensnared in the trap of identifying evil with the person who is doing it, in order that we might have someone to unload on—physically or verbally? Will we permit ourselves the pleasure of manufacturing in our consciousnesses an embodiment of evil in order to have a person to attack and bring down like Saddam's statute even if it is just in our own minds?

If a Christian is employed in murder or if a Christian leader is engrossed in supporting murder, he or she must be told to stop and must be told to stop with all the seriousness with which Jesus told the Pharisees to knock off their phony pietism, nit-picking moralizing and entrepreneurial manipulation of peoples' desire to know God. A Christian or Christian leader directly involved in or directly supporting murder must be informed of his or her Judas' discipleship with the clarity, intensity and perseverance with which Mahatma Gandhi informed one of the most brutal men of the Twentieth Century, Winston Churchill, that Churchill's choices *vis-à-vis* India were evil. For his moral truthfulness Gandhi earned Churchill's hatred. However, upon the death of the man that Churchill demeaningly referred to as that "little fakir" he said, that in all his dealings with Gandhi he never felt that Gandhi lost a concern for him personally. Resoluteness in naming homicidal violence and enmity evil must in no way undermine resoluteness to maintain the Christic perspective that those doing the evil are also the beloved of God.

VIOLENCE AND ENMITY ARE CONTAGIOUS

Let us beware and be aware, because the evils of violence and enmity possess a magnetic power that can drag people into their spirits. They can induce people to imitate them internally and externally and to initiate reciprocal dynamics of escalating hostility and cruelty. Those who are committed to the Nonviolent Jesus of the Gospel as Lord must not allow this to happen within themselves or within their communities. There is truly a feature to evil that enrages the souls of those who see it, after they have broken through the contrived facade constructed to obscure its horror. The Christian in obedience to his Nonviolent Lord must vow eternal hostility towards evil but he or she must be on guard not to become hostile towards the evildoer. If he or she does, then the Christian minimizes his or her effectiveness, for the devil cannot and will not ever drive out the devil. Satan cannot be victorious over himself. (MK 3:23; MT 12:25,26; LK 11:17-18) What is portrayed as the Victory of Violence, whether the victory takes place in thought, word or deed, is just the furrowing of the most fertile ground imaginable for the planting and the cultivation of the seeds of violence. Down the line these seeds will produce the bitter fruits of further violence and enmity with all their powers for generating transgenerational contagion by evil. A follower of the Nonviolent Jesus must work unsparingly so that he or she is not conquered internally or externally by the very spirits of violence and enmity which they are committed to resisting. He or she must not become an infected carrier of the virus of violence masking itself as Gospel nonviolence.

THE PRACTICE OF THE PRESENCE OF THE LOVING PARENT OF EACH AND OF ALL

The power and courage to unrelentingly proclaim the full Gospel of the Nonviolent Jesus and His nonviolent Way emanates directly from a constant and committed conscious relationship with the God of Peace as revealed by Jesus, with God who is love (*agapé*), with God who is the infinitely and eternally loving Father, Mother, Parent of each person and of all. Without the determination to maintain this conscious relationship we lose our courage, we lose our energy, we lose our Way, we lose our peace, we lose our awareness of the presence of the Nonviolent Holy Spirit of which James Nayler writes and we easily succumb to the temptation to follow a nonexistent Jesus. Without the sense of being always in the presence and under the absolute protection of Nonviolent Holiness, Nonviolent Love and Nonviolent Consciousness itself we will be drained of our faith in the power and efficaciousness of the cross of nonviolent love and will gradually by word, deed or desire turn the cross upside down into some kind of a sword. Without this relationship with the never ceasing Self-communication of the Nonviolent Holy One, the person who we see doing evil will cease to be a human being loved forever by God and will become a "thing" interfering with our survival or our ideas on how the world or the Church or others should act. However, for those who struggle to remain conscious of God as revealed in, by and through Jesus, a fall into such spiritual degeneracy is unlikely to take place—and if it does, it will not be justified but will provoke immediate repentance.

The mind of Christ which Christians are called to put on and from which, and only from which, Christlike acts can flower is a mind saturated from its center to its circumference with the Self-communication of God as Father/Mother/Parent "of all, over all, through all and within all" (EP 4:6). This Father/Mother/Parent God revealed by Jesus must pervade our conscious life if we are to unambiguously proclaim by word and deed, for all the remaining days of our lives, the Lordship of the Nonviolent Jesus of the Gospel, as well as, His Way of nonviolent love. This may require dying to parts of ourselves that we wish to robustly affirm. It may require picking up so many little, almost imperceptible, crosses of nonviolent love that we fall 70 x 7 times under the martyrdom of their seeming insignificance. It may demand a lifetime of unseen warfare on the battlegrounds of the mind and the heart. It may necessitate, as it did for Mahatma Gandhi, a child-like repeating of the name of God in order to stay attentive to the presence and protection of our eternal Father/Mother/Parent. However, once summoned by the power of Truth to proclaim the Nonviolent Jesus to the Churches and to the world, we only have two choices: either we must do what must be done in order to proclaim Him, or we must follow a nonexistent god into the sound and the fury that leads to nothing but suffocation in the totally perishable.

BE A REALIST

Let me conclude with a final reflection on an aspect of a nonviolent spirituality that, it seems to me might be helpful. Let us name it "perspective spirituality." Each human being comes into this world like a person who enters a movie 1/4 of the way through it. He or she leaves this world like a person who exits the same movie 1/3 of the way through it. The person has only the most superficial of conjectures about what went on before his or her arrival and only the wildest of speculations about what will come after departure. However, he or she does know there is a before and after.

Now, the evils of violence and enmity invariably catalyze anguish in those who see them for what they are. Herein hides the uncanny cleverness of evil that enables it to manipulate good to its own odious ends. It is natural, almost biological, for people to be passionately disturbed when they become aware of the ugliness of evil that lurks behind the cosmetics it wears. Evil is hideous when seen out of costume. But, this very anguish over evil is what evil utilizes to try to draw distressed souls into itself.

A "2 BY 4" WORLD

The Latin root from which the word anguish is derived is *angustia* (tight place). Anguish over evil perceived or done has a potential to constrict the mind, to narrow consciousness. In a state of anguish a person's time-space-reality awareness can shrink to the size of a molecule. Perspective and context are lost. The person finds himself or herself imprisoned in a narrow "2 by 4" world where values, attitudes, beliefs, emotions, judgments and truths are generated within a speck of reality that is experienced as the entire universe. The person may have known at one time that there are a 100 billion galaxies of a 100 billion stars, that he or she has not been present for most of the movie that came before and won't be around for most of the movie that comes after, that the Incarnation of God has taken place, that the life, teachings, death and resurrection of Jesus have been in history for 2000 years, that when he or she has "been dead 10,000 years" the nonviolent I AM who is Parental Love and Perpetual Peace will still be. The anguished person may have known that "neither life nor death, no angel, no prince, nothing that exists, nothing still to come, not any power or height or depth, nor any created thing, can ever come between us and the love of God made visible in Christ Jesus our Lord" (RM 8:38,39). However, none of this registers in the "tight place" of anguish.

THE WORD OF THE CROSS, THE WORDS FROM THE CROSS

All that envelopes consciousness in the "2 by 4" world of the hour of anguish is the overpowering experience of evil out of control and winning. Despair or hate or meaninglessness or paralysis or fury or even abandonment of the Nonviolent Messiah and His Nonviolent Way are easily surrendered to when the repercussions of violence and enmity invade the psyche. It is in this tiny "2 by 4" world that idols, false gods and anti-Christlike spirits approach us with offers of diabolical powers and promises of "effective" solutions, if these powers are accepted and the power of the cross rejected. When this state of temptation threatens our fidelity to the Nonviolent Jesus and His Nonviolent Way we must grasp the cross of nonviolent love and hold it before us by the grace of raw will as the Absolute Truth about God's reality, will, way, nature, wisdom and power. In these times we must remove the plugs from our ears that the "2 by 4" world gives us and listen to the truth about the depth of reality being communicated by the "Word of the Cross" (1 COR 1:18). We must allow God's Word from the Cross, as well as, His Word from the empty tomb to super-abundantly enlarge the perspective and the context in which we make our judgment about which way to follow in the face of seemingly unconquerable evil. We must also permit God's words from the Cross of nonviolent love of friends and enemies to reach us, for they too are His Self-communication. "Father forgive them for they know not what they do" and "I promise you, this day you will be with Me in paradise" are words whose source is a Reality that predates the "Big Bang." They are words of Nonviolent Love that overcome the illusion of a "2 by 4" universe that appears to proclaim the omnipotence of evil. They are words that Tiberius Caesar and all his spiritual heirs down the centuries never said and never could have said. They are words that can only arise out of the Nonviolent Holy Spirit in which James Nayler lived and died.

Only the atheist despairs. "Impossible" is not a word in the dictionary of Christianity. After the Resurrection of Jesus Christ nothing is impossible—not even the inconceivable! So let us with ever increasing fidelity march on in communication and in communion with the Nonviolent Lord of lords, knowing with the certainty of faith, that God will provide all that is necessary for us to plant the micro-seeds of nonviolent Christic love that He desires us to plant for the salvation of all humanity—even if He wants them planted in the worst of all possible soils, the rancid dirt of the Hill of Golgotha. Let us listen to and confidently follow the Producer, who knows how the movie begins and how it ends. He is the Alpha and the Omega, the Lord of history, the Lamb who has conquered. Let us also go forth with that larger than cosmic perspective that communicates to us that most of what is most important in existence happens on the invisible side of existence and therefore we should be concerned primarily with fidelity, not visible success. Let us persevere in faith in the nonviolent Jesus, abandoning forever all nonexistent Jesuses. Then, let us begin to sow deeds of Nonviolent Christic love, with the help of the Nonviolent Gardener, knowing that all the new flowers of all the tomorrows in time and in eternity are today seeds that have to be planted.

The Refusing Churches and New Testament Scholarship

If the interpreter is faithful to his sources, he will at least avoid distorting them; and acquaintance with biblical literature is a quick way to learn how easy it is to distort them. But (scholarly) interpreters are not the only Christians who distort the Gospel.

—Rev. John L. McKenzie
The Power and the Wisdom

The discovery of a deceiving principle, a lying activity within us, can furnish an absolutely new view of all conscious life.

—Jacques Riviere

Law students are taught that "anything can be argued" and are trained in the methodology necessary for persuasively arguing any side of any issue. Lawyers, of course, are not unique in developing such skills. This "sickness of language," as it is termed by Thomas Merton, presently infects all forms of communication. It is the contaminated lifeblood of military and "intelligence" propaganda machines, politicians, advertisers, corporate journalists, academic mandarins, used car salesmen and carnival barkers to name but a few. Conjectures, grammar, rhetoric, logic, irrelevancies, omissions, half-truths and sometimes known falsehoods are jumbled together in such a way as to validate or invalidate, to confuse or castrate or "viagratize" any idea, as the needs of the self may call for. To employ Eric Fromm's term for this solipsistic phenomenon, truth is "mobile," as mobile as the dollar bill: "what I require for truth is truth; what does not serve my interest as truth is not truth."

It is perhaps an unfortunate fact of life, but nevertheless it is a fact of life, that New Testament scholars, individually and collectively, are as disposed as any other group to the temptation "to argue anything" that is within their individual or collective self-interest to espouse. Biblical scholar Gerhard Kittel of THEOLOGISCHE WORTERBUCK ZUM NEUEN TESTAMENT fame and Die Judenfrage infamy, and the illustrious pro-Nazi philosopher, Martin Heidegger, are probably the most conspicuous modern examples of the proposition, sometimes referred to as *The Blue Angel* syndrome, that concupiscence can drive and manipulate the highest levels of cognitive competence. However, there are uncountable numbers of equal or lesser intellectual lights, ancient, medieval and modern, who can also be considered outstanding witnesses to this syndrome. In George Orwell's novel about a fear-ridden, high-tech national security state, NINETEEN EIGHTY-FOUR, he coins a word, "doublethink." It is a new word but a hoary activity. It means the acceptance as true of contradictory ideas at the same time. In NINETEEN EIGHTY-FOUR there is hardly a scholar or scrubwoman to be found who would not argue with zest on behalf of the Party's three slogans: "War is Peace. Freedom is Slavery. Ignorance is Strength." And, in today's Churches, whether they be conservative, liberal or radical Churches, how many *de facto* doublethinkers are there on the issues of violence and nonviolence, enmity and Christic love, sword and cross, Caesar and Christ?

DOES AIR EXIST?

Debating whether air exists or not can be for a moment an invigorating cognitive workout, much, as say, toying with a Rubik's cube. One may also try to respond rationally to the presentation that "air does not exist" in order to be courteous to the person who is advocating such a position. But, outside of gamesmanship and etiquette, the never ending slicing and dicing of concepts in order to deny the obvious is a crafty ploy. Arguing over what there is nothing to argue over is a stratagem of evasion. It is a scheme for drowning out truth under wave after incessant wave of chimerical polemics. For those who have an interest in having Jesus on their side when engaging in violence and enmity, this is the artifice of preference. The Aquinas dictum, *"contra factum non argumentum est"* (there is no argument against fact), is brushed aside in favor of a cornucopia of specious speculations. The argument that "air does not exist" never runs out of breath. There is always one more conjecture, one more postulation, one more assumption, one more possible interconnectedness that the intellectually nimble can dream-up for keeping the bogus argument going and thereby keeping the reality of air in doubt and the air of doubt in reality. Spurious hypothesizing is the intellectual scoundrel's last bastion of defense against unwanted truth.

Doubt gives birth to indecisiveness, fence straddling, hesitancy, and an overall undermining of the ability of the will to choose. Doubt is good and proper if there is a well-grounded basis for doubt. Without this basis the sowing of doubt is either mental illness or a gambit to decoy people away from truth and its offspring, resoluteness.

Kicking around ever more dubious and abstruse theories as to why Jesus could have engaged in violence and enmity and why He could have justified violence and enmity as God's Will on some occasions is not worthy of the history, effort and life that men and women have invested in the discipline of New Testament scholarship. It is a subterfuge. There is much to be genuinely debated in New Testament studies, but the nonviolence of Jesus and His Way of nonviolent love of friends and enemies is not on the list. Arguing over the unarguable is not what New Testament scholarship in the Twenty-First Century should be contributing to the life of the Church and the life of humanity. If what Gandhi says about Christians being the only people on earth who do not see Jesus as nonviolent is accurate, imagine what the non-Christian world thinks of the quality of a New Testament scholarship that cannot state with intellectual confidence that the Jesus of the New Testament and the primitive *kerygma* is nonviolent and teaches a Way of nonviolent love of friends and enemies.

CONSTANTINIAN CHRISTIAN MISSIONARIES AND SCHOLARS

Basically the Churches—Catholic, Orthodox, Protestant and Evangelical—take as their own, the "proclamation" of the Gospel that underlies the story about a group of Christian missionaries in a far-away land some 400 years ago. After decades of catechesis, all members of the society convert to Christianity. As the missionaries are departing, the local chief in order make them feel good and to show the depth of his and his peoples' Christian faith emphatically declares: "Know this for certain, if I and my men were around at the time, they never would have crucified Jesus, they never would have stoned Stephen, and they never would have martyred our fellow Christians—at least not without first paying a high price in their own blood." Before being summarily dismissive of this vignette, please consider what in fact the Churches of Christianity have been doing and justifying these last 1,700 years. Then explain how their proclamation and its effect differ from the proclamation of our story's missionaries and its effect. Does Twenty-First Century New Testament scholarship really want to be associated with validating and defending this kind of proclamation as being even possibly consistent with the New Testament and the primitive *kerygma*?

"X AND NOT X"

So let me try to say it with transparency. As stated in a prior article on violent versus nonviolent monotheism, between two meaningful statements, "X and not X", there is no middle ground. If one is true, the other is false. The person who says, "I am nonviolent but... is not nonviolent. He or she is justifying violence at the point of the "but". The Jesus of the New Testament and the primitive kerygma is either a justifier of violence and enmity or He is not. Now, if Jesus in His person or in His teaching is a justifier of violence and enmity then He is the most inept justifier of violence and enmity in the history of the world—and one might add that the same would hold true if He is a justifier of adultery or pedophilia. A Jesus, who endorses or legitimates violence, simply passes beyond all bounds of credibility. As one of the most esteemed Biblical scholars of the Twentieth Century, the late Rev. John L. McKenzie, former president of The Society of Biblical Literature and Exegesis and of The Catholic Biblical Association, states with unflinching clarity: "If Jesus did not reject any type of violence for any purpose then we know nothing about him" and "No reader of the New Testament, simple or sophisticated, can retain any doubt of Jesus' position towards violence directed to persons, individual or collective, organized or free enterprise: he rejected it totally."

DOUBLESPEAK AND SOLIPSISM

Yet, despite the manifest obviousness of the New Testament and the primitive *kerygma* on this issue, it is equally obvious that in the world of Christian theological and moral discourse, in the world of Christian catechesis and in the world of operational Christianity doublethink prevails. Both nonviolence and violence are presented as morally in accord with Jesus and His Way, as are non-retaliation and retaliation, love of enemies and annihilation of enemies, "put up your sword" and "take out your sword", laying down one's life for one's friends and taking other people's lives for one's friends, picking up the cross and picking up the sword, etc.

Since doublethink, and its linguistic derivative "doublespeak," are by structure solipsistic, evidence-dismissing thought processes, it can be "argued" that "War is peace," and that "Caesar's way is Christ's Way." Solipsism permits anything to be "argued"—even that adultery and pedophilia are part of Christ's Way. Indeed, there is no idea that, by slick, solipsistic, jesuitical doublethink, cannot be portrayed as being the same as its opposite, e.g., the way of the sword is the way of the cross.

So, is it any wonder why for the vast majority of people Jesus is an irrelevancy? The reason that Jesus is a non-concern for so many in the world is due to the fact that what the Churches have been proclaiming about Him has so often not been the Gospel. Central to this failure of the Churches to proclaim the Gospel truthfully, clearly and powerfully is their steel-willed *refusal* to accept what is self-evidently available to any literate person, namely the nonviolence of the Jesus of the New Testament and the primitive *kerygma*, and His Way of nonviolent love of friends and enemies. These Refusing Churches thereby broadcast an enfeebled and most unattractive mixed message to humanity: "Jesus is God, the Savior of the world and the Messiah but you do not have to believe Him when He unequivocally teaches the rejection of violence and the love of enemies."

This spiritual hodgepodge of a proclamation becomes outright doublespeak to the ordinary non-Christian and many Christians when participation in the mass homicidal violence and enmity of war is taught, with or without the veneer of scholarship, to be compatible with following Jesus and His Way, i.e., when homicidal military activity is taught as faithful discipleship. The human family may not yet be a community of Einsteins, but it is not about to become very excited spiritually over a God whose followers do not even believe He knows what He is talking about on the basic human problems of violence, retaliation and enmity.

Theology as Atheism

Now, whether or not theology, as has often been suggested, is the subtlest form of atheism is open to discussion. However, there is no question that a theology that is forever searching for new avenues by which to reject its God's teachings is an expression of agnosticism, atheism or idolatry. Humanity in its longing to know if God exists and to know God is not about to be duped by Churches, which feel they must resort to linguistic legerdemain in order to get around what they consider God Incarnate's embarrassingly dopey understanding of the real world and how to live in it. Most human beings, who have heard and will hear this inherently self-contradictory proclamation of the Refusing Churches, never have and never will respond to it by exclaiming, "It is He!"

For most of humanity the proclamation of a solipsistic gospel is anti-magnetic. Private, non-scriptural, make-believe "Jesuses" justifying, endorsing, encouraging, or supporting violence and enmity are repulsive—except for those who want to draft a non-Jesus masquerading as Jesus in order to religiously prop up their violence and enmity. For non-Christians and more than a fair share of Christians the Refusing Churches' proclamation is spiritually unintelligible and feeble. To announce that Jesus is God Incarnate and then to announce that He does not know of what He speaks when He speaks on the issues of violence and enmity is intrinsically incongruent; it is just plain daffy. Of course, many are not so gracious as to limit their evaluation of the Refusing Churches' proclamation to unintelligibility. Many simply see the faith of the Refusing Churches, whether they be fundamentalist Churches or "high" Churches, as a phony privatized faith of enlightened terrestrial self-interest, selling itself as the way to an eternity of happiness.

The failure of the Gospel to reach and empower with the Life of Christ-God contemporary humanity should be a concern for anyone who is a Christian. It is not that contemporary humanity is not in crying need of all that Jesus has to offer. It is that the Church created by Jesus in order to make available all that He has to give to humanity, refuses to make it available. If most of humanity pays no attention to Jesus, it is because most human beings see no spiritual reason for paying attention to Churches that live by and teach as God's will private "truths" that their Divine Founder irrefagably rejects.

THE COLOR OF JESUS' HAIR

The motivating desire behind this essay is to make the Gospel intelligible and arresting for men and women. The Gospel is a proclamation not a philosophy. It proclaims the awesome act of God in Jesus Christ, which is known only by revelation. This proclamation is meant to make the God event in Jesus perpetually present here and now to human beings across time and space, culture and geography. In Jesus Christ the person encounters the true God and receives the definitive revelation of the Holy Will to which he or she is called to convert. The Jesus Christ as presented in the New Testament and in the primitive *kerygma* and not the Jesus Christ of personal imagination and concupiscence is the ultimate embodiment and revealer of the true God and His Way. But, this Jesus is a nonviolent Jesus, who teaches and lives a nonviolent love of enemies and friends unto a horrifying death at the hands of lethal opponents. Conversion to and trust in this Jesus is where salvation is found.

Is the Way the Redeemer lived, what the Lord taught and how the Anointed One died not integral to "the decisive eschatological event" in Jesus Christ? For the Refusing Churches the nonviolence of Jesus and His Way of nonviolent love of friends and enemies is as inconsequential as the color of his hair. But, is it even conceivable that the God revealed by Jesus could reveal Himself, redeem the world and offer human beings a Way of encountering Him in time and in eternity in a Jesus who is the moral equivalent of a Rambo, a Julius Caesar, a Mao Zedong, a John D. Rockefeller or a Winston Churchill?

To herald the saving act of God in Jesus Christ without reference to His nonviolent love of friends and enemies is to fail to herald the Gospel in all its fullness, truth and power. Any human being, including Jesus, is only known, beyond its mere existence or raw being in time and space, through his or her words and deeds. Remove the words and deeds of Jesus and there is no discernibly unique person to know, to love, to serve, to imitate, to hear or to follow. The divinity in Christ is gracefully discovered and encountered by knowing His humanity. What He is reported to have said and what He is reported to have done is the *sine qua non* for understanding His meaning, purpose and value in the human situation. As the major Catholic moral theologian of the Twentieth Century, Rev. Bernard Haring writes, "It is not possible to speak of Christ's sacrifice while ignoring the role of nonviolence." Or, as Rev. Frederick McManus, Professor Emeritus at The Catholic University of America and one of the most influential and scholarly Catholic liturgists of our time, states regarding the Eucharistic anaphora: "The centrality of the mission of peace and nonviolence in the Gospels needs to be acknowledged in the confession of the great deeds of God in the Lord Jesus, and the Christian people need to see this essential dimension of Eucharistic peace in the prayer which they confirm and ratify with their Amen." A proclamation of a Jesus who, directly or impliedly, justifies violence and enmity by his words and deeds or who has nothing detectable to say on the subject is a pseudo-proclamation. It is a repelling proclamation. It is an anti-proclamation. However, it is the proclamation that the Refusing Churches are adamantly making daily.

Jesus is not a Vacuum

A private, solipsistic proclamation of the Gospel is a contradiction in terms. The herald of the Gospel announces what he or she has been commissioned to announce by another, namely Jesus. The content of the proclamation is the Word of God received through Jesus, the Word of God who is Jesus. The purpose of the proclamation is faith in Jesus Christ and conversion to Him. But, what is the content of this faith and conversion to which people are called? It is Jesus Christ—body and blood, soul and divinity, word and deed. It is a conversion to a Jesus Christ who is not a Biblical Phinehas, a Torquemanda, a Constantine, a Pope Julius II, an Audie Murphy, a Robespierre or any of the other violent and enmity-laced people, conservative, liberal or radical, who have walked on the face of the earth justifying themselves and their life-choices in the name of the Holy One. The Jesus of the primitive *kerygma* and the New Testament is also not a content-devoid name or person. He is not a vacuum into which individuals or Churches can shovel whatever they wish and then convert to their own content and herald it to the world as the Gospel. The Jesus of the apostolic *kerygma* and the New Testament is nonviolent and teaches a Way of nonviolent love of friends and enemies. This is who and what the herald of the Good News of the great and salvific deed of God in Jesus is commissioned to announce. This Jesus and to this Jesus alone is the chosen proclaimer of the Gospel commissioned to call others to convert.

It is in the truthful proclamation of the Good News that unfathomable reservoirs of grace, truth, peace, hope and meaning reside for attracting men and women to Jesus. Churches, incarnationally unified around the heralding of this tremendous act of Divine Love in the nonviolent Jesus, will be magnets to humanity. Even if Churches are institutionally separated in other ways, if they accept the imperative, "to love one another as I have loved you," (JN 15:9-12) that flows from the indicative that Jesus Christ is the nonviolent Divine Savior of the World, who teaches a Way of nonviolent love of friends and enemies, they will be Christic magnets. This they will be because they are proclaiming the Truth of the Nonviolent Word of God from which, in which and for which humanity is created. It is time, indeed it is 1,700 years beyond time, for violence-justifying and enmity-validating solipsistic Christians and Churches to die to themselves and to their cherished private proclamations, so that the nonviolent Jesus Christ of the New Testament and the apostolic *kerygma* can live in them and in those to whom they are called to witness and minister.

"Jesus, I don't Trust You."

Each generation, each Church, each spiritual movement within a Church e.g., Pentecostal, Marian, Benedictine, Franciscan, Carmelite, Ignatian, etc., and each individual Christian has his, her or its own reasons for refusing, distorting or discounting the full Gospel of the nonviolent Jesus and His Way of nonviolent love. However, in the end all the distorting and discounting, all the dexterous "argumentation" in support of doublespeak, solipsistic proclamations boils down to one ringing public declaration: "Jesus, I don't trust you." This is the unspoken but thunderous testimony of the Refusing Churches and all subdivisions thereof. No wonder the overwhelming majority of human beings do not take the Jesus of the Refusing Churches or the Refusing Churches seriously—except as institutions of vulgar political and economic power with which they must wheel and deal. And so, it is not so much that the Gospel of the nonviolent Jesus Christ of the primitive *kerygma* and the New Testament has been proclaimed and refused by most of humanity, it is rather that most of the Churches of Christianity have refused to proclaim it for a long, long time.

A Transmogrified Proclamation

After more than half a century of active Church participation, it is this writer's conviction that most of the bishops, priests, ministers and congregants of the various Churches are too chained to a nurtured *nomos* of a violence-enmity justifying Christianity to free themselves from fear of the nonviolent Jesus and His Way of nonviolent love of friends and enemies. Beyond this social-psychological reality, there is almost no limit to the support systems that are in place to keep Christians of every ilk shackled to this transmogrified proclamation of a violence-enmity justifying "gospel". However, behind it all, there is a primeval piece of mythology on which this social-psychological state and its support systems feed and through which they are able to do their work of enslaving Christians to palpable sophistry. This myth, which continually re-energizes the Refusing Churches, their leaders and their congregants, so that they are able to exclude the nonviolent Jesus from their proclamation of the Gospel, has at its core a pernicious falsehood. The unuttered but stupefying pivotal untruth on which this mendacious mythology relies and which the Refusing Churches propagate hourly is this: The Jesus who does not exist, that we know, is better and safer for us than the Jesus who does exist who we do not know!

Medicinal New Testament Scholarship and Remedial Truth

It is a second conviction of this writer that in the contemporary world the axial agency for the graceful liberation of the Refusing Churches from their bondages to this sham security mythology is New Testament scholarship. **If a substantial majority of**

New Testament scholars could find the courage to collectively and publicly declare what they know is true, namely, that as the result of their persevering labors in New Testament studies it must be concluded that it is incontestable that Jesus is nonviolent and that He is totally opposed to the use of violence and enmity for any purpose, then the chains would snap.

From the instant that such a declaration is made no Christian or Church, high or low, high-tech or low-tech, would ever again be able to say without denial of intellect that, "Follow Me," can include violence and enmity, that deciding for Jesus leaves open the options of violence and enmity. Both the Church and all humanity would be irrevocably changed by such a public pronouncement. Where it leads both the Church and humanity cannot be forecast, but such is the case with the entire Christ event or with the initial statement of $E=mc^2$. All that the society of New Testament scholars can do here is plainly and coherently state what the New Testament and the primitive *kerygma* graphically and incontrovertibly state about the nonviolent Jesus and His Way of nonviolent love of friends and enemies—and then let the strings of consequences vibrate throughout human consciousness.

Note, it is not a proclamation of the Gospel that is being asked of New Testament scholars. It is rather a definitive scholarly statement about what the New Testament and the primitive *kerygma* communicate concerning Jesus, violence and enmity. Surely enough time has passed and enough scholarly energy been expended since the days of Richard Simon, that New Testament scholars can at least tell humanity and Christianity this much about Jesus and His Way with intellectual and moral certainty. Again, what humanity and individual Christians do with such a statement of scholarly truth is in their hands and God's. But, what is for certain is this: Neither humanity nor individual Christians can accept or act on truth they have never heard communicated forthrightly and intelligibly.

If after this declaration Christians and Churches choose to proclaim and practice a "gospel" of justified violence and enmity, they and the world will know that their proclamation and practice is not based on anything that the Jesus of the New Testament and the primitive *kerygma* ever was, said or did. They and the world will be fully cognizant that their chosen stance, rather than being an act in conformity with intellect is an act that perverts intellect. They and the world will also be acutely aware that their transmogrified proclamation rather than being an act of sound exegesis is in reality a raw act of the will—a ***committed refusal*** to accept, obey and proclaim the Good News as proclaimed in the New Testament and the primitive *kerygma*.

PUSILLANIMITY AND PERFIDIOUSNESS

Finally, let me conclude on a note that according to cultural standards of persuasiveness and etiquette is precisely the wrong note on which to conclude. Perhaps, it is an especially wrong note when one considers the two groups principally, but not exclusively, being addressed and critiqued in this essay: New Testament scholars and institutional Church officials. Both live in closed-shop worlds that vigilantly guard their turf from the intrusions of pesky outsiders. Such worlds almost universally experience a critical analysis by a non-member as hectoring by the not fully enlightened. However, because of the spiritual, physical, moral and theological magnitude of what is at stake for so many, I feel that I must risk, hopefully without a scintilla of mean-spiritedness, this final stern word.

Truth cannot be defended by falsehoods or by being unconcerned about falsehoods. Falsehoods are no less falsehoods because they are popular falsehoods or traditional falsehoods. The explicit or implicit scholarly ratification or ecclesiastical canonization of existing popular error by ignoring it or by obfuscating known truth is a dereliction of integrity by the scholar, as well as, by the Church leader. The late Canon Joseph Coppens of Louvain, a distinguished Twentieth Century Biblical scholar, once wrote that professional exegetes may have little to say in the Church, but they ought to have the courage to say it. Indeed, where more is intrinsically required and vitally needed from the scholar or the Church leader, silence is perfidious.

The Nonviolent Spirituality of St. Maximus The Confessor

St. Maximus the Confessor is born in 580 A.D. in Constantinople. He lives for 82 years. Between his birth and death lies a physical life of which relatively little is known. As with many who gain renown after their deaths, the life of St. Maximus, as it is popularly known, is permeated with pious legend. Therefore, we must be content with knowing only a few of the larger and fewer of the smaller events of his time on earth. Yet this is sufficient, for the information we have confirms that this man, who is known as the "Father of Byzantine Theology," is no mere academic speculator. What we have left of his life verifies what we have left of his writings. He speaks primarily about a reality that is alive in him. Thus we can enter into his teachings knowing that what we are reading is not the work of a compulsive theological wordsmith, but rather is the innermost thought of a person who in the end chose to die, not kill, for the truth he has, rather than purchase an extension of earthly life by living in untruth.

A Life and Death Struggle

St. Maximus is born into an upper class family. His formal education is of the highest quality. When it is completed, he takes employment at the imperial court. In the year 610 Emperor Heraclitus names him his First Secretary. However, in 614 he resigns from this prestigious position and enters the monastery at Chrysopolis.

By 618 he has at least one disciple, a monk named Anatasius who is to stay with him until they are both martyred more than forty years later. In 625 he leaves his first monastery and goes to the Monastery of St. George at Cyzicus. It is from this monastery that his earliest writings come. In 632 he moves to the Monastery of Euchratas in Carthage. The abbot of this monastery is Sophronius, a significant figure because he is one of the first to recognize the problems involved with monothelitism,[1] the aberration of the Gospel that would eventually be responsible for taking Maximus' life. It is during this stay in Africa that Maximus completes two of his major works—*Questions to Thatassius* and *Ambigua*.

Maximus appears to have stayed in Africa until 646 at which time he travels to Rome to continue his efforts for dyothelitism.[2] Pope Martin I calls a Lateran Council in 649 in order to confront monothelitism. This Council at which Maximus is present as a monk, rejects monothelitism. When the Emperor Constans, himself a monothelitist, hears this, he arrests the Pope and Maximus. Pope Martin I is tried in 654 and is sentenced to exile in Cherson, where he dies in 655.

The trial of St. Maximus begins in 655. Consistent with the course of suffering his Master had to endure, Maximus is first subjected to trumped-up charges of crimes against the state. When this course of action proves unsuccessful, he is sent into exile for six years. In 662, at the age of 82, he is hauled back to Constantinople where a Church Council of hierarchs, more loyal to the Emperor than to Christ, anathematizes and condemns him. The traditional sentence of mutilation of those members by which "false" doctrine is expounded, is carried out. Maximus' tongue is cut out and his right hand is amputated. He is then carted about the city of Constantinople so, like his Lord, the people he is trying to serve can mindlessly ridicule him on cue from civil and ecclesiastical politicos. After this exercise of legalized viciousness and "justified" punishment, he is sent off to exile in Lazica, where he dies on August 13, 662.

THE PERDURING EMBRACE OF LOVE ENGENDERS DEIFICATION

Having now seen the historical milieu in which Maximus lives, let us zero in on the central theme from which he derives his thoughts on Gospel nonviolence: the goodness, and above all, the love of God:

> *God alone is essentially good, and only a person who imitates God is good in the disposition of his soul; for this person's chief aim is to unite the wicked with Him, who is essentially good and thus make them good. To this end, being reviled, he blesses; being persecuted, he suffers it; being defamed, he brings comfort; being slain, he prays for his slayer. He does all, lest he fall from his chief aim—love...[3] For he who has love has God himself, for 'God is Love'. To Him be glory unto ages of ages. Amen.[4]*

With the above concluding words, St. Maximus, the Father of Byzantine Theology, summarizes and closes his spiritual classic, *Four Centuries on Love*. These words could equally be a summary for his entire theology. Indeed, they encapsulate Byzantine spirituality. For beyond all realities, experiences and concepts in Byzantine spirituality, the truth that "God is Love" reigns supreme. No aspect of theology, no dimension of liturgy, no practice of spirituality is outside this primal insight. All existence is a mystery in the perduring embrace of Love. "God is Love" is the quintessential notion of Byzantine theology.

> "God is Love"...No aspect of theology, no dimension of liturgy, no practice of spirituality is outside this primal insight.

The second most important theme in the Byzantine spiritual tradition is one which might strike the Western mind as absurd, if not blasphemous. The idea is that of "deification." The formula, which has been universally employed to embody this notion, is "God became human, so that human beings may become God."[5] St. Maximus, in explaining the concept of deification, says:

> *In the same way in which the soul and the body are united, God should become accessible for participation by the soul and, through the soul intermediary, by the body, in order that the soul might receive an unchanging character, and the body immortality; and finally that the whole person should become God, deified by the grace of God-become-human, becoming whole person, soul and body, by nature and becoming whole God, soul and body by grace.*[6]

To "become partakers of the divine nature" (2 PT 1:4) is the reason why men and women were created and the reason why God became a human being in Jesus, the Christ. Deification is so central to Byzantine spirituality because it represents the purpose and meaning of all human history, individual and collective.

Since God is Love, another way of formulating the notion of deification is by saying that "Love became human so that human beings may become Love." However, the only way to become Love is by Loving. One can no more become a loving person by hating than one can become a truthful person by lying. There must be consistency between the end to be achieved and the means of achieving it. One becomes Godlike by living like God. The living God is living Love. To love, according to Maximus, is not merely to imitate God; to love is to participate in the very life of God here and now. Participation here in the Divine Life is the Way to participation in the Divine Life hereafter. "The mystery of Christ is the mystery of Love."[7] Love is Divine Life and Divine Life is Love, here and hereafter.

> "Love became human so that human beings may become Love." However, the only way to become Love is by Loving.

DEIFICATION—SYNERGY BETWEEN DIVINE WILL AND HUMAN WILL

It is not exclusively through a person's own activities, however, that he or she is deified. The process of deification occurs when the individual freely chooses to use his or her own energy in obedience to the uncreated divine energy of Love, which is the Divine Will, which is God. The synergy of these two energies finds its ontological root in Jesus Christ, the man who is God—the Person in whom this cooperation or synergy between divine will and human will is perfected. To follow Christ, then, is not merely to follow an external ethic; it is to literally live in Christ, to be one with the new reality of Immortal Love made accessible to all people. Thus, it naturally follows that when Jesus is asked what is the way to eternal life, He simply proclaims, "Love!" "Love the

Lord your God with your whole heart, whole mind and whole strength." Love your neighbor as yourself" (LK 10:25). The Kingdom of God is the Kingdom of Love. More precisely, Love is both the Kingdom and the Way to the Kingdom. More precisely still, Love is both the Reign of God and the Way to the Reign of God.

> **Love is both the Reign of God and the Way to the Reign of God.**

But what is this love? Of what does it consist? How can one judge whether one is living it? After all, the atrocity cannot be imagined that at some time and place has not been committed in the name of love.

TO LOVE AS CHRIST LOVES IS THE ENTIRE LAW OF THE GOSPEL

It is the understanding of Byzantine theology that Jesus Christ is the icon or image of the Father of all—the image of God, who is Love. The person who sees and hears Jesus Christ, sees and hears the Father (JN 10:30; 14:9). "Christ is the icon of the invisible God," says Paul (COL 1:15). Therefore, St. Maximus writes:

> *'If you love me, keep my commandments' says the Lord* (JN 14:15). *'This is my commandment, that you love one another as I have loved you'* (JN 15:12). *Thus he who does not love his neighbor, does not keep the commandments; and he who does not keep the commandments cannot love the Lord.*[8]

Here Maximus is expressing with acuity the concrete meaning and daily practical implications of the great commandment of love that is proclaimed by God Incarnate. To love God means to love one's neighbor (1 JN 4:20-21). To love one's neighbor means to love him or her as Jesus would have loved

> **To love God means to love one's neighbor....as Christ does love him or her.**

him or her, as Christ does love him or her right now. Christ, not the law; Christ, not social custom; Christ, not secular wisdom is the standard by which one determines whether he or she is loving God and neighbor.

The only commandment unique to Jesus in the entire New Testament is the one just quoted above: "Love one another as I have loved you." Love Incarnate, Jesus, is the living Icon to which anyone who wishes to do God's will must constantly refer in order to discern what the love of God and neighbor means in each situation in life. To love as Christ loves is the sum and substance of the entire moral life of the Christian—the entire law of the Gospel. It is the purpose of every life, the goal of every moment of life. It

> **To love as Christ loves is the sum and substance of the entire moral life of the Christian...the goal of every moment of life.**

is the means to be employed at every instance of life in order to accomplish every task in life. An act, which is not an act of love as Christ defines love by word and deed, is an act that is morally worthless (CF 1 COR 13). Any act that cannot be done with Christ-like love is an act that neither God nor humanity has any need.

If, therefore, one wishes to burn witches or engage in the mass slaughter of war in good Christian conscience, all one has to do is honestly prove to oneself that the loving Christ would have burned witches or engaged in the mass slaughter of war.

But if a person cannot see our Lord thinking, speaking or acting in a particular way, then he or she obviously cannot "love as He loves" by thinking, speaking or acting in such a fashion. When one does not love as Christ loves, one neither loves God nor one's neighbor. When a man or woman does not love as Christ loves, he or she cannot grow in Divine life. The name for the choice of refusing to grow in Divine life, for refusing to love as Christ loves, is sin.

SIN—CHOOSING FREELY TO REVOLT AGAINST LOVE

In Byzantine spirituality, sin is a revolt against God, a revolt against Love. Sin is a thought, word or deed that misses the mark of being in conformity with the mind, the spirit and the heart of Christ. The origin of sin is freedom, which is also the necessary condition for love. Christian love is free love or it is not Christian love. Maximus states that human beings are morally free: "Since the human being was created according to the image of the blessed and supra-essential deity, and since, on the other hand, the divine nature is free, it is obvious that a human being is free by nature, being the image of the deity."[9]

> Sin is a thought, word or deed that misses the mark of being in conformity with the mind, the spirit and the heart of Christ.

Sin has no other source than the freedom of the human being who sins. The problem of evil is the problem of the evildoer. In Byzantine spirituality, Original Sin, "The Fall," does not mean that a baby is born full of evil. There can be no sin, Original or personal, no revolt against the God of love, without the individual's free choice.

Indeed, human nature incurs the consequences of Adam's sin, which is mortality. "The shadow of death is human life," says St. Maximus.[10] Having become mortal, Adam and Eve conceived mortal children and "because of death all people have sinned" (ROM 5:2). Human beings inherit mortality from The Fall and from mortality is born the fear of non-being, the fear of death. From this fear, which arises from the desire for bodily preservation for ourselves and those whom we love, comes the temptation to sin, to be un-Christ-like and to choose unwise forms of self-love.

> From this fear [of death]... comes the temptation to sin, to be unChrist-like and to choose unwise forms of self-love.

Thus, in Byzantine spirituality the Baptism of a baby, is not to forgive sins, which the newborn has never committed, but to communicate to the infant the new Immortal Life and Love, which Christ brought into the world by His Incarnation, Teaching, Death and Resurrection. This guarantee of Eternal Life and Love liberates the human being from the fear of death and thereby liberates him or her from the attractiveness of sin and the un-Christ-likeness that seems to be required for survival. Because of faith in Jesus Christ a person is now clothed in the garment of immortality and need no longer concern himself or herself with the horrifying possibility of ceasing to be, or of being nothingized in an indifferent universe. St. Paul illuminates this good news, which is above all good news, majestically when he proclaims:

> *For I am certain of this: neither death nor life, no angel, no principality, nothing that exists, nothing still to come, not any power, or height or depth, nor any created thing, can ever come between us and the love of God made visible in Christ Jesus our Lord* (RM 8:38-39).

In Byzantine spirituality, however, freedom is never removed from persons, therefore the "origin of sin" remains. Human beings are offered by Love (God) all that makes love possible. They are offered Love itself, but it is a gift. It can only be offered. Love cannot be imposed or coerced. A person always remains free to say "Yes" or "No" to a union in Love. In the end, without the agreement of the will of the person and the will of God, salvation is not possible. People are made in God's image, which means that they are to some degree free for as long as they exist. Even if a person exists forever, this does not change. But how far a person advances into or separates himself or herself from God's likeness, that is, from loving as God loves, from being like God, from participation in the very Life of God, depends on how the person exercises his or her freedom.

Christ's resurrection can liberate us from death and sin if we allow it to do so. But under no circumstances does Christ's resurrection liberate us from freedom. For to take away freedom would be to simultaneously take away the possibility to love. Once freedom and love are no longer part of human existence, life, even immortal life, is at best a compulsive movement from one meaningless now to the next in an eternal Pavlovian Disneyland. Men and women are freely deified through the gift of Love accepted. Only by freely loving as Christ loves can the human being and all humanity be united ever more deeply in a communion of love with each other and with that eternal Communion of Love, the Trinity.

THE DISCIPLINE OF LOVE

But to love as Christ loves requires taking seriously the very first word that Jesus speaks at the beginning of his public ministry: "Repent" (MT 4:17). Repentance is not mere sentimental sorrow for sins. It is a significant change of mind, a fundamental change of heart. It means becoming a new person by putting on the new mind of Christ, and thereby loving what Christ loves and as Christ loves. St. Maximus sees that for people to live the life that Christ invites them to live necessitates that each person freely enter into a discipline of love. This discipline of love is essential, not because discipline saves, but because love saves. However, the love that saves is so contrary to the values and desires that society nurtures in people, that only the most serious work to put off one's old mind in order to put on the mind of Christ can possibly be effective. Maximus understands that the human mind is a bloody mess, and that the bloody human activities and institutions that abound are the fetid fruits of mind-styles which have chosen to do other than think, desire and love as Christ thinks, desires and loves. St. Maximus has no prescription on how minds that overflow with anger, hostility, vainglory and cupidity can create institutions that are anything other than reflections of themselves.

> Repentance is not mere sentimental sorrow for sins. It is a significant change of mind, a fundamental change of heart.... for people to live the life that Christ invites them to live necessitates that each person freely enter into a discipline of love.

Maximus is concerned with the mind, the soul and the spirit of the person. He recognizes that a person becomes what he or she thinks, desires and loves, and on a larger scale, that a community becomes what its individual members think, desire and love. Thus, each person must enter into the process of changing his or her mind and heart into the mind and heart of Christ. The discipline of love which Maximus discusses amounts to insights and suggestions on what it is necessary to do and what it is necessary to avoid in order to move more deeply into the life of God Who is Love (*Agapé*), and thereby participate more fully in the salvation of the world.

THE PROBLEM OF VIOLENCE

Because of the perimeters of this article, I shall limit my discussion of Maximus' reflections on the discipline of love to those that relate specifically to the problem of violence. This is, regrettably, a somewhat artificial treatment of his spirituality because he sees an irrevocable connection on many levels between other forms of evil and violence:

Let no man deceive you by the thought that you can be saved while serving lustful pleasure...[because] a mind that falls away from God and forms friendship with material things, surrendering to lustful 'pleasure, becomes bestial and fights with men for such things.[11]

Sin generates a further propensity to sin. Therefore, it is a fatal spiritual illusion to believe that sin can be compartmentalized and contained. "It is the greatest deception of evil," instructs the renowned Jewish theologian Martin Buber, "that it gets people to believe that once they have chosen it, they can control it." Violence is a manifestation of evil and cannot be effectively understood or overcome as an isolated form of evil.

For St. Maximus, loving God with one's whole heart, whole soul, whole mind and whole strength is everything. All emanates from this first great commandment, including the second great commandment, to love one's neighbor. The very first sentence of St. Maximus', *Four Centuries on Love*, reads: "Love is that good disposition of the soul in which it prefers nothing that exists to the knowledge of God."[12] This coincides with Mahatma Gandhi's explicit statement in his autobiography concerning the North Star that guides his every act:

What I want to achieve—what I have been striving and pining to achieve these thirty years—is self-realization, to see God face to face. I live and move and have my being in pursuit of this goal. All that I do in the way of speaking and writing and all my ventures in the political field are directed to this same end.[13]

Knowledge, for Maximus, does not refer to the product of abstract cognitive speculation, but is rather knowledge in the biblical sense of knowing and being known in a face to face communion of love. "But," adds Maximus, "no person can come to such a state of love if he be attached to anything earthly."[14]

"[H]e who has torn the mind away from love of God and from His presence and lets it attach to anything sensory prefers the body to the soul"[15] and "self love, the mother of passions, is love of the body."[16] "What a person loves, he or she desires to grasp with all their strength and all that obstructs them in this they push aside, lest they lose it."[17] Thus a love of God "casts out every passion which hinders this end."[18] "Passions taking hold of the mind attach it to material objects and separating it from God force it to be occupied with them. On the other hand, love of God, when it takes possession of the mind, severs its bonds, persuading it to value neither objects of the senses nor even temporal life itself."[19]

THE VOLUNTARY RELINQUISHING OF VIOLENCE

It would be very easy and very wrong to relegate Maximus to the category of a non-realist who simply espouses a doctrine of passive pietism. One of the most obvious meanings of nonviolence is the voluntary relinquishing of the protection of violence. What are the dynamics of consciousness and conscience that are necessary in order to genuinely accept this way of existence, this way of living without the protection of violence? Certainly most people who say they espouse nonviolence do not equate nonviolence with the total rejection of violence in human affairs. They may reject the more obnoxious and brutal forms of violence. They may reject all violence that is not socially condoned. They may reject all violence that does not seem to serve, advance or protect their earthly interests. For instance, the pacifist church, which calls on the police power of the state to protect its personal and real property, possesses worldly prudence, but is not nonviolent. Maximus says that "Love of God disposes a person to scorn all transitory things."[20] Without this state of detachment, which issues from loving the God of Love, nonviolence is impossible:

> *If one loves someone, one strives to please him or her in all possible ways. Thus if a person loves God he or she will certainly strive to do what pleases Him.[21]...To love Him is to keep His commandments.[22]...But if you are indeed keeping the commandment of loving your neighbor, why do you implant in yourself the bitterness of annoyance against him? Is it not clear that instead of active love you prefer the transitory and in protecting it you wage war against your brother or sister?[23]*

The love of the transitory always results in war against someone, in some way, because, knowingly or unknowingly, some neighbors assist a person in her or his particular love of the transitory, while other neighbors inhibit her or him. Those who provide assistance, usually receive good will; those who hinder them, usually receive something other than love. Only the love of God can result in love of all neighbors—enemies as well as friends—for no neighbor, regardless of her or his desire for the transitory, can separate one from the love of God. However, all neighbors, even the lethal enemy neighbor, can provide assistance in a person's progress in his or her journey "to see God face to face."

SEPARATING PASSIONS FROM REPRESENTATIONS

Transitory things in themselves are not evil. It is the way the individual apprehends and judges them that causes problems. People develop according to what they think and according to how they respond to what is thought. "An object is one thing, a representation another, passion yet another. An object is, for example, a man, a woman, gold and so forth; a representation, a simple thought of some such object; passion, either an irrational love or undiscerning hatred of one of these things."[24] "The mind of a lover of God arms itself not against things and their representation, but against the passions connected with the representation. In other words, it rises not against the man nor against the woman who has offended it, nor against their image, but against the passions connected with these images."[25] "The whole struggle against the demons consists in separating passions from representations."[26] Or, as St. Isaac the Syrian explains it: "If you want to love your enemy, attack yourself."

> The mind of a lover of God arms itself not against things and their representation, but against the passions connected with the representation....The whole struggle against the demons consists in separating passions from representations.

Dissolve the desire and the act never happens. Countermanding the consciousness of hate and lust ensures that murder and adultery never occur. Nurturing the consciousness of hate and lust increases the probability that murder and adultery will increase. The conquest of the only enemy a Christian has, evil, in all its forms, is in the first instance a conquest of the enemy within:

> *When you see that your mind acts rightly and justly amidst worldly thoughts, know that your body will remain pure and free of sin also. But if you see your mind occupied by sinful thoughts and do not stop it, then know your body too will not fail to succumb to them.*[27]

For St. Maximus the struggle against evil cannot be piecemeal. Human freedom ultimately resides in one's ability to choose which thoughts one retains and with what disposition they are retained. The Christian life, that is to say, the effort to put on and live from the mind of Christ, is a very active, intense use of intellect and will. It is an ongoing commitment to choose a particular mindstyle, a mindstyle consistent with the mindstyle of Christ. As the Christian mindstyle is chosen, the Christian lifestyle will organically follow. And, where two or more have the same mindstyle and the same behaviorstyle, a community-style comes into being. As St. Maximus conveys:

> Human freedom ultimately resides in one's ability to choose which thoughts one retains and with what disposition they are retained.

> *As things are the world for the body, so representations are the world for the mind. As the body of a man commits adultery with the body of a woman, so the mind of a man commits adultery with the representation of a woman....In the same way he revenges himself through a mental image of his body on a mental image of the man who has offended him. It is the same with all other sins; for what the body does in deed in the world of things, the mind does in the world of images.*[28]

The battlefield for the Christian, then, is the mind. Stop the enemy, evil, on the threshold of consciousness and victory is assured. Fidelity to the metanoic struggle to "put on the mind of Christ" is the war against the source of all the wars. The refusal to fight this hidden war on this internal battlefield is tantamount to spiritually disempowering all external activity (1 COR 13).

> Fidelity to the metanoic struggle to "put on the mind of Christ" is the war against the source of all the wars.

There is a danger of interpreting Maximus as only offering another form of "Christianized" stoicism, that joyless good news of "not this—not that," that unhappy, self-righteous mental universe of detached lovelessness. In "Christian" stoicism the primary value is control. In St. Maximus' thought, the prime and only value is Christic love. "If we truly love God, by this very love we shall banish passion. And to love Him means to prefer Him to the world."[29] This preference amounts in the first instance to preferring thoughts of Him and His will to passionate representations of the transitory.

"Therefore," St. Maximus says, "one must observe his mind."[30] Nonviolence requires that one first be vigilant and watchful of one's own heart:

> *Thus when one's inner perception of a brother or sister who has offended you is that of bitterness, guard against rancor in yourself. The way of those who remember injuries leads to death, because to remember an injury is also to become a transgressor.*[31]

Maximus encourages Christians to pray for those toward whom rancor is felt. By doing so they separate their:

> *distress from the memory of the wrong the person has done to [them] and [thereby] arrest in themselves the movement of the passion. Such passion is banished from the soul by feelings of friendliness and affection. Kindness, humility and efforts to live at peace with someone who bears malice against you will free that person from his or her passion.*[32]

THE REFUSAL TO ABANDON CHRISTIC LOVE

How total is the nonviolence that St. Maximus espouses?

> *A person who loves Christ is certain to imitate Him as much as he can. And Christ never ceased doing good for people; was long suffering in the face of ingratitude and revilement; and when He was scourged and put to death, He endured this, imputing evil against no one. These three actions are acts of love for the neighbor, without which a person deceives himself or herself if he or she asserts that they love Christ or that they will gain His kingdom.*[33]

It is hard to envision a clearer statement regarding the centrality of nonviolence to Christ's teaching, to the Christian life and to a genuine love of Christ. The totality of the requirement of nonviolent love under all circumstances is evident when Maximus says, "Christ does not wish you to feel hatred or malice, anger or bitterness against anyone, in whatever manner or for anything. The four Gospels preach this to all people."[34] "He who abandons love for any such reason has not yet understood the aim of Christ's commandments."[35]

> Christ does not wish you to feel hatred or malice…He who abandons love for any such reason has not yet understood the aim of Christ's commandments.

Nonviolence is either total or it is non-existent. An ethic of justified violence, that is, violence made acceptable when certain conditions are present, is not nonviolence. It is precisely at the moment when violence is justified for some reason that nonviolence becomes an operational option. Nonviolence is a total approach to all life—internal and external, private and public—or else it does not exist. As Maximus says:

> *The friends of Christ love all people sincerely, but are not loved by all. Friends of the world neither love all, nor are loved by all. Friends of Christ keep the bonds of love to the end: but friends of the world love only until some discord arises between them about some earthly thing.*[36]

What St. Maximus is indicating here is that Jesus Christ authorizes no one, under any circumstances, to choose violence and enmity, by whatever name, over Christic love.

A Nonviolent Mindstyle and Lifestyle Invite the Cross

The nonviolence being spoken of by Maximus here, is far removed from the nonviolence of which I once heard a peace activist speak. When this nonviolent leader was asked if he thought that the hundreds of people he was encouraging to occupy government property were, in fact, believers in nonviolence, he said, "I just hope that they believe in it enough to be nonviolent while they are on government property." For Maximus, such nonviolence would not be nonviolence. It would just be a method of doing evil under the guise of nonviolence, what Gandhi called "the violence of the weak." It would be the traditional absurdity of using evil to try to conquer evil by re-naming evil good.

St. Maximus himself says, "No," to civil and ecclesiastical authorities when he feels "No" has to be said. He also suffers imprisonment and torture for his stand. But his "No," his imprisonment and his torture are the culmination of an entire mindstyle and lifestyle. A life commitment to the daily discipline of nonviolent love is a Via Dolorosa with a high probability that a Golgotha awaits at the end of the Way. However, the postponement of gratification in order to love, the breathing out of one's happiness in order to breath life into others is what the Way and the Cross of Nonviolent Suffering Love call for daily. Without such personal commitment by all who engage in acts of nonviolent civil disobedience, it is hard to see how authentic nonviolent civil disobedience is possible.

> [T]he postponement of gratification in order to love, the breathing out of one's happiness in order to breath life into others is what the Way and the Cross of Nonviolent Suffering Love call for daily.

This is not to say or in any way imply that nonviolent civil disobedience cannot be a valid Christian activity. On the contrary, nonviolent civil disobedience can be an awesomely effective force against evil in many of its most heinous manifestations. Indeed, nonviolent civil disobedience can be an imperative of Christic love. It is only to underline for clarity's sake, that nonviolent civil disobedience in order to be the powerful agent against evil that it is capable of being, must proceed from the moment to moment struggle to live a disciplined nonviolent lifestyle out of a disciplined nonviolent mindstyle. To voluntarily and secretly traffic in thoughts of resentment, envy, anger, hate, self-righteousness, hostility, retaliation, re-

> [N]onviolent civil disobedience in order to be the powerful agent against evil that it is capable of being, must proceed from the moment to moment struggle to live a disciplined nonviolent lifestyle out of a disciplined nonviolent mindstyle.

venge, etc., is to abandon nonviolence. It is to use nonviolent tactics as a cover for violence, as an instrument to hurt and/or impose one's will on others. Such nonviolence has no relationship to Christic nonviolent love and this has catastrophic implications for its ability to accomplish anything that really needs to be accomplished in the human situation (1 COR 13:1-13). In other words, a commitment to a nonviolent spirituality is that without which authentic and powerfull nonviolent tactics and strategies cannot be created and implemented.

THE REJECTION OF ALL VIOLENCE—INTERNAL AND EXTERNAL

Christ does not just condemn illegal violence;
He condemns all violence.
Christ does not simply condemn sordid violence;
He condemns romantic violence.
Christ does not merely condemn personal violence;
He condemns social violence.
Christ does not only condemn external violence;
He condemns internal violence.

Gospel nonviolence is the rejection of violence at all levels because violence is evil; it is contrary the will of the God of Unconditional and Everlasting Love as revealed by God Himself, Jesus Christ.

Gospel nonviolence is not merely the rejection and condemnation of those forms of violence—usually found in "the other"—that a person feels particularly upset over at the moment. Whether violence is chosen in the name of self-interest, self-defense or social responsibility—violence in thought, word or deed is incompatible with loving as Christ loves. Maximus knew the power that human institutions such as the family, state, religion and school have to nurture mindstyles and lifestyles of selfishness, retaliation, revengeful justice, enmity and violence. He knew the transitory loves to which the human heart can give itself and how clever the powers of this world are at manipulating these. He knew the extremes to which people go in order to get or to protect the totally perishable realities they desire. It is precisely because Maximus is under no self-created or socially created delusions about the power of evil that he is so unambiguous about the effort that has to be made and the price that has to be paid to love as Christ loves privately and publicly, internally and externally.

> Gospel nonviolence is not merely the rejection and condemnation of those forms of violence…that a person feels particularly upset over at the moment…. [It is] the effort that has to be made and the price that has to be paid.

Building an External Commonwealth of Love for All

Yet, St. Maximus' spirituality is not difficult to comprehend. Its five essential points are these:

1. God is Love,

2. God became human so that human beings may become God,

3. Love became human so that human beings could become Love,

4. The only Way to become Love is by Loving, and

5. Love as Christ-God loves.

"Relate all happenings to the ultimate end,"[37] advises St. Maximus. The ultimate end of existence is deification—gracefully reaching eternal union with Holy Immortal Love. Nonviolent Christ-like love in thought, word and deed is the Way to this end—there is no other. So, when Maximus says, "Do not wound your brother or sister, even with insinuations, lest you receive the same in return and thus banish a loving disposition from both,"[38] and "Do not regard as well-meaning those who repeat to you words which engender in you vexation or enmity against a brother or sister—even if they appear to speak the truth. But turn away from such, as from deadly snakes,"[39] he is talking about

> Relate all happenings to the ultimate end…[which] is deification—gracefully reaching eternal union with Holy Immortal Love…. [Maximus] is talking about more than the power of positive thinking. He is speaking of how to build the eternal Commonwealth of Love for all humanity.

more than the power of positive thinking. He is speaking of how to build the eternal Commonwealth of Love for all humanity.

That lesser commonwealths are able to be built on enmity, on greed, on the sword, on hostility, on calumny and on many other evils is obvious. But, to relate the morality of all choices, to whether a commonwealth of the transitory will arise or be sustained, would be for Maximus deadly folly. It is the equivalent of elevating the purely transitory to the level of an ultimate criterion by which to judge the goodness of thoughts, words or deeds. The five principles that embody St. Maximus' spirituality are easy to understand; and provided one is willing to accept a Christianity with a cross, they are possible to apply and to execute on a daily basis. Nevertheless, one has to have one's priorities straight. One must seek first the Kingdom of God, the Commonwealth of Love, and its righteousness and then live in the firm faith that all else will be given in God's good time, good place and good way (MT 6:33).

THE HUMAN MIND—THE HOLY PLACE, THE TEMPLE OF GOD

For Maximus, "the holy place, the temple of God is the human mind."[40] It is here that the demons "have devastated the soul by passionate thoughts, have erected the idol of sin."[41] Here also is the primary field of battle on which the war against evil must be fought. Refuse to combat evil here and all is lost. Actions that are not the consequence of having put on the mind of Christ, that are not the fruit of Christ-like love, are simply the sound and fury signifying nothing morally (1 COR 13). "For God's judgment," says Maximus, "looks not only on what is done, but also on the intentions with which it is done."[42]

> [T]he holy place, the temple of God is the human mind.... Here also is the primary field of battle on which the war against evil must be fought.

Yet, for Maximus, not only intentions, but also "what is done," is of axial importance. Putting on the mind of Christ is not some sort of mental game or contrived peak religious experience. The only way one can know if one has, in fact, put on the mind of Christ is if one is living "a love testified by deeds."[43] "Do" is the most used verb by Jesus in the Gospels says Maximus. For St. Maximus, a person who is living a mindstyle that is not testified to by deeds, is a stranger to love and "'a stranger to love is a stranger to God, for God is Love'" (1 JN 4:8).[44]

DROPPING ALLEGIANCES THAT ARE IMPEDIMENTS TO LOVE

The spirituality of nonviolence of St. Maximus the Confessor is probably not the first presentation of Gospel nonviolence to which people are normally introduced. However, as other constructs of nonviolence show themselves to require greater depth in order to be able to do battle efficaciously with the powers of darkness, the Wisdom present in the spirituality enunciated by St. Maximus becomes more manifest. "He loves all men and women who loves nothing human," says Maximus.[45] There is, of course, no end to the distortions to which such a statement is subject. But, does it not mean something as simple and as profound as dropping all allegiances to the transitory and thereby quieting all nurtured, acquisitive desires for the transitory, desires that can operate as impediments to loving all neighbors, friends and enemies? Is not this level of awareness and commitment pertinent to maximizing the power of Gospel nonviolence?

Since the Gospel is about God and since God and His Love are of infinite depth, to search continually for new depths in one's understanding of Christic Nonviolent Love and its applications should be spiritually natural. St. Maximus is not the last word along the Way of Nonviolent Love but, it seems to me, he does have very important insights to ponder at various points along the Way. The nonviolent spirituality of St. Maximus is predicated on the understanding that the microcosmic act of Christic love is all humanity has to work with in its struggle against evil, and that this act of love is all humanity needs to work with in order to be all it was created to be—to do all it was created to do. Where Love is God is, because God is Love. Where Love is, Power is—the only Power capable of conquering evil and death and bringing all humanity into an eternally graced union with God.

> The nonviolent spirituality of St. Maximus is predicated on the understanding that the microcosmic act of Christic love is all that humanity has to work with in its struggle against evil, and that this act of love is all humanity needs to work with in order to be all it was created to be—to do all it was created to do.

> Where Love is, Power is—the only Power capable of conquering evil and death and bringing all humanity into an eternally graced union with God.

One of the most extraordinary Christian characters in world literature is Dostoevsky's Byzantine staretz, Fr. Zosima. He is the literary embodiment of the epitome of Byzantine spirituality. Fr. Zosima is probably best known in a popular sense for his statement that "Love in action is a harsh and dreadful thing, compared with love in dreams."[46] But there is another reflection that the staretz made that magnificently captures the spirituality of nonviolent love of the "Father of Byzantine Theology." Let us conclude this exposition of the nonviolence of St. Maximus the Confessor with that meditation:

> *At some thoughts a person stands perplexed, above all at the sight of human sin, and he wonders whether to combat it by force or by humble love. Always decide: 'I will combat it by humble love.' If you resolve on that once and for all, you can conquer the whole world. Loving humility is a terrible force: it is the strongest of all things and there is nothing else like it.*[47]

NOTES

1. The theology that Christ was not as the Council of Chalcedon had stated "true God and true man," but, in fact, had one will (divine), not a human will and a divine will.

2. The doctrine that Christ had two wills, and therefore, had to make choices as all human beings must.

3. St. Maximus the Confessor, Four Centuries on Love, The Early Fathers from the Philokalia, ed. by E. Kadlouovsky and G. E. H. Palmer (London: Faber and Faber Ltd., 1954) IV, p. 90.

4. Ibid., IV, p. 100.

5. For example: St. Irenaeus, Adversus Haereses, V, Preface, PG 7, col 1120; St. Athanasius, De Incarnatione Verbi, 54, PG 25, col 192B; St. Gregory Nazianzen, Poema Dogmatica, 10, 5-9, PG 37, col 465; St. Gregory of Nyssa, Oratoria Catechetica Magna, 25, PG 45, col 65D. All these references to "God became man that man might become God" can also be found in: In the Image and Likeness of God, ed. by Vladimir Losskey (Crestwood, NY: St. Vladimir's Seminary Press, 1974).

6. St. Maximus the Confessor, Ambigua, PG 91, Col 1237AB.

7. Lars Thunberg, Microcosm and Mediator: The Theological Anthropology of Maximus the Confessor, (Lund: C. W. K. Gleerup, 1965), p. 20.

8. Maximus, Four Centuries on Love, I, p. 16.

9. St. Maximus the Confessor, Disputations with Pyrrho, PG 91, col 304C.

10. Maximus, Four Centuries in Love, II, p. 96.

11. Ibid., II, p. 63.

12. Ibid., I, p. 1.

13. Mohandas K. Gandhi, An Autobiography: The Story of My Experiments with Truth, (New York: Dover Publications, Inc., 1983), p. 8.

14. Maximus, Four Centuries of Love, I, p. 1.

15. Ibid., I, p. 8.

16. Ibid., II, p. 8.

17. Ibid, II, p. 7.

18. Ibid., II, p. 7.

19. Ibid., II, p. 3.

20. Ibid., II, p. 58.

21. Ibid., III, p. 10.

22. Ibid., I, p. 16.

23. Ibid., III, p. 15.

24. Ibid., III, p. 42.

25. Ibid., III, p. 40.

26. Ibid., III, p. 41.

27. Ibid., III, p. 52.

28. Ibid., III, p. 53.

29. Ibid., III, p. 50.

30. Ibid., III, p. 79.

31. Ibid., III, p. 89.

32. Ibid., III, p. 90

33. Ibid., IV, p. 55.

34. Ibid., IV, p. 84.

35. Ibid., IV, p. 81.

36. Ibid., IV, p. 98.

37. Ibid., IV, p. 24.

38. Ibid., IV, p. 32

39. Ibid., IV, p. 31.

40. Ibid., II, p. 31.

41. Ibid., II, p. 31.

42. Ibid., II, p. 37.

43. Ibid., I, p. 39.

44. Ibid., I, p. 38.

45. Ibid., III, p. 37.

46. Fyodor Dostoevski, The Brothers Karamazov, (New York: Bantam Books) 1981, Book II, Part 4.

47. Ibid., Book IV, Part 2.

Behold
The Nonviolent Lamb of God

*The Lamb
is the Lord of lords,
the King of kings.*

Rv 17:14

A symbol points to something other than itself or stands for something other than itself. St. Augustine writes that a symbol or sign "is a thing which, over and above the impression it makes on the senses, causes something else to come into mind as a consequence of itself." Signs and symbols are like the footprints of an animal that has passed-by. The footprint is a thing in itself but it can lead to knowledge about something other than itself. "Conventional signs," notes Augustine, "are those which human beings mutually exchange for the purpose of showing the feelings of their minds, or their perceptions, or their thoughts."

The quality of a symbol depends on how accurately or fully it communicates the reality of what is in the mind of the one who employs it to the mind of the one who receives it. A pyramid can be a symbol of Egypt, as a shamrock can be of Ireland. However, a pyramid would fail as a symbol of Ireland, as a shamrock would be experienced as an absurdity as a symbol of Egypt. In both these instances the object employed as a symbol could not function as a symbol because of the incongruity between the symbol chosen and the reality that one is attempting to communicate. A symbol can also atrophy into non-communicative meaninglessness over time by non-use or by the deadening effects of unthinking, mere rote use. For a symbol to function as a symbol it must have living significance for its communicator and its receiver. In order to have living significance a symbol must be worked at, pondered, analyzed in terms of reality, allowed to create the anxiety it was intended to create, permitted to generate new commitments or to intensify prior commitments. An animal's footprint can be a warning of danger ahead or it can be a sign pointing the way out of a jungle in which a person is hopelessly lost. Or, an animal's footprint may be viewed as just a depression in the soil.

THE LAMB

A lamb is not a snake, a rat or a tiger. A lamb is not a predator. It does not prey on others so it can live; others prey on it in order to serve their interests. The lamb is never a victimizer, it is always the victim. Fear and terror are completely absent from the experience generated by a lamb. On the contrary, a lamb elicits a non-threatening, welcoming experience. Even in the face of mortal threat there is nothing exhibited by the lamb that is the equivalent of the fang- or claw-bearing of a snake, rat or tiger.

Hence, the lamb is an unequivocal and universal symbol of gentleness, nonviolence, meekness and innocence. "As meek as a lamb" and "as gentle as a lamb" are clichés common to innumerable cultures, yesterday and today. There is no vagueness in what this symbol communicates. Hundreds of years before Jesus in another part of the world, the legendary storyteller, Aesop, wrote "The lamb prays to the Lord in the time of creation: Lord do not give me any weapons of defense, because if I have the means to hurt I shall wish to do so."

HEBREW SCRIPTURES

Among the Jewish people of Old Testament times the lamb is the animal to be taken in sacrifice to God for the benefit of the people. When the Father of Faith, Abraham, is taking his son, Isaac, up Mt. Moriah to sacrifice him, Isaac inquires, "Where is the lamb?" Abraham answers, "God will provide." When God tells Moses that on a certain night an angel of judgment will take the first-born in Egypt, God also informs him that every Jewish household should kill and eat a lamb and put its blood on the doorposts, and if this is done the angel will pass over that house and the Jewish people will be preserved from death. Hence, the Passover Feast that stands at the very heart of Jewish religion as a remembrance of God's saving, delivering and rescuing power requires the sacrifice of a lamb for the meal. By extension of these memories, the lamb becomes the offering at other major Jewish Feasts, as well as, the offering for those who wish to make atonement for personal sin. It is the lamb that is the twice-daily sacrifice (morning and evening) in the Temple until it is destroyed in 70 A.D.

Finally, in the Old Testament there is that mysterious figure of the Book of Isaiah, the Servant of Yahweh or the Suffering Servant. In Hebrew Scriptures he is the Mt. Everest of nonviolent love for all. He is gentle, does not break the crushed reed nor quench the wavering flame, does not raise his voice in the street, is a man of sorrows, afflicted and thought guilty by others, surrendering himself to death, but "praying all the time for sinners":

> *"Yet, ours were the sufferings he was bearing*
> *ours the sorrows he was carrying,*
> *while we thought of him as someone being punished,*

and struck with affliction by God
whereas he was being wounded for our rebellion,
crushed because of our guilt;
the punishment reconciling us fell on him,
and we have been healed by his wounds.
We had all gone astray like sheep
each taking his own way
and Yahweh brought the acts of rebellion
of all of us to bear on him.
Ill treated and afflicted,
he never opened his mouth,
like a lamb led to slaughter..."

Isaiah 53:4-7

New Testament

Although, Julius Caesar like Jesus Christ suffers and dies at the hands of the power elite of his day, no sane person would ever consider designating Caesar by the symbol of a lamb even though he is a victim being killed, as most victims are, for some "greater good." Caesar as scapegoat, perhaps—Caesar as lamb, never! However, in the Apostolic Tradition and in the New Testament, the lamb symbol is utilized over and over again as a direct reference to Jesus. The characteristics of the person that are intended, when the early Christians delineate Jesus by the figure of the lamb, are self-evident: meekness, innocence, nonviolent self-sacrificial love for the benefit of others.

In the New Testament the Last Supper and the Crucifixion take place at the time of the Passover. The symbolism of the Lord's Supper as the new Passover Meal and of Jesus as the new Passover Lamb is obvious. Indeed in the Gospel of John, Jesus is crucified at the very hour when the priests are slaughtering the lambs for the Passover in the Temple. The Jesus of the New Testament is the new Passover Lamb whose blood saves, delivers and rescues not just from the evils of Pharaoh-like political and economic oppression, but also from all the satanic powers of evil and death. As St. Paul explicitly says, "Christ our paschal (Passover) lamb has been sacrificed" (1 Cor 5:7). As St. Peter explicitly says, "You know you were ransomed from the futile ways inherited from your fathers, not with perishable things such as gold or silver, but by the precious blood of Christ the unblemished lamb" (1 Pt 1:10). What is clear from all this is that whatever the mystery of what God did through Jesus, God did not do it through a person, a personality or a personal "modus operandi" that could be symbolized properly and accurately by a snake, rat or tiger. The Lamb is God's chosen symbol for revealing the person and work of Jesus and for communicating the Way

Jesus' followers are to envision Him and to continue to advance the cause of God throughout history: "Remember, I am sending you out like sheep among wolves." (MT 10:16)

BAPTISM

It is in the Gospel of John the Evangelist, that John the Baptist first speaks those words which billions of Christians over the centuries have heard just prior to Holy Communion: "Behold the Lamb of God who takes away the sins of the world" (JN 1:29). Then the Baptist says "I saw the Spirit come down (on Jesus) like a dove from the sky."

In the Gospels of Matthew, Mark and Luke, when John baptizes Jesus, the Spirit descends on Him as a dove and a voice, a revelation from heaven says, "This is my beloved son upon whom my favor rests." It is understood in Scripture scholarship that this sentence directly refers to the opening line of the Hymn of the Suffering Servant (IS 42:1). At His baptism at the beginning of His public ministry, the identity which Jesus receives and accepts is as the Suffering Servant: the gentle, nonviolent "lamb led to slaughter" for the good of others.

In the Gospel of John, when John the Baptist points to Jesus and proclaims "Behold the Lamb of God," the same truth, that Jesus is the Suffering Servant (IS 53:7,12), is being communicated. In fact, the words, "Behold the Lamb of God" in Aramaic, the native language of Jesus and John, are exactly the same words in Aramaic as "Behold the Servant of Yahweh (the Suffering Servant)." Therefore, Christians, when they "Behold the Lamb of God," are not just only looking upon Christ, the new Passover Lamb, they are also gazing upon Christ, the Suffering Servant, the nonviolent "lamb led to slaughter" into whom they are baptized.

It is critical to ponder, to struggle with sincerity to comprehend, that to be baptized into Christ is to accept to be baptized into the baptism into which He was baptized (MK 10:38; LK 12:50)—and no other. That baptism, as has been said, is explicitly referenced by all four gospels to the nonviolent, gentle lamb of sacrificial suffering love on behalf of others that is found in Isaiah's Hymn of the Suffering Servant. The Greek word baptism means "immersion." At Baptism the catechumen is totally immersed into the new Lamb-like life of the Suffering Servant Messiah (Christ), which simultaneously is total immersion into the very life of God who is love (1 JN 4: 7-8, 16) and in whom "violence and hatred have no part." (*Roman Catholic Sacramentary Mass for Peace and Justice*) St. Paul explains this by saying that "as many of you as have been baptized into Christ have put on Christ" (GAL 3:27). To put on Christ is to truly put on the Lamb of God. Baptism is not a ceremonial propaganda gimmick whereby a person puts on sheep's clothing to camouflage a wolf, snake, rat or tiger's heart. Indeed, theologically and spiritually, personally and communally, it makes little sense to receive the nourishment of the Lamb of God in the Eucharist until one has put on the Lamb of God in Baptism and thereby united oneself with the Lamb and with one's fellow Christians in the Community of the Lamb, the Body of Christ (1 COR 12:1).

Eucharist

The Eucharist is the celebration of the Community committed to the Lamb of God, the community of the Suffering Servant. The Passover Meal of the Old Testament is bread and the lamb; the Messianic Passover Meal of the New Testament is bread which becomes the Lamb of God, the Body of Christ. In the ancient sister Churches of the East, Catholic and Orthodox, the consecrated bread is called not the Host, but the Lamb. Immediately prior to Holy Communion in the Western Church the community prays three times, "Lamb of God who takes away the sins of the world have mercy on us... grant us peace." The priest then raises the Host for the people to see and exclaims, "This is the Lamb of God who takes away the sins of the world, happy are those who are called to His Supper." This dramatic moment in the Western Eucharistic Liturgy goes back at least to the seventh century. The designation of the sanctified bread as the Lamb goes back well beyond that in the Eastern Church's liturgy. The Lamb is and has been the Church's Eucharistic symbol *par excellence* because the Eucharist, the summit of Christian worship, is the celebration of the Community of the Lamb in the presence of the Lamb.

Now when a Christian beholds and consumes the Lamb in Communion, it should be in order to sustain and deepen the New Life of the Lamb within him or her and within the Community. St. Augustine commenting on the worthy reception of Communion states, "If you receive well, you are what you receive... (therefore) be what you see and receive what you are." Each worthy reception of Communion should draw the Christian ever more profoundly into the Life of the Lamb. Every Eucharist that is what it is supposed to be should build up the Community of the Lamb through Communion with the Lamb. As each Christian approaches the moment of Communion, he or she should bow reverently before the Lamb of God desiring whole-heartedly to imitate the One who is presently being adored. What other disposition could possibly be proper and right for the worthy reception of the Lamb of God, other than the unreserved desire and commitment to become what one consumes?

Church

The Church is composed of human beings who accept to be baptized into the Baptism in which the Lamb of God is baptized and who thereby chose to unreservedly follow the Lamb. The Church is set apart by God as the privileged place where Jesus Christ, the definitive revealer of God and God's Way, can be recognized. The Lamb of God and the truth of the Lamb of God is proclaimed in time and space by those who follow the Way of the Lamb and who are empowered to do so by consuming in the Community's Eucharist celebration the One they are proclaiming by imitation and by word. The Church follows this Way because she believes that the values, attitudes, beliefs and powers symbolized and effected by the Lamb are the axis on which the Church and history must be ordered, as well as, the Archimedean fulcrum from which to move the world spiritually—and hence in every other way. She believes that the Lamb has conquered (REV 17:14). Therefore, She knows the Heart of the Lamb must be the Heart of the Church as well as the heart of each believer, because the Heart of the Lamb is the Heart of God who alone can vanquish evil and death and bring humanity that peace for which each soul longs.

SOCIAL RESPONSIBILITY

Three times Jesus asks Peter, "Do you love me?" Three times after Peter replies in the affirmative Jesus says, "Feed my lambs." The Church is the "little flock" of Jesus that is given at the Last Supper a *new commandment* (JN 15:12) that all should love one another as the Lamb of God loves them. The mystical Body of Christ is the mystical Body of the Lamb of God. The Heart of the Lamb, therefore, is at the Heart of the Way of Jesus and must therefore be at the Heart of the Way taught by the Church. A lamb's heart can never move a snake, rat or tiger's body, physically, spiritually or mystically, and the impression that it can, must never be allowed to exist as Gospel truth is in the Holy Eucharist that the Church primarily nourishes the Lamb's lambs, and it is in the Holy Eucharist that the Church makes its greatest contribution to the creation of a truly human society. If the Eucharist is permitted to be all that it can be, then by the presence, action and operation of the Holy Spirit of the Lamb of God it will create and empower ever new incarnations of the Way of the Lamb of God in each communicant, as well as, in each Church. If the Eucharist is permitted to be what it is, it will renew fidelity to the new commandment of the Eucharistic Lamb. Then, through the communicants' Lamb-like lives, the Eucharistic Lamb of God will become the Divine leaven in the human dough and the face of the earth will be renewed. Said succinctly, the legitimate fruits of Communion with the Lamb of God are mustard seed deeds of Lamb-like Divine Love, that release the power of God in the soil of history for the life, healing, peace and salvation of all. And perhaps above all else, by the Eucharistic Lamb of God being incarnated in the lives of Christians the true face of God will be magnified (glorified), so that all people will be able to "see" and thereby find eternal security in His Peaceful Smile. *Deo Gratias!*

The Nonviolent Eucharistic Jesus: A Pastoral Approach

Twelve frightened men, who feel that death is hovering over, crowd around the Son of Man whose hand is lifted over a piece of bread and over a cup.

Of what value is this gesture, of what use can it be?

How futile it seems when already a mob is arming itself with clubs, when in a few hours Jesus will be delivered to the courts, ranked among transgressors, tortured, disfigured, laughed at by His enemies, pitiable to those who love Him, and shown to be powerless before all.

However, this Man, condemned to death does not offer any defense; He does nothing but bless the bread and wine and, with eyes raised, pronounces a few words.

François Mauriac

The Eucharist is not only a mystery to consecrate, to receive, to contemplate and adore. It is also a mystery to imitate.

Raniero Cantalamessa, O.F.M.Cap.

Outside of Jesus Christ, the Eucharist has no Christian meaning. Everything about it must ultimately be referenced to Him and then through Him to Abba. The same is true of the Christian life. Jesus is the ultimate norm of Christian existence; everything must be referenced to Him. If He is not the final standard against which the Church and the Christian must measure everything in order to determine if it is the will of God or not, then who or what is?

The Ultimate Norm of the Christian Life

What would Christianity or the Church mean for the Christian if Jesus' Way or teachings were made subject to, or were measured for correctness by whether Plato, Hugh Hefner, or the local emperor happen to agree with them? Since for the Christian Jesus is the Word of God, the Son of God, the Son of Man, the

Self-revelation of God: "The one who sees me sees the Father" (JN 14:9), since for the Christian He is "the Way and the Truth and the Life" (JN 14:6), it is senseless to maintain that the Christian life can ultimately be modeled on anyone or anything except Jesus. Even the saints must be measured against Jesus and His teachings to determine what in their lives is worthy of Christian honor and what is not.

New Commandment Contains the Entire Law of the Gospel

Jesus, Himself, unequivocally commands precisely this when He says, "I give you a new commandment: Love one another. As I have loved you, so you also should love one another" (JN 13:34). As the one the Church calls "the greatest saint of modern times," St. Thérèse of Lisieux, says in her autobiography, *The Story of a Soul*:

> *Among the countless graces I have received this year, perhaps the greatest has been that of being able to grasp in all its fullness the meaning of love...I had striven above all to love God, and in loving Him I discovered the secret of those other words "Not everyone who says Lord, Lord shall enter into the kingdom of heaven, but the one who does the will of my Father." Jesus made me understand what the will was by the words he used at the Last Supper when He gave His "new commandment" and told His apostles "to love one another as He had loved them"...When God under the old law told His people to love their neighbors as themselves, He had not yet come down to earth. As God knows how much we love ourselves, He could not ask us to do more. But when Jesus gave His apostles a "new commandment, His own commandment," He did not ask only that we should love our neighbors as ourselves, but that we should love them as He loves them and as He will love them to the end of time. O Jesus, I know you command nothing that is impossible...O Jesus ever since its gentle flame has consumed my heart, I have run with delight along the way of your "new commandment."*

The *Catechism of the Catholic Church* states that "The entire Law of the Gospel is contained in the *new commandment* of Jesus, to love one another as he has loved us" and that "This *commandment* summarizes all the others and expresses His [the Father's] entire will." Now if, as the biblical scholar, Rev. John L. McKenzie, echoing the understanding of modern Biblical scholarship, says, Jesus' rejection of violence is "the clearest of teachings" in the New Testament, then that love that is in the Spirit of Christ, that love that is imitative of Christ, that love that is Christ-like, that love that is "as I have loved," that love which "contains the entire Law of the Gospel," that love "which expresses His entire will" is a nonviolent love of friends and enemies.

> The entire Law of the Gospel is contained in the new commandment of Jesus, to love one another as he has loved us...this commandment summarizes all the others and expresses His [the Father's] entire will.

Both Biblical scholarship and a common sense reading of the Gospel tell us that this *new commandment* of Jesus to "love one another as I have loved you," is not a throwaway line or an arbitrary insertion of a thought into the Gospel. On the contrary, the *new commandment* is so placed in the Gospel as to be presented as the supreme and solemn summary of all of Jesus' teachings and commands. The importance of all this for Eucharistic understanding and Eucharistic unity is this: Jesus' solemn *new commandment* is given and proclaimed not on a mountain top nor in the Temple, but, as St. Thérèse notes, at the Last Supper, the First Eucharist.

> [T]he New Commandment is so placed in the Gospel as to be presented as the supreme and solemn summary of all of Jesus' teachings and commands. It contains the entire Law of the Gospel

Poised between time and eternity and about to be pressed like an olive by religiously endorsed, rationally justified and state executed homicidal violence, to which He knows He must respond with a love that is neither violent nor retaliatory, with a love that forgives and that seeks to draw good out of evil, He proclaims, "I will be with you only a little while longer. You will look for me and as I told the Jews, where I go you cannot come; now I say to you, I give you a new commandment: Love one another. As I have loved you, so you also should love one another" (JN 13:33-34).

LITURGICAL AND OPERATIONAL INDIFFERENCE

It is hard to conceive of a more dramatically powerful context to communicate the importance of a truth to people for an indefinite future. Imagine how the world would be today if this *new commandment* as taught on the first Holy Thursday and lived unto death on the first Good Friday was continuously remembered in Catholic, Orthodox, and Protestant Eucharistic Prayers throughout the ages. For one thing, there would be no Catholic, Orthodox, or Protestant division of the Church because, whatever the intellectual reasons were that promoted each division and each division of a division, the one thing that predates all of them and postdates most of them is a thoroughgoing liturgical and operational indifference to the *new commandment* that Jesus proclaims by word at the First Eucharist and by example at the Sacrifice of Calvary.

All the major modern divisions in the Church follow by centuries the Church's justification of violence and homicide with all the distortion of perspective and spirit that persistence in such activities brings to individuals and communities. And, after each division all of the Churches—minus a few of the 'Peace Churches'—continue to teach, to endorse and to employ violence and homicide as part of their Christian way. This necessitated that in these Churches, or any subdivision thereof, the Eucharistic liturgy be not too explicit in remembering the details of the Gospel-given history of the Lord's Supper, of the Lord's Passion and of the Lord's Death.

> [C]ould any Church that justified and participates in violence and homicide afford to be continually Eucharistically emphatic in remembering Jesus' New Commandment given at the Last Supper and the clear relationship between it and the way He in fact historically responded to violence and enmity?

Less still could any Church that justifies and participates in violence and homicide afford to be continually Eucharistically emphatic in remembering Jesus' *new commandment* given at the Last Supper, and the clear relationship between it and the Way He in fact historically responds to violence and enmity. What one does not underline is what one does not want to remember.

A Eucharistic Prayer that Embodies Nonviolent Love

So until this very day, in the Eucharistic Liturgies of such Churches, a solitary word, "suffered" or "death," has normally been quite enough memory, commemoration, remembrance, or anamnesis for fulfilling the Lord's Command, "Do this in memory (anamnesis) of me." Of course, technically the words "suffered" and "death" are theologically correct, but are they pastorally sufficient for the sanctification of the Christian, the Church, and the world? What would the condition of the Church and hence the world be like today if the Eucharistic Prayers of the Churches of Christianity had read at their most sacred point, "the institution narrative-anamnesis (remembrance)," something like the following over the last 1700 years:

...On the night before He went forth to His eternally memorable and life-giving death, like a Lamb led to slaughter, rejecting violence, loving His enemies, and praying for His persecutors, He bestowed upon His disciples the gift of a New Commandment:

"Love one another. As I have loved you, so you also
should love one another."

Then He took bread into His holy hands, and looking up to You, almighty God, He gave thanks, blessed it, broke it, gave it to His disciples and said:

"Take this, all of you, and eat it: this is my body
which will be given up for you."

Likewise, when the Supper was ended, He took the cup. Again He gave You thanks and praise, gave the cup to His disciples and said:

"Take this, all of you, and drink from it: this is the cup of my blood, the blood of the
new and everlasting covenant. It will be shed for you
and for all so that sins may be forgiven."

"Do this in memory of me."

> *Obedient, therefore, to this precept of salvation, we call to mind and reverence His passion where He lived to the fullest the precepts which He taught for our sanctification. We remember His suffering at the hands of a fallen humanity filled with the spirit of violence and enmity. But, we remember also that He endured this humiliation with a love free of retaliation, revenge, and retribution. We recall His execution on the cross. But, we recall also that He died loving enemies, praying for persecutors, forgiving, and being superabundantly merciful to those for whom justice would have demanded justice. Finally, we celebrate the memory of the fruits of His trustful obedience to thy will, O God: the resurrection on the third day, the ascension into heaven, the enthronement at the right hand, the second and glorious coming. Therefore we offer You your own, from what is your own, in all and for the sake of all...*

The explicit inclusion of the memory of Jesus' *new commandment*, Jesus' rejection of violence, Jesus' love of enemies, Jesus' prayer for His persecutors, and Jesus' return of good for evil in the Eucharistic Prayer of the Churches at the point of "institution-anamnesis" is not a whimsical or arbitrary insertion of haphazard events from Jesus' life. This is what happens from the Cenacle to Calvary. This is the memory given to us to revere by the ultimate historical, theological and pastoral documents on the subject: the four Gospels.

Maundy Thursday—A Mandate to Love as Christ Loves

The very name for Holy Thursday, Maundy Thursday, comes from the Latin "mandatum," which means a command, commission, charge, order, injunction. It is a direct and exclusive reference to the *new commandment* given at the Lord's Supper. The inclusion of the *new commandment* in the Eucharistic Prayer is not riding one's own theological or liturgical hobby-horse into the Church's public prayer life. The *new commandment* is there from Day One of the Eucharist and it is there in maximal solemnity and seriousness.

So, also, rejection of violence, love of enemies, and prayer for persecutors are an irrevocable part of the history, Scripture, and authentic memory of the Sacrifice of Love on Calvary. Refusing the protection of the sword (MT 26:52), healing the ear of the armed man who is to take Him to His death (LK 22:51) and crying out for God's forgiveness for those who are destroying Him (LK 23:34) is the memory the Gospels give to humanity of the victimization of Christ. To side-step these authentic Apostolic memories in order to get to a more profound or holy or "deep" spirituality is sheer folly. One has to have the humility to accept revelation as God offers it. If one does not want to prayerfully enter into revelation as presented by God, then one has no access to revelation; for who but God can author revelation?

EMACIATED REVELATORY REMEMBRANCE SUBVERTS DIVINE LOVE

Jesus does not die of a heart attack. He dies when His heart is attacked by human beings inebriated with the diabolical spirit of justified, religiously endorsed homicide—and He dies giving a definite, discernible, and consistent response to that satanic spirit. This reality cannot be insignificant in discerning the Truth of the revelation God is trying to communicate to humanity for the good of humanity in Jesus. The Sacrifice of the Cross is not about mere animal pain that is meant to assuage the lust of a sadistic, blood-thirsty, parochial god. It is about the revelation of the nature and meaning and way and power of a Divine Love that saves from an Enemy and a menace that the darkest phenomena of history can only but hint at. To consistently dismiss and to structurally ignore major facts in the God-given revelatory memory is to assure that little of what God intended to be communicated by this costly revelation will be communicated by it. So, while use of an isolated word, "suffered" or "death," in the Eucharistic Prayer is theologically passable, pastorally speaking it is emaciated revelatory anamnesis (remembrance).

> The Sacrifice of the Cross...is about the revelation of the nature and meaning and way and power of a Divine Love that saves from an Enemy and a menace that the blackest realities of history can only but hint at.

However, it does not take much reflection to perceive how these detail-devoid Eucharistic Prayers—that do not mention Jesus' *new commandment* given at the Last Supper, that do not mention His rejection of violence, that do not mention His love of even lethal enemies, that do not mention His prayer for persecutors, and His struggle to overcome evil with good—serve a critical function in amalgamating Christianity into the local national or ethnic violence-ennobling myths, as a religious legitimizer. Intentional forgetfulness, structured inattentiveness, and a cavalier disparaging of Jesus' teachings of nonviolent love have always been part of this process of religious validation by evasion. Without this cultivated liturgical blind spot Jesus could not be drafted as a Divine support person for the home team's homicide and enmity.

AMNESIA ABOUT TRUTHS IN THE SUFFERING AND DEATH OF CHRIST

It is possible today, as it has been possible for 1700 years, for a normal person to spend a lifetime listening to the Eucharistic Prayers of all of the mainline Christian Churches and never apprehend that what is being remembered is a Person—who at the moments being remembered in the Prayers—rejects violence, forgives everyone, prays for persecutors, returns good for evil. In other words, in most Christian Churches, the anamnesis has become an agency for amnesia about truths in the suffering and death of Christ that if consistently brought to consciousness at the sacred time of the community's Eucharist would stand in judgement on a multitude of community activities, past and present.

> It is possible…to spend a lifetime listening to the Eucharistic Prayers and never apprehend that what is being remembered is a Person—who rejected violence, forgave everyone, prayed for persecutors, and returned good for evil?

The Rev. Frederick R. McManus, Emeritus Professor at The Catholic University of America and one of the two or three most influential Catholic liturgists of the 20th Century, writing on this issue says:

> *The Nonviolent Eucharist is a valuable and viable proposal to augment eucharistic anaphoras with some direct reference to the ministry and teaching of Jesus concerning peace and love, with concrete mention of the nonviolence of the Gospel message. The tradition of variety in the Eucharistic prayer, longstanding in the East and happily introduced into the Roman liturgy in the light of Vatican II's mandate to reform the Order of Mass, is ample reason to study this proposal. The centrality of the mission of peace and nonviolence in the Gospels needs to be acknowledged in the confession of the great deeds of God in the Lord Jesus, and the Christian people need to see this essential dimension of Eucharistic peace in the prayer which they confirm and ratify with their Amen.*

The most renowned moral theologian of the Catholic Church in the 20th Century, Rev. Bernard Häring, states emphatically that, "It is not possible to speak of Christ's sacrifice while ignoring the role of nonviolence." Yet, this is precisely what most Christian Churches have been doing in their Eucharistic Prayers since Constantine first employed the cross as an ensign to lead people into the enmity and homicide called war.

FACT: *Catholics, Orthodox, and Protestants all believe they have authentic Eucharistic communion within their own Churches and often the same belief holds for communion between different Churches. This, however, has not prevented them from sojourning into slaying their own and other Christians on a grand scale and then exonerating themselves by some fantastic contortion of the Gospel.*

THE KEY TO EUCHARISTIC UNITY AND CHRISTIAN UNITY

Now what I am about to suggest I am sure could sound more than farfetched, but I believe it is the pivotal decision for Christic Truth on which a future of Christian unity and Eucharistic unity wait. At this time in history, the key to Eucharistic unity and Christian unity is for Churches—each by whatever process of authority is internal to it—to compose new Eucharistic Prayers

> [T]he key to Eucharistic unity and Christian unity is for churches to compose new Eucharist Prayers which vividly call to mind the New Commandment…

which vividly call to mind the *New Commandment*, and the actual details of the historic confrontation between homicidal violence and Jesus' Nonviolent Love of friends and enemies that took place at the moment being remembered.

This is not one among many things the Churches can do for peace and unity—it is what they must do. The present meagerness of Scriptural and historical memory, while it does not render the Eucharistic Prayers invalid, does make them pastorally deceptive by omission. Harnessed by nationalisms around the world, Christians do not hear the broad terms "suffered" and "death" as they were engaged in 33 A.D. Pastoral responsibility before God and pastoral integrity before the community insist that the fitting and right textual adjustments be instituted because there is a radical spiritual danger that the *paucis verbis* of the present remembrance in the Eucharistic Prayers of all the mainline Churches is unwittingly serving those forces which the Eucharistic Jesus comes to conquer.

> [T]here is a radical spiritual danger that the *paucis verbis* of the present remembrance in the Eucharistic Prayers of all the mainline churches is serving those forces which the Eucharistic Jesus comes to conquer.

It is Archimedes who states that there is a point outside the world that if he could locate it, he could move the world from it. The "institution narrative-anamnesis" of the Eucharistic Prayer of the Churches is that spiritual Archimedian point—if the truth of Christ's Sacrifice is allowed the fullness of its historical revelatory reality there. It is not magic I speak of here. It is the hidden power of the cross that is released when those who are in Christ respond to the offer of grace through Christ—an offer made through a unique and unequaled "salvation device" when He said, "Do this in remembrance of me."

For the leadership of each Church to authorize text clarifications in its Eucharistic Prayer would not be magic. For said leadership to explain the changes to the community would not be magic. For each community to consciously stand or kneel daily, weekly, or monthly in the presence of such a Nonviolent Eucharistic Lord would not be magic. All would necessitate human choice, but choice aimed at cooperating more faithfully with the incalculably powerful and mysterious reality of the Divine Design for salvation in Jesus—choice on behalf of a more authentic expression, experience and encounter with the Saving Presence of Divine Love as revealed through, with and in the Nonviolent Eucharistic Christ.

NEW TIME OF CHRISTIAN AGAPÉ

A more truthful Eucharistic Prayer is the starting point of "the fair beginning of a nobler time." For certain this is the point from which to move the world into a New Time of Christic Agapé because, from this point on, the Christian and the Church will derive their Life from the Bread of Life of an Agapé Meal that is reverently respectful of the "last wish" of Jesus—that the love (*agapé*) which He showed His disciples be remembered and lived in the community as the unbreachable standard of all Christian interaction. This is the spiritual Archimedian point because there is infinitely more Power in that Mysterious Meal in the Upper Room than meets the eye—if the choice is but made to embrace it.

What is equally true is this: there is infinitely more to the *new commandment* than meets the mind. As each Church Eucharistically remembers more lucidly the truth of Jesus' life of Nonviolent Love, His death in Nonviolent Love, and His resurrection through Nonviolent Love, Jesus' *new commandment* will disclose its depth of meaning, purpose, and power to the Churches of Christianity in a manner that will gift them with an experience of new reality. Out of this new reality will come new insight and new spirit—and from this new reality and new insight and new spirit will come new words, new phraseology, new language, new thoughts that will resolve aged and serious problems of truth. Rising from this new level of Eucharistic fidelity will come a new convergence of Christic Love and Truth that will engender an existential unity beyond present imagination. It is not magic I speak of here. Prayer changes people, and people change things, but the "Yes" for a more pastorally accurate remembrance narrative in the Eucharistic Prayer must first be given by pastors. As at Nazareth of old, God, who desires to renew the face of the earth, holds His breath and awaits His chosen servant's *fiat*.

BETRAYAL OF BAPTISMAL AND EUCHARISTIC UNITY

In a 1969 article for the *Notre Dame Alumnus*, I wrote: "To paraphrase a student slogan, 'Suppose someone gave a war and the Christians refused to kill or harm one another'...It would be a giant step forward for humanity if the Church would preach as a minimum standard of morality, the absolute immorality of one follower of Christ killing another follower of Christ."

In 1969 I lost on all fronts with this. For the conservatives it was "just ridiculous"; for the liberals, it was too absolutist; and for the radicals, it was Christianist and anti-humanist. But, I know more surely today than I did fifty years ago that this is the truth of the matter. Homicide-justifying Christianity cannot dialogue itself out of the snare into which it has fallen. It must first unreservedly desire to be obedient to Jesus' new commandment; then from this wholehearted desire will issue the grace, insight and power to do the other tasks committed to the Christian and the Church. Now, this desire to be faithful to the new commandment would at least seem to mean that as a dimension of Baptism and Eucharist, the Christian would always say "No!" if called upon to kill other Christians. He or she would do this in order not to be reduced to a 'Judas-Christian'—a betrayer of one's gift of Baptismal unity in Christ and a betrayer of one's task of Eucharistic unity in His *New Commandment*.

How could this not be what Jesus intended for His disciples by His *New Commandment* at the Last Supper? How could this not be what Jesus intended His followers to teach, nurture, encourage, foster, energize, and command when bringing people into Baptismal and Eucharistic unity with Him and through Him with each other and God? The Church will be the servant it is meant to be to God and to humanity only to the extent that it is faithful to what it has been commanded to do internally, namely to "Love one another. As I have loved you, so you also should love one another." Absent an unswerving commitment to Jesus' *New Commandment*, the Church will become a body tearing itself apart limb by limb—and anti-sacrament of disunity, the public incarnational denial of its own truth.

DISUNITY EMANATES FROM SEPARATION OF DIVINE MANDATES

A commandment that is consigned century after century to the doorsteps of oblivion is a non-thought in a community. Obedience to a non-thought is a patent impossibility. Yet, it is at the very same Supper that the Lord commands for all time "Do this in memory of me" that He pronounces for all time His *New Commandment*. How can these Divine Mandates be honestly separated? How can one be obeyed religiously while the other is religiously ignored?

It is this separation between the two great Eucharistic Commands that is the source of and the sustaining power for separation within Christianity—ecclesiastically and Eucharistically. It is this separation in Christianity between the two great Eucharistic Commands, whose mutually complementary purpose is to unite, that has reduced the Church in confrontation with the horrid reality of evil to a coping dinosaur rather than a conquering Spirit. Disunity disempowers to the detriment of all—except the Fiend.

For mercy's sake, the pastors of Christianity must relinquish their stance of calculated inattentiveness to the unbreakable unity of Word and Sacrament. They must simply stop managing the Eucharistic Prayer in a manner that spiritually short-circuits the process of repentance—and hence unification—by perpetually camouflaging the unwanted truth of Jesus' nonviolent love of friends and enemies and His command to follow His example of love. There are not two Jesus Christs: the Eucharistic Christ of faith on one hand, and the historical Jesus on the other. John Paul II states in his Encyclical, *Redemptoris Missio* (1990), "One cannot separate Jesus from the Christ or speak of a 'Jesus of history' who would differ from the 'Christ of faith'...Christ is none other than Jesus of Nazareth." The only Jesus Christ present at the Eucharist, the only Jesus Christ to remember and receive in the Eucharist is the Jesus Christ who taught and lived unto death a Way of nonviolent love of friends and enemies and who commanded His disciples to "Love one another as I have loved you"—and to "Do this in memory of me."

> For mercy's sake, the pastors of Christianity must relinquish their stance of chosen ignorance. They must simply stop managing the Eucharistic Prayer in a manner that spiritually short-circuits the process of repentance, and hence unification...

A Pastorally Truth-Filled Eucharist

Having recently concluded a Century in which more people have been killed by rationally-justified, religiously-legitimized war, revolution, abortion, and capital punishment than all the centuries of humanity combined; having recently concluded a Century that has by the billions mercilessly murdered "the least" (MT 25:14-46) by squandering on the technology of violence and homicide the most lavish gifts of intelligence and learning ever granted a century of humanity; having recently concluded a Century that has brought a planet of humanity to the lip of a cauldron bubbling with the brew of nuclear plagues and war-generated diseases; having recently concluded a Century where Christianity has been a major player in all these evils—it is a moral imperative for Christian pastors to begin to lead their Churches away from evasive Eucharistic Prayers and into remembering the Way God committed to them for salvific and revelatory remembrance on Holy Thursday-Good Friday, 33 A.D.

A pastorally truth-filled Eucharistic institution narrative, as enunciated above, initiated in the beginning by the authority of each of the Churches for its own community, is the key not only to the resolution of Church divisions and Eucharistic disunity, but also the key to that New Pentecost which is the only Power that can transfigure the relentless agonia humanity has made of history. From a New Holy Thursday shall shine a New Pentecost because Eucharistic prayer is the most powerful prayer to which humanity will ever have access. This means that, entered into with an honest, humble and contrite heart, Eucharistic prayer in all its forms—adoration, contrition, thanksgiving, and supplication—is the supreme instrumentality available to the human being and to the

> A pastorally truth-filled Eucharist...is the only Power that can transfigure the relentless agonia humanity has made of history... [It] is the supreme instrumentality available to the human being and to the human community for their sanctification...

human community for their sanctification—which can only express itself in time and space as deeds of Christ-like love of God, friends, and enemies.

To love the Eucharist is to live the Eucharist. A Nonviolent Eucharistic Prayer is a mandatum of Truth, a mandatum of Peace, a mandatum of Love.

(Rev.) Emmanuel Charles McCarthy

The Nonviolent Eucharistic Jesus: A Scholarly Approach

Is faith a narcotic dream in a world of heavily armed robbers, or is it an awakening?

THOMAS MERTON, O.C.S.O.

We know how the Eucharist makes the Church: the Eucharist makes the Church by making the Church Eucharist! The Eucharist is not only the source and cause of the Church's holiness, it is also its model.

RANIERO CANTALAMESSA, O.F.M.CAP.

The **Nonviolent Love** of Jesus for both friends and enemies is historically at the heart of His passion and death, it must therefore be communicated as being ineradicably at the heart of the Eucharist. It is the nonviolent Lamb of God, who is worshipped and consumed in the Eucharist. It is the nonviolent Lamb of God, whom the Eucharist empowers us, individually and as a Church, to imitate, to become and to proclaim. The passion narrative is about the Lamb, who goes to His death rejecting violence, loving enemies, returning good for evil, praying for His persecutors—yet conquers and reigns eternal. It is not about a snake or a rat or a tiger who goes to his death with bloody fangs or claws bared. It is also not about dying of natural causes. As Bernard Häring, C.SS.R., the most prominent Catholic moral theologian in the second half of the Twentieth Century, writes, "It is not possible to speak of Christ's sacrifice while ignoring the role of nonviolence…Nonviolence belongs to the mystery of the Redeemer and redemption." The sacrifice of Christ is not about salvation through mere physiological pain. It is about salvation through the nonviolent suffering love of Jesus toward all and for all, even lethal enemies. It is about revealing the true nature of Divine love, the true and authentic Face of God. As the United States' Catholic Bishops teach in their Pastoral, *The Challenge of Peace* (1983):

> *In all of his suffering, as in all of his life and ministry, Jesus refused to defend himself with force or with violence. He endured violence and cruelty so that God's love might be fully manifest and the world might be reconciled to the One from whom it had become estranged.*

Atonement and redemption, sanctification and salvation are the fruits of nonviolent, unconditional love made visible at a terrible cost to Jesus from Gethsemane to Golgotha. Therefore, what is made visible in the Gospels at the spiritual and revelatory apex of the life of Jesus should be made luminously visible in the re-presentation of the passion and death of Jesus in the Eucharistic Prayer.

ENCOUNTER WITH GOD

The Eucharist is the principal means that the Church offers to the world for meeting the true God and the truth of God through Jesus Christ, as well as for overcoming evil and death in all their manifestations. The Eucharist is God's gift of Himself through Jesus and His Church to humanity for its liberation from enslavement to any and all of the powers of darkness and for its entering into an eternal union with the Giver and Sustainer of Life.

Ultimately the grace that is given in the Eucharist is God, Jesus. To use Schillebeechx's phraseology, "Jesus is the sacrament of the human encounter with God." Jesus is this because He is God incarnate. The Eucharist is not a "salvation gimmick." It is relating to an existing person, Jesus Christ. This person, however, not only has a divine reality but also has a human identity. He has a history of thoughts, words and deeds. He has a history of acting and being acted upon. He has a history of joys and sorrows, choices and responses, all of which make Him and identify Him as the unique totally human—totally divine person that He is.

PRINCIPAL WITNESS AND MUNDANE SPECIFICS

The Second Vatican Council (*Dogmatic Constitution on Divine Revelation*, 18) declares the Gospels to be, "the principal witness of the life and teaching of the incarnate Word, our Savior." It further states that the Gospels "have a special pre-eminence among all the Scriptures, even those of the New Testament," and that they "faithfully hand on what Jesus Christ, while living among people, really did and taught for their eternal salvation." Now, the Gospels leave not a scintilla of doubt that certain facts, which some would dismiss as merely the "mundane specifics" of Jesus' life, are vital communications for knowing the Way and the work, the person and the being of Jesus and of God.

> The Gospels leave not a scintilla of doubt that certain facts, which some would dismiss as merely the "mundane specifics" of Jesus' life, are vital communications for knowing the Way and the work, the person and the being of Jesus and of God.

Remove these so-called "mundane specifics" from His life and there is no Jesus to be known; there is no Jesus who can serve as the sacrament of the human encounter with God. The bracketing out of segments, especially major themes, of Jesus' life results spiritually in diluting, or in some cases falsifying, the knowledge of God which is supposed to be revealed through, with and in Him. Diluted encounters with God obviously do not bear the same fruits, for the human being or for the human community, as do unmodified, unedited, unexpurgated, unsparingly truthful encounters with God through the Jesus of the New Testament. Hence, a Eucharistic Canon anemic in its remembrance of the "mundane specifics" of the historical Jesus' passion and death, of the Way He suffers and dies, must result at best in a very watered down relationship with the true God and with the truth of God. If too many of the "mundane specifics" of Jesus' passion and death are left out of the Eucharistic Prayer, it is possible that those present at the Eucharist may hardly recognize Him "in the breaking of the bread" (LK 24:35; AC 2:42) or worse, may not recognize Him or His pertinence to their lifeworld at all.

> If too many of the "mundane specifics" of Jesus' passion and death are left out of the Eucharistic Prayer, it is possible that those present at the Eucharist may hardly recognize Him "in the breaking of the bread" or worse, may not recognize Him or His pertinence to their lifeworld at all.

A Eucharistic Canon that pushes aside the "mundane specifics" of Jesus' passion and death, *ipso facto* eviscerates the power of the Eucharist by not making available to the faithful significant dimensions of the gift of Divine Love which is made visible in Jesus' journey from the Upper Room to Golgotha. Bernard Lonergan, S.J., who has been called the Apostle of the Specific, again and again throughout his writings makes the following point: "[T]o know the concrete in its concreteness is to know all there is to be known about each thing. To know all there is to be known about each thing is, precisely, to know being." This may sound a bit esoteric but what Lonergan is communicating is that human beings encounter the real via the concrete and the specific of existence. It is therefore spiritually and theologically impermissible to bypass or downplay, as being of little or no significance, the **Nonviolent Love** of friends and enemies that permeates the entire drama of Jesus' preaching, passion and death for the salvation of the world. As the renowned biblical scholar and the first Catholic ever to be elected president of The Society of Biblical Literature and Exegesis, the Rev. John L. McKenzie, states with maximal scholarly authority:

> *If Jesus did not reject any type of violence for any purpose, then we know nothing of him.*

No Toleration of Ambiguity

It is sheer spiritual folly to believe that one can minimize the historical humanity of Jesus and thereby arrive at a deeper experience of the Christ of faith or the Second Person of the Holy Trinity or God. Nothing in the Eucharistic Celebration must allow in the least for such a spiritually destructive misinterpretation of Christian faith and prayer. As Lonergan notes, "[V]ague verbal claims that help us ignore the specifics of the particulars in which we are enmeshed" serve to assist people in their flight from understanding and from commitment. "The Eucharist," proclaims John Paul

II in *Ecclesia de Eucharistia*, "is too great a gift to tolerate ambiguity and depreciation." But, is not the Eucharist pastorally depreciated and rendered precariously ambiguous when the Nonviolent Love of friends and enemies, that Jesus steadfastly adheres to throughout his passion and death, is treated as so minor as to merit only disregard?

It is left to the Church to orchestrate the re-presentation of the salvific gift of Christ-God in the Eucharist to the world. It is the Church that is responsible for making the Eucharist pastorally available in the fullness of its truth and power so that humanity can reap all the benefits of this wholly holy sacrifice of love. This pastoral process of re-presenting Christ's saving passion and death to humanity involves human judgment, evaluation, creativity, learning and discernment in order to insure that there is no discrepancy between Word and Sacrament. No contradiction can objectively exist between the Jesus of the New Testament, who teaches and lives unto death on the cross a Way of Nonviolent Love of friends and enemies, and the Jesus encountered in the Eucharist. Christians have a Baptismal birthright to worship in the presence of this consistency of Word and Sacrament and to be straightforwardly apprised of it by their pastors. Word and Sacrament must be conspicuously one in the Church because Word and Sacrament are one in reality, in God. So whether a disciple looks upon Jesus in the Gospels or looks upon Jesus in the Eucharist, he or she must see, indeed has an unqualified right to vividly see, the same Jesus. That Jesus is a Jesus, who in obedience to the will of the Father, teaches by word and deed a Way of Nonviolent Love of friends and enemies—even when in direct confrontation with lethal enmity and violence.

It requires the exercise of pastoral acumen by the Shepherds of Jesus' flock to ensure that the gift of the Holy Eucharist is seen, is accepted and is used for the purposes for which it is created. We all know how fear or ignorance or arrogance can be the cause of the most precious gift being rejected. We likewise are aware that the most benign and salubrious gift can be misused to the point of becoming an agent of destruction, e.g., the gift of a car that is then operated by a driver under the influence of drugs. All this then immediately poses two questions. First, in the context of a human community ravaged by an unprecedented and ever-escalating firestorm of violence and enmity, what pastoral dynamic does the Eucharist intrinsically possess to confront and to conquer this satanic eruption, fueled by the reckless squandering of human life and resources on the technology of destruction? Second, what is the proper, most effective way of offering this gift, this grace, to the world so that it will be a divinely efficacious means for subduing and binding the diabolical spirits of violence and enmity across cultures and nations, time and space?

VIRULENT PLAGUE

It is not being an alarmist or a self-righteous prophet of doom to recognize and to call to the attention of others that science, technology and money today are, above all else, at the service of the evils of violence and enmity. Science and technology represent power over nature. Power over nature can be an avenue to power over people, since the human being is body, as well as, soul and spirit. Science and technology can heal or hurt. The arms industry, which is premeditatedly organized to deliver pain and destruction efficiently for a profit, is by far the single largest and most profitable business on the planet at this time and it is completely at the service of enmity and violence. Trillions of dollars a year are spent on creating, manufacturing and distributing the raw instrumentality by which human lives are made subject to unspeakable levels of pain and unfathomable levels of destruction, whether or not the weapons are ever actually employed. Hundreds of billions of dollars more are invested annually in devising and implementing ever new schemes and methodologies for nurturing, promoting and sustaining the spirits, the mindstyles, the ideologies and the value systems that make these weapons and the tidal waves of misery to which they continuously doom the *"anawim,"* appear not only desirable but necessary, not only praiseworthy but of God! Yet, as Pope Paul VI says in 1976 in his statement on disarmament to the United Nations: "The armaments race is to be condemned unreservedly…It is in itself an act of aggression which amounts to a crime, for even when they are not used, by their cost alone, armaments kill the poor by causing them to starve." In such a world as this—where the evils of violence and enmity are so normalized—the Second Vatican Council's (*Gaudium et Spes*, 81) solemn warning is many times more dire and urgent today than when issued: "[T]he arms race is a virulent plague" (*gravissimam plagam*).

> "The armaments race is to be condemned unreservedly…It is in itself an act of aggression which amounts to a crime, for even when they are not used, by their cost alone, armaments kill the poor by causing them to starve."

POWER MADE VISIBLE

So, is it possible that in a little piece of Consecrated Bread and in a little cup of Sanctified Wine there exists a power, indeed the only power, that is able to extricate Christians and all humanity from the ever tightening iron grip of that spirit that induces Cain's enmity toward and destruction of his brother? Faith answers this question with an emphatic, "Yes!" Even in the face of all evidence to the contrary—including the stranglehold that the arms industry has on governments, economies and media worldwide—faith in Christ firmly proclaims that in the Eucharist abides the power (MT 28:18) to prevail over the most deeply-rooted, most extensively-organized and most highly-financed manifestations of evil.

The Eucharist has an innate and indelible, temporal and eternal solidarity with the nonviolent Jesus—the victim of violence and enmity in His passion and death and the victor over violence and enmity in His resurrection. Indeed the Eucharist, among other things, would seem to be purposely created by Intelligent Design to free humanity from the wickedness and snares of that spirit that was behind the destruction of Abel and Jesus and is behind every expression of enmity and homicidal violence in history—from Cain to this very hour. But, this inherent dimension of the Eucharistic Sacrifice must be made visible by the pastoral decision of those who are chosen by Jesus Christ to be overseers of His Church's sacramental life and to be pastors of His people's moral life.

UNIVERSAL PUBLIC EDUCATION

Remember, 200,000 years ago the human brain possessed, because of God's graceful design, everything necessary in order to read. However, it was not until a mere 200 years ago, when humanity began to organize itself in a way that made universal public education available, that universal literacy began to take hold country after country. By the gift and grace of God the capacity to be literate objectively existed for hundreds of millennia, but until human beings chose to do what was necessary in order to access it, it remained in the realm of almost pure potentiality. Prior to universal public education releasing this God-given endowment, only a miniscule number of human beings were able to become what they had the capability of becoming, i.e., literate.

So also is the case in the Church today and by extension in humanity today in relationship to the objectively present but latent power of the Eucharist to conquer violence and enmity and to release humanity from the diabolical trap of the normalized reciprocal destruction of human beings by human beings. A Eucharistic Prayer in the model suggested below would be the human decision for the spiritual equivalent of "universal public education" in the Way of Jesus. It would be a manifestation of a Gospel-grounded liturgical catechesis that would expand forever not only the Christian's but also all humanity's consciousness of the true nature of the true God and hence of the truth of God's Way—the only

Way of vanquishing violence and enmity. In the context of what has just been said and to underline what has been previously stated, a historically, theologically, liturgically and pastorally accurate addition to the institution narrative-anamnesis of the Eucharistic Canons could read as follows:

> ...On the night before He went forth to His eternally memorable and life-giving death, like a Lamb led to the slaughter, rejecting violence, loving His enemies, praying for His persecutors, He bestowed upon His disciples the gift of a New Commandment:
>
> > "Love one another. As I have loved you, so you also should love one another."
>
> Then He took bread into His holy hands, and looking up to You, almighty God, He gave thanks, blessed it, broke it, gave it to His disciples and said:
>
> > "Take this, all of you, and eat it: this is my body which will be given up for you."
>
> Likewise, when the Supper was ended, He took the cup. Again He gave You thanks and praise, gave the cup to His disciples and said:
>
> > "Take this, all of you, and drink from it:
> > this is the cup of my blood, the blood of the new and everlasting covenant.
> > It will be shed for you and for all so that sins may be forgiven."
>
> > "Do this in memory of me."
>
> Obedient, therefore, to this precept of salvation, we call to mind and reverence His passion where He lived to the fullest the precepts which He taught for our sanctification. We remember His suffering at the hands of a fallen humanity filled with the spirit of violence and enmity. But, we remember also that He endured this humiliation with a love free of retaliation, revenge and retribution. We recall His execution on the cross. But, we recall also that He died loving enemies, praying for persecutors, forgiving, and being superabundantly merciful to those for whom justice would have demanded justice. Finally, we celebrate the memory of the fruits of His trustful obedience to thy will, O God: the resurrection on the third day, the ascension into heaven, the enthronement at the right hand, the second and glorious coming. Therefore we offer You your own, from what is your own, in all and for the sake of all...

This simple, short, incisive addition to the Eucharistic Prayer would release power that would dwarf in history the power released by the splitting of the atom. The Jesus of history, the Christ of faith, the Jesus of Gethsemane, the Christ of Calvary, the Jesus of the Gospels—the only Jesus Christ there is, was or ever will be—explicitly confronts the diabolical spirits of enmity and homicidal violence in all their fury at the very hour of His passion and death. By His words and deeds during this New Passover event He teaches humanity how to conquer these evils, while at the same time revealing once and for all the true face of God—a Father "who is rich in mercy," who "lets His rain fall on the wicked and the righteous," who "lets His sun rise on the good and the evil," who forgives limitlessly and in whom "violence and cruelty can have no part" (*Roman Missal, The Sacramentary*, Mass for Peace and Justice). The Eucharist is the mind-changing, converting, healing, empowering, life-saving Divine gift given to a humanity being shredded by evil presenting itself as inevitable and inescapable violence and enmity. However, the Eucharist can only be this transforming Presence if it is made fully visible and available to Christians and through Christians to the world. Made available, that is, in a ritual atmosphere that permeates the senses and the consciousness, the will and the heart, the soul and the conscience of Christian after Christian, person after person, generation after generation with the specific Gospel details of the Nonviolent Love and the Nonviolent Lover who saves.

Undeveloped Remembrance in the Acting Person

Is it not the liturgical absence of the nonviolent Way in which Jesus lives the Paschal Triduum that is the "missing piece" pastorally in contemporary Eucharistic anaphoras? Is there not a pastoral oversight of Gospel and Eucharistic truth here, to which the Overseers of the Divine Liturgy should respond? Is not the willingness to overlook self-evident elements of truth in a situation in which we are absorbed perilous at any level of existence? Bernard Lonergan has shown in his work, *Insight*, that when human activity settles down into routines of partial, vague or ambiguous truths, unconcerned with concrete specifics, then "initiative becomes the privilege of violence." Habituation to a patterned blind spot results in the tragic—and not just for the person or persons missing the indisputably present reality. John Paul II states in *Ecclesia de Eucharistia*: "The Eucharist is indelibly marked by the event of the Lord's passion and death, of which it is not only a reminder but the sacramental re-presentation." What is indelible can never be erased, but it can be concealed, rendered invisible or ignored, thereby assuring that it will never be stored in the heart.

The act of remembering requires that an event has already taken place in history before the moment of remembrance. Prior to a person reasonably interpreting an event, or deriving meaning from it, or determining why it took place, the person must re-member—put back together—what took place. The definitive documents that tell humanity what took place from the Cenacle to Calvary are unquestionably the Gospels. To re-member the Last Supper, which "is indelibly marked by His passion and death," is to re-member the accounts of these events as recorded in the Gospel. For, as Vatican II (*Dei Verbum*, 18) affirms, it is these accounts that are of "apostolic origin," are "the foundation of faith" and are "what the apostles preach in fulfillment of the commission of Christ." To re-member the "Me," who is to be remembered, only as one who "suffers and dies" but not to re-member the Way the "Me" suffers and dies—rejecting violence, loving enemies, forgiving superabundantly, returning good for evil, praying for persecutors—is not to re-member. It is to dis-member by the omission of overwhelmingly critical facts. At best it is to barely re-member. It is the narrowing of the re-membrance of what took place, which in turn narrows the interpretation of why it took place and how people are to respond to it. Pastorally, it should be transparent that a remembrance narrative, drained of nearly all historical particulars, cannot yield the bounteous spiritual fruits that a remembrance more generous in Passion-specificity could.

> To re-member the "Me," who is to be remembered, only as one who "suffers and dies" but not to re-member the Way the "Me" suffers and dies—rejecting violence, loving enemies, forgiving superabundantly, returning good for evil, praying for persecutors—is not to re-member. It is to dis-member by the omission of overwhelmingly critical facts.

The New Testament itself is specific about the content of the Eucharistic memorial: "As often as you eat this bread and drink this cup you proclaim the Lord's death" (1 CO 11:26). The content is Christ's death. Does death, however, mean only the moment when permanent cardiac arrest occurs, when brain waves cease, when pulmonary function totally collapses? Of course not! Death here means all that brings about that moment, all that is part of "mortifying" Him: the humiliations, the beatings, the berating, the hate manifest toward Him, the lies concocted to destroy Him, the manhandling, the betrayal by friends. And, death here also means the Way He responds to all these "mortifications"—with nonviolent suffering love toward unfaithful friends and ruthless enemies. The Altar of Calvary is an Altar of Agapé, not merely an altar of raw mammalian pain. Identification with Jesus' suffering is identification with Jesus' loving as God loves, and as God desires His sons and daughters to love (JN 13:34). The kind of love with which Jesus loves throughout His passion and death is not incidental to

> Death here means all that brings about that moment, all that is part of "mortifying" Him...death here also means the Way He responds to all these "mortifications"—with nonviolent suffering love toward unfaithful friends and ruthless enemies.

a truth full re-membrance, to the proper fulfillment of His Eucharistic precept: Do this in remembrance of me.

A Eucharistic narrative-anamnesis of minimum specificity pastorally weakens the revelation to, as well as, the call to the Eucharistic assembly from God through Jesus "to become what you behold, worship and consume." This arbitrary liturgical abridgement in the Eucharistic Prayer leads to a telling experiential rupture between Gospel content and anamnesis content. It is as if these two exist side by side divested of any demonstrable connections except for the most attenuated of cognitive bridges: words like "suffers," or "passion," or "dies for us." The whole Way that Jesus suffers and dies in His passion is made all but invisible in one Eucharistic Prayer after another. This is in contra-distinction to the Gospels, which give a detailed and absolutely consistent presentation of the Way that Jesus confronts evil, enmity and homicidal violence. Why a liturgist would consider the Way of Nonviolent Love of friends and enemies that Jesus chose as His Way during His passion to be unworthy of illumination in the Eucharistic Prayer is difficult to fathom. Indeed, why a liturgist would not consider this as a pastorally crucial dimension of all Eucharistic Prayers is perplexing. Certainly, they must be aware that ambiguity in language is resolved in the definitiveness of the human act. It is the acting Person, that the institution narrative-anamnesis is primarily supposed to assist the Christian and the Christian Community in encountering. It is the acting Jesus in the "mundane specifics" of His passion and death who gives flesh and blood, body and soul—and divinity—to such open-ended words as "suffers," "dies" and "passion."

HARMFULNESS OF INCOMPLETE EXPRESSION

What is not difficult to comprehend and to prove is the harmfulness of this pared-down approach to the institution narrative-anamnesis. The harmfulness consists in the danger of secularization. Minimalist remembrance narratives have historically shown themselves capable of allowing countless Christians to participate in the Eucharist and thereafter pledge allegiance to *der Führer* of the hour—without any spiritual uneasiness or qualms of conscience. This is a fact of scandalous proportions, which moved Bernard Häring to write: "At this juncture in history, to neglect the message and practice of [Christ's] nonviolence could easily make the Church and Her teaching seem irrelevant." This is a fact of prior Church life that must be viewed anew in the shadow of the on-going "virulent plague" condemned by Paul VI, which is expressing itself in unprecedented carnage. It is a fact that pastorally cries out for a Eucharistic Prayer that calls forth a more fulsome institution narrative-anamnesis that will ignite the desire and steel the courage to imitate the nonviolent Jesus of the Gospel.

Do not Christians, leadership and laity, liturgists and theologians, have to be extremely careful not to do with the Eucharistic Jesus what the Hebrews and Romans did with the historical Jesus—remove Him and His Way from their midst in order to avoid the truth of God, which His full presence would mightily proclaim and beckon others to follow? A nonviolent historical and Eucharistic Jesus who is kept out of sight is a nonviolent Jesus who is kept out of mind. But what is the cost to the Church and to humanity, yesterday, today and tomorrow, for liturgically enshrining the absence of such critical Paschal memory?

EVASION OF UNWANTED TRUTH

Might this not be an ecclesial spiritual problem of the highest order? Human beings, even the most saintly, must constantly struggle against the temptation to evade unwanted truth. Is there not more than ample evidence available to permit with moral certainty the rational deduction that a Christian Community, whose historical record is entangled in nationalistic and ethnic enmity and violence, could very, very easily not want to honestly and to continually face the theological, spiritual, ethical and cognitive dissonance between its past and/or present and the nonviolent Jesus of the Gospels and the Eucharist?

In other words, does not a continuous *de minimis* Eucharistic Prayer, institution narrative-anamnesis, serve the purpose of promoting an equally continuous *de minimis* call to repentance (metanoia)? Does not this approach to Eucharistic Prayers interfere with Christians "more copiously receiving His grace" (*Sacrosanctum Concilium*, 33) at the Eucharistic celebration? Note the issue here is not that the Church *qua* Church has failed in Her mission. Indeed in Her Vatican II Constitution on the Sacred Liturgy (*Sacrosanctum Concilium*) She could not have been more forthright and open, when She declares that, "The Council desires that where necessary the rites be carefully and thoroughly revised in the light

> [D]oes not a continuous *de minimis* Eucharistic Prayer, institution narrative-anamnesis, serve the purpose of promoting an equally continuous de minimis call to repentance (metanoia)? Does not this approach to Eucharistic Prayers interfere with Christians "more copiously receiving His grace" at the Eucharistic celebration?

of sound tradition, and that they be given new vigor to meet the circumstances and needs of modern times" (*Sacrosanctum Concilium*, 4). She is equally transparent in Article 33 of *Sacrosanctum Concilium* that the sacred liturgy is supposed to "contain abundant instruction for the faithful."

John Paul II accurately portrays the God-given, intrinsic structure of human consciousness when he states that "All human beings desire to know...[no one is] genuinely indifferent to the question of whether what they know is true or not." Granting then that the desire to know truth is indelibly impressed in the human person by God, does it not now have to be assiduously communicated by those responsible for the health of souls in the Church, that it is theologically, spiritually, pastorally and liturgically indisputable that a Jesus, who would be engaging in defensive or retaliatory homicidal violence, hating enemies, taking an eye for an eye and cursing persecutors, would be a Jesus engaging in his passion and death in a way that is radically different from the Way of the Jesus of the Gospels? Does it also not now have to be said that the knowledge of God that such a Jesus would communicate about the kind of God God is and what God expects of people would be radically different from what is received in the Gospels and what should be received through every Eucharistic Prayer? Certainly this matter is now exposed as serious enough, as axial enough, as pastorally urgent enough in its implications to warrant immediate attention. The generalized terms "suffers," "dies," "passion" have a distinct and definite meaning in relationship to Jesus. Emaciated re-membrance that generates vagueness or nebulousness—contrary to Gospel specificity—does not seem to be fitting or right any longer. Indeed, if one takes seriously the phenomenon of concupiscence in human life, then it is almost self-evident that anything less than well-defined, straight-forward, unmistakable Gospel-fixed language in the institution narrative-anamnesis invites false understandings. Abstruseness, ambivalence or equivocalness at the apogee of Christian worship is dangerous. For, as Cardinal Joseph Ratzinger has said, "[C]ontradictory things cannot be means to salvation. The truth and the lie cannot be ways of salvation in the same sense."

Is there not unseen, yet immense tragedy, operating in the "forgetfulness" of Eucharistic Prayers on this critically and historically incontrovertible dimension of Jesus' passion and death? If the Divine Liturgy is meant to instruct, as it is, then how is it possible to know the Way of the Father in order to "keep the ways of Yahweh" (PR 119; WS 6:18; IS 26:8; JN 13:34; 15:10), if in the crowning revelatory moment of the Father's Way in the passion and death of Jesus, the Father's Way is all but hidden behind the veil of a minimalist institution narrative-anamnesis? The issue here is not Eucharistic validity. But, as the Second Vatican Council states: "[W]hen the Liturgy is celebrated, more is required than the mere observance of the laws governing validity" (*Sacrosanctum Concilium*, 11). The issue here is allowing the Eucharist to be the fountain of grace and the empowering source of those copious fruits that a humanity, chronically living in a wasteland of enmity and violence, absolutely requires. For ordinary people to be able to see and to encounter with ease the Eucharistic sacrifice of Jesus on Golgotha as a sacrifice on the Altar of Nonviolent Unconditional Love for All—friends and enemies—would seem to be vital. It would therefore also seem to be a given that those chosen to oversee such matters accept responsibility for revising whatever must be revised in order to insure that Jesus' Way of nonviolent self-sacrificial love be in fact remembered—that inchoate memory no longer be fueled under the rubric of "sufficient remembrance for sacramental validity."

> For ordinary people to be able to see and to encounter with ease the Eucharistic sacrifice of Jesus on Golgotha as a sacrifice on the Altar of Nonviolent Unconditional Love for All—friends and enemies—would seem to be vital.

WAY AND PURPOSE

The Way Jesus suffers and dies is as much a part of the eternal unchanging essence of His Passion as is the Purpose of His suffering and death. Indeed, as noted above, His Way is intrinsic to His Purpose and vice versa. This being the case, both Way and Purpose should be re-membered, re-presented, celebrated and given thanks for in the Eucharistic Prayer. Is it not incumbent upon all at a Eucharistic assembly to pay attention to what is in fact in front of them? Therefore, and again, does not the love of Christ compel those, whose duty it is to see to it that the Eucharist is all that it is supposed to be for the Christian Community, to make sure that matter and form are so arranged that the average person can with reasonable effort be attentive to what he or she is objectively in the presence of? And, should not this duty always include assuring attentiveness not only to the objective fact that Jesus suffers and dies for us, but also should it not foster attentiveness to the objective fact of the Way He suffers and dies for us, namely, rejecting violence, forgiving and loving His lethal enemies? Are not Way and Purpose historically and objectively, physically and metaphysically, theologically and spiritually, forever inseparable from each other? How then can a pastorally integral Eucharistic Prayer not honestly and self-evidently include both Way and Purpose?

> The Way Jesus suffers and dies is as much a part of the eternal unchanging essence of His Passion as is the Purpose of His suffering and death...[D]oes not the love of Christ compel those, whose duty it is to see to it that the Eucharist is all that it is supposed to be for the Christian Community, to make sure that matter and form are so arranged that the average person can with reasonable effort be attentive to what he or she is objectively in the presence of?

KNOWER AND KNOWN

Without intending to embark upon an area that is outside the focus of these reflections on the Eucharist Prayer, I nevertheless think it appropriate to here point out that the Eucharist, like the Gospels, originates in a predominantly oral culture. Therefore the memory or remembrance that the original Apostolic tradition would have been preserving, narrating and passing on would have been an oral memory. Walter Ong, S.J., in his magisterial work, *Orality and Literacy: The Technologizing of the Word* (1982) demonstrates that

> *For an oral culture learning or knowing means achieving close, empathetic, communal identification with the known; writing (however) separates the knower from the known and thus sets up conditions for 'objectivity,' in the sense of personal disengagement or distancing...Writing fosters abstractions that disengage knowledge from the arena where human beings struggle. By keeping knowledge embedded in the human lifeworld, orality situates knowledge within the context of struggle.*

It is difficult and may even be dangerous to try to love a text-based abstract concept, even if it is theological. It is, of course, possible to be grateful for a written abstraction. Most people are grateful for $E = mc^2$ or for the poet writing:

> *The brain is wider than the sky,*
> *For put them side by side*
> *The one the other will contain*
> *With ease, and you besides.*

But, the kind and degree of gratitude that flows from love for a person is beyond the ability of expository writing to elicit. Written narrative, however, can partially overcome the disengaged distance and depersonalization that exist between knower and known in expository discourse, and can evoke levels of identification between knower and known that open the door to a deeper and more grateful person-centered love. The Eucharistic Prayer, institution narrative-anamnesis, in the primitive, oral Christian Community, obviously calls forth wholehearted love between the knower and the Known and obviously should call it forth in the contemporary literate Christian Community. But, does it?

The Preface for Christmas exhaltingly explains and proclaims: "In Him we see our God made visible and so are caught up in love of the God we cannot see." How probable is it that a Eucharistic Prayer with a minimalist institution narrative-anamnesis can generate and nurture a love of God in which the Community will be "caught up" in love and gratitude? Must not the Eucharistic Community see and hear more of the nonviolent, long-suffering, forgiving love of friends and enemies "made visible" by the Incarnate Word at the supreme moment of the manifestation of such love, before it can be "caught up in love of the God we cannot see"?

> Must not the Eucharistic Community see and hear more of the nonviolent... Incarnate Word... before it can be "caught up in love of the God we cannot see"?

Ong writes: "Oral cultures must conceptualize and verbalize all their knowledge with more or less close reference to the human lifeworld. A chirographic (writing) culture and even more so a typographic (print) culture can distance and in a way denature even the human." The Second Vatican Council states: "Liturgical services are not private functions, but are celebrations of the Church" (*Sacrosanctum Concilium*, 26). This is important because while it is true that the facticity of human existence requires that each person encounter reality uniquely to some degree, it is nevertheless clear that encountering reality alone in one's room by the process of reading a printed page is not the same as encountering reality as a full participant in a celebrating-thanking faith Community that is struggling to know, love and serve God through His Incarnate Word. Eucharistic Prayer, that contracts the entire Gospel narrative of God's great deed of love in Jesus' passion and death into a few minimally descriptive printed words, which are then recited to the Community, simply cannot be evaluated as pastorally sound for a Eucharistic Community longing for and struggling for a deeper "closer, empathetic identification with the Known." Certainly introducing into the institution narrative-anamnesis of the Eucharistic Prayer awareness of specifics of the Way of Nonviolent Love of friends and enemies that the Incarnate Word enfleshed throughout His passion and death is as important and as needed a revision today as at another time was the revision that made the public presentation of the Eucharistic Prayer in the vernacular normal.

Mandatum for Change

Vatican II teaches: "The liturgy is made up of unchangeable elements divinely instituted and elements subject to change. The latter not only may but ought to be changed with the passing of time, if features have by chance crept in which are less harmonious with the intimate nature of the liturgy or if existing elements have grown less functional" (*Sacrosanctum Concilium*, 21). The mandatum for the change being suggested in this essay is therefore contained in the Constitution on the Sacred Liturgy. However, Vatican II's mandatum is intrinsically and perpetually tied to the *novum mandatum*, "new commandment," spoken by Our Lord at the Last Supper and proclaimed by the Catholic Church to "contain the entire Law of the Gospel" (*Catechism of the Catholic Church*, §1970): "I give you a new commandment: love one another. As I have loved you, so you also

> "I give you a new commandment: love one another. As I have loved you, so you also should love one another" (Jn 13:34). Without an explicit and constant re-presentation of how Jesus loves, how is it possible for His new *"mandatum"* to be followed?

should love one another" (JN 13:34). Without an explicit and constant re-presentation of how Jesus loves, how is it possible for His new "*mandatum*" to be followed? Since the Eucharistic re-presentation of the passion and death of Jesus is ordained to action, to life, to the renewal of life, a faithful re-membrance is a *sine qua non* for fidelity to "the ways of Yahweh"—for fidelity to the *novum mandatum*. In the Christian life an accurate re-membrance of the past is an indispensable condition for a correct orientation in the present and for the future. Beyond this, if as St. Augustine rightly states in the *City of God*, "[In the Eucharist] the Church itself is offered in what is offered" then does it not have to be made explicit what the nature and content of this Christ/Church offering is? Is it not the total offering of Community and self in, with and through Christ to unconditionally do the will of the Father, regardless of the sacrifice that may be required? But, it is the *novum mandatum* that "expresses the Father's entire will" (*Catechism of the Catholic Church*, §2822). So, how can the Eucharistic Community reasonably be expected to be "caught up in love of the God we cannot see," and with full awareness and commitment make the offering it is called to make, if the love and truth of God "made visible" in Jesus' passion and death is not "made visible" in the Eucharistic re-presentation of His passion and death—except for a compressed re-membrance devoid of any mention of the Way of sacrifice. Indeed, what does the petition to the Father to send down His Holy Spirit so that those who take part in the Eucharist may "become one body, one spirit in Christ" (Eucharistic *epiclesis*) mean, if it is not a request to empower the Eucharistic Community to live the *novum mandatum*? Surely, a truncated institution narrative-anamnesis is an "existing element" that can now be seen as "less functional" than other options, and hence "ought to be changed."

Again, the validity of an abruptly concise, emotionally insulated, ethically colorless Eucharistic Prayer, institution narrative-anamnesis, is not the question. The issue is pastoral, which should not be taken to mean it is any less significant than the issue of validity (*Sacrosanctum Concilium*, 11). The issue is what does a Eucharistic Prayer do which concerns itself in only a most cursory fashion with the Way of nonviolent suffering love of friends and enemies that Jesus undertook for the salvation of all? Does it help or hinder the intensity and the quality of the relationship between the knower and the Known? Does a terse institution narrative-anamnesis help or hinder the individual Christian and the Eucharistic Community in following the *new commandment* of love "as I have loved" that is embedded in the Eucharist *in aeternum*? Does it help or hinder the reconciliation of people with each other, which is incontestably the will of God? Does it help or hinder our love for Jesus whom we can see, and through Him our love for "the God we cannot see"? Does it help or hinder growth in gratitude to the Father for all that has been done for us in love and out of love? Does a bland, detailed-depleted Eucharistic narrative help or hinder the Christian in establishing heart-to-heart contact with God?

EUCHARIST: THE ARENA OF STRUGGLE

Pope John Paul II in his 2004 World Day of Peace Message writes that, "Christians know that love is the reason for God's entering into relationship with man. And it is love he awaits as man's response." This is incontestable truth. Indeed, the Latin word for "remember" is *recordari*, which literally means to bring back again (*re*) to the heart (*cor*). As Raniero Cantalamessa shows, Eucharistic remembrance "is not just an activity of the intellect, it is also one of the will and the heart; to remember is to think with love." The issue is how deeply do Christians grasp this, and how much more profoundly could they realize it with a Eucharistic Prayer that daily and weekly enunciated the "mundane specifics" of the Way Jesus chose in obedience to the will of the God who is love (1 JN 4:16). Surely, a deeper, "closer, empathetic identification" with the Known (Jesus) would be established by a more fulsome institution narrative-anamnesis simply because it would generate new bonds of solidarity between knower and Known. It would bring the passion of Jesus into the very lifeworld of the Christian, "the arena where human beings struggle" against the very same spirits of evil with which Jesus contends in Gethsemane and on Calvary. It would bring to mind for the Christian, through the acting person Jesus—possibilities that are easily forgotten in this world. This in turn would open doors in "the arena where human beings struggle" to alternatives that would never otherwise be considered.

> Surely, a deeper, "closer, empathetic identification" with the Known (Jesus) would be established by a more fulsome institution narrative-anamnesis simply because it would generate new bonds of solidarity between knower and Known. It would bring the passion of Jesus into the very lifeworld of the Christian, "the arena where human beings struggle" against the very same spirits of evil with which Jesus contends in Gethsemane and on Calvary.

THE CIVILIZATION OF LOVE AND THE BANALITY OF EVIL

Enmity, violence and the lies, personal and systematic, which support these satanic realities, are the powers against which people struggle in their lifeworlds, personally and socially. Hannah Arendt, in her writing on the trial of Adolph Eichmann, Eichmann in Jerusalem, coins the now famous phrase—"the banality of evil." In what does this banality consist? It consists in a vast machine of ordinary people engaging in brutal enmity and violence without any explicit intention to do evil and without any pressing conscious awareness that evil is being done. When Bernard Häring writes, "The good news of peace and nonviolence plays a central role in Jesus' proclamation of salvation…Redemption can no longer be treated without particular attention to the therapeutic and liberating power of nonviolence, as embodied and revealed by Jesus," he is pleading that the Way of love "embodied and revealed by Jesus" be raised up before the world with persistence and clarity in order that "the murderous reign of hatred, violence and lies" be unmasked and denied allegiance. Where better to raise it up than in the Eucharistic Prayer, which is the very re-presentation of the unmasking of the diabolicalness of normalized enmity and violence, as well as the revelation of the power of the Way and the Person who unmasked and conquered it.

> Redemption can no longer be treated without particular attention to the therapeutic and liberating power of nonviolence, as embodied and revealed by Jesus.

Does a Gospel-oriented mind need do any more than be in contact with the daily fare of news and entertainment via local and globalized mass media to be aware of the manner in which and the degree to which sanitized and sweetened enmity and violence are daily fed into the spiritual bloodstream of ordinary people in order to anesthetize them to what they are making of their own souls and the lives of others? The Church cannot match the powers of this world, mass-media minute for mass-media minute, in order to counteract this ceaseless input of utterly destructive images, mythologies and ideologies. But, the Church has a nonpareil power that is omnipotently superior to anything that mass media and well-financed propaganda on behalf of the spirits of enmity and violence have available to them.

As an antidote to the poisonous parade of enemies that is manufactured almost daily through mass-media propaganda by governments, militaries and weapons-related industries, the Church has the Eucharist. The Church has the sacramental re-presentation of the passion, death and resurrection of Jesus. The Church has the Mass-medium of Jesus choosing a Way of nonviolent suffering and forgiving love of friends and enemies all the way to resurrection. The Church has a historical and Eucharistic Jesus who unmasks all forms of violence and enmity, for the ugly, sordid, anti-human, anti-God realities that they are. The Church has the Mass which can re-present daily to the peoples of the world the one and only Way to that vision of a

> As an antidote to the poisonous parade of enemies that is manufactured almost daily through mass-media propaganda by governments, militaries and weapons-related industries, the Church has the Eucharist. The Church has the Mass-medium of Jesus choosing a Way of nonviolent suffering and forgiving love of friends and enemies all the way to resurrection.

"civilization of love" that Pope John Paul II—despite the disparaging reception he receives on this matter from the devotees of the realpolitik of enmity and violence—so vigorously insists must reign if humanity is to enjoy authentic and lasting peace. In the last paragraph of his 2004 World Day of Peace Message, the Pope offers an alternative vision of truth and hope to the narcotic glories of enmity and violence into which people are daily dragged and drugged:

> *At the beginning of a new year I wish to repeat to women and men of **every** language, religion and culture the ancient maxim: 'Love conquers all.' Yes, dear brothers and sisters throughout the world, in the end love will be victorious.*

The love of which the Successor of Peter is speaking and to which he is calling human beings to awaken, is the love "embodied and revealed by Christ"—and no other. It is the love made visible in Gethsemane and on Calvary. It is the love that should be made readily visible, indeed magnified, at the Eucharist.

A Priority Task

Perhaps it should be considered a priority task by those in authority in each Church to act pastorally so as to give the Eucharistic Prayer "new vigor to meet the circumstances and needs of modern times" (*Sacrosanctum Concilium*, 4). This can be done by a simple Gospel addition to the Eucharistic Canon. This addition would assure that the nonviolent Spirit of the Holy, which guided and guarded Jesus through the violence and enmity of Gethsemane and Golgotha to His resurrection, is easily accessible through the Eucharist to all those human beings who, in solidarity with Jesus, long for peace and eternal life now and forever—but who are daily bedeviled by the cunning, ferocious and well-financed spirits of enmity and violence. In presenting to the Church at this hour in history a Eucharistic Canon that is specific about the Nonviolent Love of friends and enemies—which Jesus lives in conformity with the will of the Father from the start to the finish of His passion and death—Church leaders need have no fear that they are introducing something that is historically, biblically, spiritually or liturgically out of place. On the contrary all that is being done here is the pastoral "fleshing out," via the presentation of incontestable Gospel specifics, truth that is already present in embryonic form in every Eucharist. As succinctly stated by Rev. Frederick R. McManus, professor emeritus at the Catholic University of America and one of the most eminent Catholic liturgists of the Twentieth Century, regarding the need to augment Eucharistic anaphoras with some direct reference to the nonviolence of the Gospel message:

> Perhaps it should be considered a priority task…to give the Eucharistic Prayer "new vigor to meet the circumstances and needs of modern times".

The centrality of the mission of peace and nonviolence in the Gospels needs to be acknowledged in the confession of the great deeds of God in the Lord Jesus, and the Christian people need to see this essential dimension of Eucharistic peace in the prayer which they confirm and ratify with their Amen.

THE CATALYTIC FACTOR AWAKENS POSSIBILITIES

Allowed by the decisions of those responsible in the Churches for seeing to it that the Eucharist confers upon lacerated and imprisoned humanity all that it was designed by its Creator to bestow, the Eucharist can be the nonviolent Exodus event for which not only Christians, but also humanity itself, will give thanks forever to the Father of all (EP 4:6). The addition of a minimal catalytic factor can ofttimes alter an entire reality. A poisonous toxin can be neutralized by the introduction of a small catalytic agent. A gene on DNA, that otherwise would be transcribed incorrectly or not at all, is transcribed correctly by the action of an integral catalytic factor. The presence of the proper catalyst has the potential for producing outcomes that are unrealizable in its absence. Catalysts, by their very nature, facilitate harmonious interactions between substrates, which ultimately make the impossible possible. A Eucharistic Prayer—candidly incorporating the Nonviolent Love that Jesus deliberately embraces throughout His passion and death—is the catalytic factor that will facilitate a union with the Divine that will awaken humanity to the way out of the "virulent plague" of ceaseless, reciprocal homicidal enmity and the preparation for ceaseless, reciprocal homicidal enmity. It is the Way out because Jesus is the Way. And, Jesus is the Way because Jesus is God, Emmanuel, "God with us" in the flesh, showing us the Way beyond enmity and violence, evil and death by the concrete "mundane specifics" of His words and deeds. Indeed, the Way He reveals to us, the Way in which we are to "pick up our cross" daily, leads ultimately to participation in the fullness of Life Eternal. The Banquet of the Lamb therefore must not only empower the Church on earth to live and to love in the Way of Jesus, but it must also reveal that Way of salvation and its Source without blemish or distortion, confusion or equivocation. To reiterate Pope John Paul II's admonition:

> *The Eucharist is too great a gift to tolerate ambiguity and depreciation.*

FEAST OF THE THEOPHANY
(REV.) EMMANUEL CHARLES MCCARTHY
JANUARY 6, 2004

EPILOGUE

The title of this book on the Nonviolent Jesus of the Gospels, ***All things flee thee for thou fleest Me***, is derived from Francis Thompson's poem, *The Hound of Heaven*. The poem is the story of the plight of a person, who spends his or her life running from God, from His Will and from His Way. It is also the story of God pursuing this runaway soul *"with unhurring chase, and unperturbed pace, deliberate speed, majestic instancy."* The poem opens with the now famous stanza:

> *I fled Him, down the nights and down the days;*
> *I fled Him, down the arches of the years;*
> *I fled Him, down the labyrinthine ways*
> *Of my own mind; and in the mist of tears*
> *I hid from Him, and under running laughter.*
> *Up vistaed hopes I sped;*
> *And shot, precipitated,*
> *Adown Titanic glooms of chasmed fears,*
> *From those strong Feet that followed, followed after.*
> *But with unhurrying chase, And unperturbed pace,*
> *Deliberate speed, majestic instancy,*
> *They beat—and a Voice beat*
> *More instant than the Feet—*
> *"All things betray thee, who betrayest Me."*

If the "I" of Thompson's poem is read not as an individual person but as that corporate person called the institutional Church, then the poem is equally the story of Christianity since the time of Constantine (272-337 AD). An enormous portion of documented Church history over the last 1700 years has been the Church fleeing the Nonviolent Jesus. An almost invisible piece of Church history has been the Nonviolent Jesus pursuing the fleeing Church *"with unhurrying chase, and unperturbed pace, deliberate speed, majestic instancy."*

Strange as it is to say, the institutional Church fears the Nonviolent Jesus, *"Lest, having Him, I must have naught besides."* "What will become of us," worry its leadership and laity, "if we cannot righteously engage in violence like other religions? Who will defend us against the dark surges of the human psyche? Our buildings, our treasuries, our achievements, our pleasures and our very lives and the lives of those we love will be cast into intolerable jeopardy if we cannot substitute violence for love, if we cannot re-name violence love?" With horrifying hypotheticals dancing in their heads and with terrifying conjectures hardening their hearts, Catholic, Protestant, Orthodox and Evangelical Christians flee the Nonviolent Jesus, "*down the nights and down the days, down the arches of the years, down the labyrinthine ways of [their] own mind[s]."*

How unfortunate is the lot of those born into one of the Churches seeking refuge from the Nonviolent Messiah. While still in the Edenic innocence of infancy, people in these communities are given to eat of the fruits of the flight from God. They, as members of a fleeing Pilgrim Church, will more than likely never know any other way than the way that avoids facing up to the Nonviolent Jesus. Yet, their Guide Book, the New Testament, will unequivocally and continuously remind them that the Nonviolent Jesus is the Way. What warping of the soul must take place when a person, young or old, is forced out of fear or out of inculcated untruth to live a falsehood about something that is of critical importance to his or her relationship with God?

Suppose a teacher is teaching his or her class about Albert Einstein. Suppose all the proper pedagogical methodologies and technologies are utilized to instruct the class about Einstein and his thought. Now suppose the teacher, because of his or her belief that the world was created 4,212 years ago, omits informing the students about Einstein's great insight, $E=mc^2$, believing that such information would undermine a 4,212 year-old-world theory. Beyond all this, suppose further that the teacher by a process of selective omission and emphasis cleverly arranges the content matter of the course in such a way as to leave students with the impression that Einstein actually supports a 4,212 year-old-world belief or is at least neutrally tolerant of it. Now I ask, "Is a '4,212 year-old-world Einstein' Einstein?" Is Einstein Einstein without $E=mc^2$? What would such a teacher really be about: communicating truth concerning Einstein or trying to place the most authoritative name in physics on his or her own view of reality? Which is more self-servingly deceptive: an Einstein without $E=mc^2$ or a Jesus without His Way of nonviolent love of friends and enemies? Which is the greater absurdity: an Einstein who endorses a 4,212 year old world or a Jesus who endorses homicidal violence?

Very few Christians flee from the Nonviolent Jesus by themselves. Most require fellow travelers in order to maintain the mirage that they are following the Jesus of the Gospel, while traveling in the wrong direction down a one-way street. Much of Christian theology over the last 1700 years is an aggregation of pep talks by Christian comrades in arms spelling out how to be at peace and how to attain peace and meaning while steering clear of the Nonviolent Jesus. Much of the remainder of Christian theology, especially moral theology, is an apologia for deserting the Nonviolent Jesus of history and faith. Yet the Nonviolent Word, enshrined forever in the Gospel for all to hear and see, unrelentingly pursues His Church across the seasons and centuries *"with unhurrying chase, and unperturbed pace, deliberate speed, majestic instancy."*

"All things betray thee, who betrayest Me." the "Hound" warns. To paraphrase Gertrude Stein: The wrong way is the wrong way is the wrong way; the Nonviolent Word is the Nonviolent Word is the Nonviolent Word. Nothing can alter what is rooted in God for all eternity. Jesus asks His apostles, "Will you also leave me" (JN 6:68)? Peter responds with the impeccable clarity that should govern every Christians' response to every temptation to repudiate the Nonviolent Jesus: "Lord, who shall we go to? You have the message of eternal life, and we believe; we know that you are the Holy One of God." If the successors of the apostles flee the Nonviolent Jesus, where would they go? Who else has the words of eternal life? Perhaps, it is appropriate and necessary to recall, and to recall persistently and in exhaustive detail, where people have gone, spiritually and historically, when they have taken their leave of the Nonviolent Jesus. The reluctance of leadership, a reluctance that borders on willful refusal to repent, to name and own the evil and misery which it has provoked and which its predecessors have sponsored when they have cut the Church off from the Nonviolent Jesus is telling. It says, with a clarity that is embarrassingly transparent to the non-Christian world, that there is something unbearably distressing to be seen.

"All things flee thee, for thou fleest Me!" the "Hound" declares. If Jesus is the Redeemer, why doesn't the world look more redeemed after 2000 years?" asks the entire non-Christian world. The answer is self-evident for those who have eyes and wish to see. The Kingdom of God can only be brought about by the means of the Kingdom of God. Not one speck of evil, not one unChrist-like act, not one act of homicidal violence, is needed for the Kingdom to come in all its fullness. To abandon the Nonviolent Jesus is to abandon the means that the Nonviolent Word of God communicates to humanity as the means by which the Kingdom (Reign) of God is to be established. The old Chesterton chestnut is apropos here: "It is not that Christianity has been tried and failed. It is that Christianity has been found too difficult and not tried." The Christianity which is "not tried" is the Christianity of the Nonviolent Jesus who

> "It is not that Christianity has been tried and failed. It is that Christianity has been found too difficult and not tried."

taught a Way of nonviolent love of friends and enemies. It is the Christianity that refuses to return injury for injury, that chooses to return good for injury, that accepts the cross of nonviolent suffering love which is the brick and mortar of the Kingdom of God. Every manner of kingdom can be built up by means contrary to the Way of the Nonviolent Jesus of the Gospel—every manner of kingdom that is except the Kingdom of God. When the Churches with their leadership and laity abandon the Nonviolent Jesus and His Nonviolent Way, it must be asked what kingdom are they committed to bringing to earth? What king are they *de facto* serving? What King are they fleeing?

Is it only when "one stone does not remain upon another" (MK 13:1; LK 21:5; MT 24:2) at St. Peter's Basilica in Rome, at St. John the Divine Cathedral in New York, at Hagia Sophia in Istanbul, in the United States, in England, in France, in Russia, in Belize that the words of the "Hound" will be understood: "*All things flee thee, for thou fleest Me!*"? Then again, maybe these words of warning can best be fathomed not by the total collapse of Westminster Cathedral, the Twin Towers or Monte Casino, but in light of the dark, sorrowful and agonizing deathbed lament of Bishop Wolsey, "Had I but served my God with half the zeal I served my king."

Stalin taught, rather successfully, that the big lie is easier to maintain and harder to expose than the small lie. In a world that operates economically on the moral acceptability of the proverb, "The rich man gains a market; the poor man loses a leg," unmasking the lie of redemptive Christian violence looks impossible. Twenty-First Century Christianity seems as if it is going to be a blood-red Xerox of Twentieth Century Christianity which, of course, was a technologically magnified encore of the sixteen prior centuries of "justified" Christian slaughter. The big lie is almost unassailable. Even when it is pointed out, it perpetuates itself by claiming it is just one among many difficulties with which the Church must deal, like communion on the tongue or in the hand, or whether drinking alcohol is contrary to the Gospel. The big lie, however, is truth in drag. It is a major distortion of the underlying reality. When a person or group succumbs to its magnetism, the ruling lie feels like "gospel truth"—even when the Gospel explicitly repudiates it.

It is important to now stop. The truth has been stated. There comes a time when the continuation of a quibbling debate about an incontestable truth is spiritually unhealthy and serves only as an escape from decision. Because a Christian or Church does not know how to implement the Nonviolent Way of the Nonviolent Jesus does not alter the fact that He and His Way are nonviolent. The only process by which $E=mc^2$ could have had the profound effect it has had on human life is the process of millions of people spending billions of hours and dollars attempting to implement it by trial and error. Without this expenditure of time, mind and money, $E=mc^2$ would be as irrelevant to the world today as the Nonviolent Jesus and His Way of Nonviolent Love are to Christianity today. Truth that is not incarnated, truth that remains only in the mind is truth that is powerless to help humanity. Known truth that is not permitted to enter human history is truth that brings judgment and pain upon humanity via the consequences that flow from its enforced absence.

One of the most faithful disciples ever of the Nonviolent Jesus is an all but unknown Protestant clergyman, Adin Ballou (1803-1890) from Hopedale, Massachusetts. Tolstoy in his masterpiece on Gospel Nonviolence, *The Kingdom of God is Within You*, writes ten pages on Ballou and quotes him extensively. Ballou concludes his little book, *Christian Non-Resistance* (1846) with this poem:

> *The earth, so long a slaughter-field,*
> *Shall yet an Eden bloom;*
> *The tiger to the lamb shall yield,*
> *And War descend the tomb;*
> *For all shall feel the Saviour's love,*
> *Reflected from the cross—*
> *That love, that non-resistant love,*
> *Which triumphed on the cross.*

Now a truth that requires the crucifixion of the Son of God in order for it to break through the sophistries of history must be of colossal importance and must have monstrous barriers to overcome in order to be seen and accepted. The Cross of Nonviolent Love of friends and enemies is the truth without which the Church cannot be the Church it is supposed to be. The Nonviolent Cross is also the truth without which human beings cannot live the lives they were created to live, that is, lives of personal and social peace in communion with and in imitation of God. "The Cross," reflects Mahatma Gandhi, "makes a universal appeal at the moment you give it universal meaning." The Cross of Nonviolent Monotheism is humanity's only hope because it is the authentic revelation of the nature and will of the Holy One, and hence is Divine Power acting in concert with the very structure of the universe. The Japanese Christian spiritual leader, Toyohiko Kagawa (1888-1960), imprisoned many times by Japanese authorities for speaking and writing about the Cross of Nonviolent Love universalizes its message and hence its invitation in these memorable words:

> *The Cross of Nonviolent Monotheism is humanity's only hope because it is the authentic revelation of the nature and will of the Holy One, and hence is Divine Power acting in concert with the very structure of the universe.*

> Love evolves perennially, never grudging sacrifice. Since love has never abhorred martyrdom, it perceives that in the process of evolution it is more effective to be killed rather than to kill. Men who fear to make the sacrifice of love will fight. Those who believe in the sacrifice through love believe in the principle of non-injury. For those who eternally evolve, there is an eternal cross.

Fleeing the Nonviolent Jesus of the Cross always remains an option. But, pursuit of the Constantinian Church, pursuit of the homicide-justifying Church, pursuit of fleeing pastors and flocks,

> *down the nights and down the days;*
> *down the arches of the years;*
> *down the labyrinthine ways*
> *of [their] own mind[s]…*

is the irrevocable and unconditional commitment of the Eternal Word of Nonviolent Love made flesh, Jesus Christ. His pursuit is our hope. Pursuit *"with unhurrying chase, and unperturbed pace, deliberate speed, majestic instancy"* is the chosen task of this tremendous Lover until that day when all the Churches of Christianity can with one mind and one heart exclaim: "Now is the winter of our flight from Truth made glorious summer by facing the Nonviolent Son of God!"

> *Do you see the eyes of the Crucified*
> *Looking at you with searching gaze?*
> *They are asking you a question:*
> *Are you, in all seriousness,*
> *Ready to enter once again*
> *Into a covenant with the Crucified?*
> *What are you going to answer?*
>
> — ST. EDITH STEIN

BIOGRAPHY

(REV.) EMMANUEL CHARLES MCCARTHY

Rev. Emmanuel Charles McCarthy is a priest of the Eastern Rite (Byzantine-Melkite) of the Catholic Church in communion with the Bishop of Rome, the Pope. He was ordained on August 9, 1981, in Damascus, Syria, by Patriarch Maximos V. He served as Spiritual Director and Rector of St. Gregory the Theologian Byzantine-Melkite Catholic Seminary and is presently a Retreat Director. Formerly a lawyer and a university educator, he is the founder and the original director of The Program for the Study and Practice of Nonviolent Conflict Resolution at the University of Notre Dame. He is also co-founder of Pax Christi-USA.

For over fifty years he directed retreats throughout the world on the issue of the relationship of faith and violence, and the Nonviolent Jesus and His Way of Nonviolent Love of friends and enemies. In 1983 he began The Annual Forty Day Fast for the Truth of Gospel Nonviolence, (July 1 to August 9), whose purpose is to pray to the Father in the name of Jesus to bestow on the Churches of Christianity whatever extraordinary graces are needed to turn from justifying violence and enmity and begin to teach what Jesus taught about violence and enmity. In 1990 he initiated the July 16 Twenty-Four Hours Day of Prayer for Forgiveness and Protection with Our Lady of Mount Carmel at Trinity Site, where the first atomic bomb was detonated, in the New Mexico desert.

He has been nominated for the Nobel Peace Prize and is author of several books, including *All Things Flee Thee for Thou Fleest Me: A Cry to the Churches and Their Leaders to Return to the Nonviolent Jesus and His Nonviolent Way, August 9*, and *The Stations of the Cross of Nonviolent Love*. He has written innumerable popular articles and theological essays on the subject of violence, religion and the Nonviolent Love of friends and enemies that the Jesus of the Gospels teaches by His words and by His deeds. His CD/DVD series, *Behold the Lamb*, is almost universally considered to be the most spiritually profound presentation on Gospel Nonviolence available in those formats.

A Christian Parent's Pledge to All Mothers and Fathers

I will not raise my precious child to kill your precious child.

And if it is within my power, I will

not hand over my beloved child to others

to kill your beloved child, or

to learn how to kill the one you cherish.